D1572059

The Extraordinary Life of

Mike Cumberlege
SOE

The Extraordinary Life of

Mike Cumberlege
SOE

ROBIN KNIGHT

FONTHILL

In memory of Michael Cumberlege,
a true hero of his time who gave his life for his country.

Fonthill Media LLC
www.fonthillmedia.com
office@fonthillmedia.com

First published in the United Kingdom and the United States of America 2018

British Library Cataloguing in Publication Data:
A catalogue record for this book is available from the British Library

ISBN 978-1-78155-732-7

All photographs are from the personal collections of the Cumberlege family with the exception of those indicated. Every effort has been made to track down and attribute the photographs used.

Typeset in 10pt on 13pt Sabon
Printed and bound in England

Acknowledgements

Many people on three continents helped with the compilation of this biography. Without their input and encouragement, the book would not have been completed.

My main assistance has come from three absolutely invaluable and generous sources: the Cumberlege family, and, in particular, Mike's son Marcus in Bruges, his granddaughter Eunice in Paris, and Marcus's half-brother John Livingstone-Learmonth; Walter Paine in New Hampshire, USA, who sailed across the Atlantic in the *Queen Mary* liner aged ninety-three carrying a priceless cache of letters written by Mike in the 1938–42 period (all the letters quoted in this book come from family collections unless otherwise stated); and Platon Alexiades in Montreal, Canada, whose book *Target Corinth Canal 1941–44* provides the core framework for the chapters covering the Second World War.

Second only to them are the uncomplaining staff in the National Archives at Kew. More than 180 files were unearthed for me over a long period. On all occasions, those I dealt with at Kew were unfailingly supportive and informative. Similarly, the staff in Humanities Room 2 in the British Library helped in many ways as I ploughed through long-forgotten accounts of peace and war stored in the warehouses.

Other input has come from some surprising places. Andy Titov in Kiev got in touch after my booklet on Mike Cumberlege was published in 2015 to inform me about a Ukrainian nationalist leader Taras Bulba-Borovets and his association with Mike. Hannah Weinberg of the Schlesinger Library at Harvard University dug out useful material from the Elizabeth David collection held there. Katharine Thomson of the Churchill Archives Centre at Churchill College, Cambridge, pointed me to the papers of Admiral John Henry Godfrey that are stored there. Ben Macintyre of *The Times* newspaper and author of many SOE-related volumes encouraged me to think in terms of a book. The photographer Ben Gibson, with whom I worked on assignments for BP in the Caucasus, gave me fresh insights into his father, Charles Gibson-Cowan.

From Greece and the United States, members of the Vergos family contributed with first-person detail about the 1941 Crete-Alexandria period. Monika Liebscher, archivist at the Sachsenhausen Memorial Site near Berlin, and the historian Professor Nikolaus Wachsmann of the University of London added important information to that part of the book. So did S. J. Spear in the Office of the Naval Secretary in London and Rachel Roberts, archivist at Cheltenham Ladies College.

Walter Paine's sister-in-law Melissa Moyer did valuable work in Belmont, New Hampshire, in 2006–08 establishing a timeline and basic source material for Mike's life and career. Noah Scott, archivist of the Brotherhood of Veterans of the Greek Campaigns, contacted me with new information. Bianka Geisler of the Users' Service Department at the International Tracing Service in Bad Arolsen, Germany, did a search of the ITS's massive archive of 50 million civilian victims of the Nazis, looking for any new details of Mike's imprisonment in Sachsenhausen.

On Mike's pre-Second World War seagoing career, Monica Blank, an archivist at the Rockefeller Archive Center in New York, helped me to unearth detail about Leonard Outhwaite and his sailing relationship with Mike in 1929–30. Author Robin Bryer and the archivist at Dauntsey's School added snippets about the *Jolie Brise* period. Three logs of *Landfall*'s cruises in 1938–39, written by Don Moffat, were handed to me by Walter Paine and Marcus Cumberlege and gave new insights into Mike's temperament. Other information came from the Cruising Association and from Janet Grosvenor, Archivist and Race Management Consultant at the Royal Ocean Racing Club.

The most difficult parts of the book to nail down proved to be Mike's childhood and early years. School magazines from the Nautical College, Pangbourne, for the 1919–22 period subsequently provided some information. Ben Strickland in London recalled stories about Mike from his teenage years as told to him by his mother who was at school with Mike's sister, Diana. Nicholas Lapthorn, head of the Field Studies Centre at Nettlecombe Court, gave me a clue about Mike's pre-Pangbourne days in Somerset. Dr Jane Harrold, archivist at the Britannia Museum, searched its records for any indication that Mike tried, and failed, to gain entry to Dartmouth in 1917–19. From Australia, David Michael and John Smith of the Naval Historical Society of Australia were most helpful. Susan Scott, archivist at the Cayzer Family Archive, scoured the records of the Clan Line for evidence of Mike's time with the company.

The digital world did not exist in Mike's lifetime but it, too, played a part. In the Netherlands, Hans Houterman of www.unithistories.com gave invaluable career information about RN and Army officers who served with Mike in the

Second World War. The historian Dr Steven Kippax, who animates an SOE Forum, was another well-informed advisor. Tony Drury of the Royal Navy Research Archive, www.royalnavyresearcharchive.org.uk, was unfailingly positive and made sure my earlier short history of Mike's life was formatted, updated, and posted on his website.

I am indebted to Lt-Col. Ewen Southby-Tailyour and to Sir John Weston for their invaluable assistance. Ewen has written an insightful Introduction, which only someone with his background working alongside the Special Boat Service and as an Old Pangbournian, an author, and a former Yachtsman of the Year could have done. John applied his forensic eye, his own skills as a poet, and his many years spent cutting through diplomatic obfuscations to critique Mike's poetry.

I am also grateful to Alan Sutton at Fonthill Media, who got behind this biography after a succession of publishers and literary agents rejected the book as commercially unviable or refused to read the manuscript. He and his team have been excellent guides through the maze that is the publishing business today.

Finally, I owe a large debt of gratitude to my ever-loyal and understanding wife, Jean, for her expert proofreading and insightful comments. Her tolerance and forbearance as I immersed myself in another unexpected lead on what proved to be a very protracted search for answers over two years never faltered.

Family memories, of course, are notoriously varied. It has proved so in this instance. Today, the Cumberlege family is spread around the world from Peru to Thailand, France, Majorca, California, and Belgium and is not in close contact. Another obstacle has been that much of the SOE Aegean/Middle East record for the 1941–42 period, once stored in a warehouse in Cairo, was destroyed in a fire in 1942.

History, and biography, can never be complete, and maybe new material will appear in years to come. Yet, as of 2018, this record of the short, but action-packed life of Mike Cumberlege is as complete as I could make it. Any interpretations of the facts as they have been unearthed are mine alone.

CONTENTS

Introduction

Truly Elizabethan in character—a combination of gaiety and solidity and sensitiveness and poetry with daring and adventurousness—and great courage.

This is the story of a remarkable man who, had he lived in the nineteenth century, would have flourished as one of the great maritime adventurers during the expansion, by sea, of the British Empire. Had he survived the Second World War, he and his adored wife, Nancy, may have become a leading partnership in exploring under sail, perhaps only matched by the Hiscocks and the Smeetons.

Mike Cumberlege joined the Nautical College Pangbourne two years after its formation and enjoyed the perfect institution to give him the confidence and self-assurance needed for almost everything that followed: the Merchant Navy, the Royal Naval Reserve in war, and life as a "professional" yacht skipper that included sailing the soon-to-be famous *Jolie Brise*. Of the utmost significance for the future were a series of cruises around the Baltic, Adriatic, and Aegean in a 71-foot ketch, the *Landfall*, during which he seldom stopped sketching and surveying out-of-the-way anchorages while finding time to compose beautiful poetry and write evocative descriptions of places he visited and sights he witnessed.

Called up for war service in 1940, again with the RNR, Cumberlege's unique character was swiftly recognised with an appointment to Marseilles on 'Contraband Control Duties' before being appointed a liaison officer to General de Gaulle and his embryo Free French Forces.

In 1941, thanks to his personal relationship with the Director of Naval Intelligence, he was sent to the Cape Verde islands as 'Consular Shipping Adviser'—a cover for further clandestine activities. Rather more in line with Cumberlege's exemplary seamanship skills, coupled with his intimate knowledge of the Aegean (and, once again, thanks to the Director of Naval Intelligence), he was appointed to command the quaintly-named, but surprisingly effective Allied 'para-naval-force' in the Eastern Mediterranean. This 'made-to-measure' work (as far as Mike Cumberlege's character was concerned) involved covert missions across the area under the control of the Special Operations Executive (SOE). This was an inspired posting for a man who was more than qualified for the task and was the precursor of much that was to ensue.

Cumberlege's duties, while exercising command from a heavily-armed, 40-ton auxiliary ketch with no sails, were wide-ranging in scope and location. They included, among many similar operations, a reconnaissance of the Dodecanese islands and Rhodes in preparation for a proposed amphibious operation and a two-week covert survey of Crete. This was work with which the modern-day Special Boat Service would be familiar.

A failed attempt to block the Corinth Canal ended with him being wounded by German dive-bombers, forcing an even greater determination to complete the task, once the reasons for the initial failure had been remedied. During the German invasion of Crete and the subsequent evacuation of Allied forces from that island, in which he played a significant and courageous part, he was captain of a caïque armed and refitted for clandestine operations: his pre-war yachting adventures coupled with his meticulous anchorage surveys made him, once more, ideal for this type of maritime warfare.

A second SOE attempt to block the canal, Operation Locksmith, concluded not only in disaster but, worst still, through clever German subterfuge and possibly thanks to his own understandable mistakes, his eventual capture.

Had he not been forced to endure years of unspeakable torture, he would, almost inevitably I believe, have been invited to join the Combined Operations Pilotage Parties for the reconnaissance of beaches prior to the Normandy landings on D-Day.

In effect, he was an SBS officer before the modern SBS was formed and had much in common in both his sailing and service life with that of Lt-Col. 'Blondie' Hasler of Operation Frankton fame. They met very briefly in October 1942—Cumberlege was Hasler's senior by nine years—but sadly never again, especially in more peaceful times, for what a gathering that would have been. Who can tell what marvellous inspirations might have emerged from subsequent collaboration that would have benefited yachtsmen in the eventual peace and servicemen conducting future asymmetric, maritime operations?

Tragically, though, Mike Cumberlege did not survive confinement and was murdered by the Nazis in, it is believed, February or March 1945 in Sachsenhausen concentration camp: neither his body nor his few meagre effects have been found. It is incomprehensible that such a noble and gentle man should have been murdered by the scum of Europe. What is equally unfathomable, to modern minds, is how he remained cheerful and optimistic to the very end, despite the outrageous indignities—beyond all sane imagination—that he suffered at the hands of history's most abominable sadists over two, long, excruciatingly-painful years.

Many of us latter-day 'military mariners' wish we had met Mike Cumberlege early in our own careers, for we would have gleaned priceless guidelines in the handling of small boats, conducting covert beach reconnaissance, and in commanding small, seaborne operations in support of the larger maritime picture.

The Royal Navy has an expression signalled by an admiral to express complete satisfaction at a job well done and which is most sparingly given. It is a two-flag hoist that reads simply *BZ* or *Bravo Zulu*. I know of few men, if any, that deserve that accolade more than Lt Cdr Claude Michael Bulstrode Cumberlege DSO & Bar, Reserve Decoration, Greek Medal of Honour, RNR.

The diligence with which Robin Knight has researched Mike Cumberlege's short but eventful life, and the subsequent manner in which his impressive achievements have been recorded by the author, will ensure that this book has a more-than-worthwhile place—indeed, an important place—in the literature of unconventional maritime operations during the Second World War.

Ewen Southby-Tailyour, March 2017
Lt-Col. Royal Marines (retired)
Author of *Reasons in Writing* and a dozen other books
Yachtsman of the Year, 1982

1

Christmas Day 1944

It is 5 a.m. on Christmas Day 1944. In the T-shaped Zellenbau, a separate solitary confinement cell block in Sachsenhausen concentration camp 22 miles north of Berlin, eighty top security British, Polish, Norwegian, Danish, Russian, Ukrainian, and German prisoners are woken up by a siren, a naked 60-watt light bulb is switched on in each cell, and morning ablutions commence at the double—part of an unvarying routine of pointless, empty monotony punctuated by moments of terror and fear that defines existence day in, day out in this cursed place. Cell buckets are emptied twice a day, one by one, in the block lavatory. A quick rinse of the pail with cold water from a running tap and a brief wash using gritty soap follows, accompanied by loud shouts and threats from the supervising warders—one of whom shows no mercy and wields a long, leather-covered whip that he uses to slash tardy prisoners on their backs or buttocks.

All contact and conversation among the prisoners is forbidden. Each cell, with its individual number, heavy iron door that only opens outward, and Judas spy hole used constantly by the guards, is then swept out by its occupant. A rudimentary breakfast of ersatz coffee made from acorns and a slice of black bread daubed with a jammy saccharine pulp and a smear of margarine is delivered by a 'trustee'—normally a German orderly jailed many years earlier for his dissident political or religious beliefs. Little fresh air seeps in to this grim, stinking hellhole; what air there is has long been polluted by the guards' endless smoking. Adding to the stresses, a radio blares out of the guards' room from dawn to midnight at maximum volume, and both words and music are unintelligible to the prisoners.

At midday, 'Christmas fare' appears: stew with a small piece of pork, a doughy lump of pudding, a sweet biscuit, and a ration of jam. In the afternoon, the short, expressionless bookkeeper-like camp commandant Anton Kaindl—'a skinny little half portion' according to one of the prisoners—pays a visit to his most honoured 'guest', the British spy Captain Payne Best.[1] 'I hardly recognised him—a tired, broken man,' Best says later.[2] Apparently, Kaindl complains that it has become impossible to run Sachsenhausen with its 42,000 inmates: 'It is too big. One man can do nothing. It is a pig sty'. Moans and sobs emanate from Cell 14 where a young SS conscript who has deserted passes his final hours before being shot the next day. That evening, the camp loudspeakers blast out the nostalgic strains of the carol '*Stille Nacht, heilige Nacht*'. Only one of the RAF's regular nuisance raids on the German capital silences the haunting words and tune.[3]

An uneasy atmosphere prevails. Since September, conditions in the cell block have got steadily worse. Outside, the thermometer has plunged below -20 degrees Celsius at night as an extreme winter gets a firm grip. Inside, extra blankets have been distributed to a few of the more favoured prisoners, but most shiver constantly in the intense cold. Supplies of every sort are running short and food is down to the very bare minimum. Cigarettes have disappeared, even on the black market. In the crematorium, the guards are beginning to burn papers as often as bodies. For many of the prisoners, it is an effort even to drag oneself out of bed.

For weeks, the distant rumble of artillery fire—'a remote drumming from the east' as one prisoner calls it—has provided a backdrop to the days and nights as Soviet ground forces slowly advance on Berlin. Third Reich officials at every level have begun to worry about their necks, and mass shootings, gassings, and hangings are ramping up across the Nazis' concentration camp empire. Although the long, low Zellenbau is sound-proofed with a kind of rubberoid flooring in the corridors, each guard's footstep is imprinted on a prisoner's mind. Whenever steps are heard approaching a cell, the insistent thought occurs: 'Where is he going to stop?' Then the noise recedes as another victim further up the corridor is dragged off for torture or interrogation most probably in the underground cellar next to the Zellenbau's boiler room.

Although all communication is banned, many of the prisoners have found ingenious ways to get around this and know that it is Christmas Day. Some have even exchanged cards made from toilet paper or torn scraps of the *Völkischer Beobachter*, the Nazi newspaper sometimes handed out to favoured captives by friendly orderlies. Those prisoners subject to 'full arrest' spend their days in darkened, icy cells, denied books to read or paper and pencils. Even lying on the iron bed and straw palaise in the tiny cell is prohibited in daytime. Most of the guards, including Kurt Eccarius, 'the Beast of the Bunker', are off duty this day, so the prisoners remain locked in their cells, denied their regular fifteen- or thirty-minute exercise walk in the small outdoor yard, diagonally crossed by a path ironically known as Hitlerstrasse, which surrounds much of the Zellenbau. This yard has a suitably grisly backdrop—half a dozen iron poles concreted into the ground on which prisoners are manacled and hung for hours at a time before being shot or gassed. On another outer wall of the

Zellenbau, there are hooks on which victims are strung up and left to die. This usually takes three to four hours and the death throes are easily audible in the cell block.

A number of notably tough-minded characters are locked up in the Zellenbau on this cold, damp Christmas Day morning. Among them are a dozen or more British servicemen, including five of the most determined Allied POW escapers of the Second World War: Wg Cdr Harry 'Wings' Day, Flt Lt Sydney Dowse, Maj. Johnnie Dodge, Flt Lt Jimmy James, and Lt-Col. Jack Churchill (a distant cousin of Winston Churchill). There is also the unlucky British spy Capt. Payne Best, kidnapped by the Germans in neutral Holland in November 1939 and treated with kid-gloves by Kaindl. In the cell next to Best is a Special Operations Executive (SOE) agent, Sqn Ldr Hugh Falconer, a wireless transmission virtuoso captured behind enemy lines in Tunisia in 1943. Other prized SOE prisoners include Maj. Francis Suttill and Capt. William Grover-Williams, both seized by the SS in France in 1943.

Barely known to anyone else in the Zellenbau due to its prolonged isolation in two successive and murderous concentration camps over the previous twenty months, there is also a four-person Allied commando team in the block. It had been captured in the Aegean Sea on 1 May 1943 after a daring and ultimately abortive Special Operations Executive (SOE) mission codenamed Operation Locksmith that was intended to blow up the Corinth Canal. Led by a Royal Naval Reserve lieutenant commander, Mike Cumberlege DSO and Greek Medal of Honour, the group also includes Rhodesian-born Sgt James 'Jumbo' Steele from the Black Watch regiment; a Yorkshire-born radio operator, Cpl Thomas Handley; and Cpl Jan Kotrba of the Czech Army in Exile, who had sailed with Cumberlege before the war and was known to the SS as John Davies.

Cumberlege and his party had been transferred to Sachsenhausen in January 1944 after a gruelling eight-month interlude in the notorious Mauthausen extermination camp in Austria, where Cumberlege was tortured 'severely' to get him to admit he had been on a sabotage mission. All four have remained in solitary confinement in the Zellenbau ever since—treated as common criminals, denied POW status, not allowed to write or receive letters, permitted no Red Cross food parcels, given no 'privileges' (such as books or cigarettes), forced to wear the standard camp 'uniform' of rough blue-striped dirty grey serge, round caps, and clogs, and fed a starvation diet of wurzels (a root crop cooked in water that is normally fed to pigs). Even by the abysmal standards of the Zellenbau, they rate as the lowest of the low, treated in this harsh way to justify, in SS minds, keeping them alive at all following Hitler's infamous order issued in October 1942 that every Allied commando captured by German forces was to be killed on the spot, whether in uniform or not. By Christmas 1944, the only remaining value of the Locksmith party to the Nazis seems to be for last-ditch surrender or negotiation purposes as the Allied net closes in on Hitler, the Third Reich, and Berlin.

In this living torment, the key to sanity and survival is to establish a disciplined routine for oneself. Many of the men (there are no women) learn to meditate, reliving their pre-war pasts or dreaming of the post-war future. If there is a clear window in a cell—many are so filthy that it is impossible to see out—by standing on tiptoe on the bed, it is possible to see through into the exercise yard and even sometimes to spot the sky or a bird in flight. Occasionally, the prisoners may hear a choir elsewhere in the camp practising taunting Nazi songs such as 'We are sailing to England'. Most inmates exercise by walking for an hour at a time up and down the cell, but once pacing the small 2-metre (6-foot, 6-inch) by 1.5-metre (5-foot) space becomes incessant, it is often the prelude to a nervous breakdown or a suicide attempt. Staying fit, though, is critical both to survival and to countering depression; one of the few ways to leave the Zellenbau alive is to visit the camp dentist in his surgery.

Some prisoners resort to prolonged mental maths calculations, listen to well-loved music in their minds, or play chess with themselves using paper wrappings fashioned into pieces and scratching a playing board on the cell floor. Some try to learn German by memorising sections of Nazi communiques read out over the Zellenbau loudspeakers. Poetry absorbed at school consoles the more creative, both that by others and poems they make up on the spot. Some spend their days obsessively trying to acquire bits of information about the Zellenbau. On one occasion during 1944, Mike Cumberlege made an esoteric request to be allowed a wood-carving knife to pass the time. The request reached Dr Otto Reichel who worked in the *Ausland* (abroad) International Law department of the *Abwehr* (German military intelligence). Reichel, who was aware that Cumberlege had won the DSO, regarded him as a 'man of distinction' and thought that the request should be granted. Whether it was or not is unknown.

A variety of guards, mostly men unfit for military service, rule every prisoner's life. Some hate Sachsenhausen and sneak favours, like cigarettes, to the prisoners, but many others revel in the sheer brutality and corruption of the Zellenbau. Chief among the persecutors during the 1943–45 period is the head guard, the swarthy and unreliable Kurt Eccarius—'a dour-looking drunkard of 35 who seldom smiled' as one prisoner puts it after the war. Franz Ettlinger is 'a good-looking sadist, bully, sycophant, thief, drunkard' aged twenty-seven. Josef Drexl, aged fifty, is 'an uncouth Bavarian peasant'. Five SS corporals, all in their twenties, report to Eccarius—Lux, a sadist who tortures prisoners for self-gratification, Hartman, Meyer, Schmidt, and Beck. Each of these thugs is egged on by the Camp Adjutant and Chief Executive Officer of the Zellenbau Heinrich Wessel, 'one of the most brutal of men'. He is in the habit of visiting the block for the pleasure of witnessing torture sessions, executions, and the stringing-up of prisoners on the poles in the exercise yard.

Even in this sewer, all humanity had not been lost. In 1940, Payne Best was given his own guard, a man called Paul Konig. The two become friendly and share Best's cell during daylight hours. Konig stays with Best to 1945 and convinces himself that it is his duty to improve his captive's lot. Similar to Konig are some of the orderlies known as 'trusties'—men like Paul Schröter, once a Hamburg car driver and member of the German Bible Society and a man of immense fortitude, Karl the barber, and Petski, who runs the clothing store (both Jehovah's Witnesses). Schröter was arrested for his religious beliefs in 1936 and has spent a decade at Sachsenhausen keeping alive in low-level orderly roles. After the war, he is to become a recognised 'Victim of Fascism'. These 'trusties', or some of them, also perform an important function in keeping prisoners in the Zellenbau informed to some degree about the world inside and outside their prison.

Messages between prisoners flow by a variety of methods and are largely tolerated by the guards. Bits of newspaper are thrown into a cell by someone taking exercise outside or concealed in the toilet buckets that are sometimes moved around by an orderly. Those allowed to exercise develop a way of tapping messages on the palms of their hands to other prisoners watching from their cells as they parade around the outdoor yard. Those who know Morse code use it to tap on the walls or radiators (if they have them) of their cells. As the warders' morale declines from the middle of 1944, more of a blind eye is turned to these activities, notwithstanding the continuing casual brutality. Each cell door is numbered, and in the interests of secrecy, prisoners have no names, much to the confusion of the poorly-educated guards who become muddled and give away identities to the orderlies. This information is then passed on surreptitiously.

Adding to the pressures on everyone in Sachsenhausen, the intensive Allied air campaign directed at Berlin, just half an hour away, has become a daily event by the end of 1943 as Cumberlege and his team reach the Zellenbau, and it continues through most of the year ahead, reaching a crescendo in February 1945. Gigantic firework displays can be viewed almost nightly by those outside the Zellenbau in camp huts such as Sonderlager A. High in the sky above the site, a 'remorseless' procession of heavy Allied bombers passes overhead; Sachsenhausen is on the direct approach to Berlin for Allied planes coming from the northwest and within the flak girdle around the German capital. When the Pathfinder bombing system is introduced late in 1943 by the RAF, red flares like strings of coloured balloons drop down to mark the four corners of the camp.

All the same, numerous bombs fall around Sachsenhausen, which borders a number of high-tariff targets: a Heinkel armaments factory less than 1,000 yards from the camp perimeter, the largest brick works in the world, a repair facility for SS vehicles in Germany, a depot which receives stolen property from all over Europe, and the headquarters of the Third Reich's concentration camp administrative centre. In the camp itself are two huts producing high-quality forged British banknotes—although whether the Allies know this is doubtful. Inevitably, there are casualties in the camp, notably after a big daylight raid in March 1944 when a USAF bomber is hit, jettisoning its load as it descends. Seven bombs fall into the Zellenbau exercise yard and two straddle the cells. Some raids during the dark winter nights last from 9 p.m. to 6 a.m. The main danger, though, comes from the many dud German shells that fall from the sky and from shot-down Allied aircraft. On one occasion in February 1945, an USAF parachutist lands on the parade ground in the very centre of the camp; an SS sergeant (condemned after the war) kicks him to death. For days after this raid, time bombs go off in the target area, sending nearby houses into the sky.

Air raid alarms in the Zellenbau are usually followed by the sound of running feet as the guards dive for cover. An unearthly hush follows, broken only by sirens sounding the full alarm. By the end of January 1945, Allied planes are flying over Berlin unopposed and a huge raid by the USAF at the start of February devastates the centre of the city:

> 'The Zellenbau swayed, like a ship on waves, but remained intact,' a Ukrainian inmate remembered. 'While SS troops hid in a bunker, the prisoners sat in their cages.... The roar of engines, bombings, gunfire, the howling sirens, the cries and laments of the slain and wounded mingled in such a terrible cacophony that it was harmful to damaged people, even those with the strongest nerves.'[4]

Until October 1944, when a new regime was adopted for a few months, the Zellenbau has been the main individual punishment and execution block of the huge camp. Close by the Zellenbau is a building known as the *Industriehof*, which specialises in mass murder and houses a gas chamber, gallows, a machine-gun sandpit, and a crematorium. Next to the sandpit, a three-room shooting range, known in German as a *genickschussbaracke* and disguised as an infirmary, is used for more discreet executions. Throughout 1944, sadistic guards run riot, beatings and public executions, especially of Russians, become a daily event, and the 'terrible falsetto screams' of badly-injured victims alternate day and night with the sharp crack of a pistol as another man is shot in his cell:

> 'Life is concentrated on one point' recalls a Ukrainian nationalist who was held in a cell next to Cumberlege during 1944. 'All the horrors of the bombing every day are like a psychological paradise compared to the endless sleepless nights. When a sunrise occurs, it brings some joyful hope ... but the desired outcome [release] does not come.'[5]

By Christmas 1944, the strain of eleven months' living under a constant aerial bombardment added to the ceaseless mental and physical pressure involved in surviving Sachsenhausen's toughest regime might have broken anyone. However, Cumberlege, by several contemporary accounts, remains upbeat and unbowed. At this time, the camp is experiencing a mass influx of prisoners from other concentration camps further to the east, food is in even shorter than usual supply, there has been a sharp rise in suicides in the Zellenbau and elsewhere in the camp, and many of the cells are now occupied by five men (usually SS deserters). Meanwhile, most of the original guards have slunk away under various pretexts to be replaced by nothing-to-lose, ruthless Balts of German origin. Day-to-day control of the prisoners beyond arbitrarily shooting or hanging them is beginning to end.

In retrospect, this Christmas period six years into the war in Europe is utopia compared to what was to follow over the next seventeen weeks. Only days after 25 December 1944, an intensified killing spree begins in the Zellenbau. This carnage is to continue to the day that the 30,000 plus remaining starving, ill, and emaciated prisoners are forced out of Sachsenhausen at the point of a gun by their guards on a suicidal SS-mandated death march to reach Allied lines to the west. Around 5,000 so-called 'political prisoners' liable to give testimony against their jailers or the Third Reich are murdered from the end of January on the direct orders of the head of the Gestapo (Heinrich Müller) and the head of the concentration camp system (Rudolf Höss; former commandant of Auschwitz) according to testimony later given by Kaindl at his trial in 1947. In late-February, clouds of thick smoke begin to pour out of the *kommandantur*, where all camp records are kept, for days on end. By April, the population of the Zellenbau has fallen from about 180 to thirteen. When Soviet troops enter Sachsenhausen on 22 April 1945, just 3,000 prisoners out of the total camp population are there to bear witness. None of them are from the Zellenbau.

By then, Cumberlege and his team are dead. Sometime in the February–April period, each man has been taken out of his cell to the *genickschussbaracke* and shot through the back of the neck in stark violation of the Geneva Convention and all norms concerning the treatment of POWs. Mike Cumberlege was aged thirty-nine when he was murdered. After the Second World War, he is awarded a Bar to his DSO posthumously for his courageous second attempt to destroy the Corinth Canal. No trace of his remains or personal belongings is ever found, and in the chaos of post-war, divided, and occupied Germany, it is not until November 1946 that the Admiralty feels able to inform his widow with a degree of certainty that he 'was presumed to have lost his life at the hands of the enemy … in Sachsenhausen'.

2

Childhood,
Boyhood, and Youth*

Claude Michael Bulstrode Cumberlege was born in London at 'St George, Hanover Square' on 26 October 1905 according to the official record. Since there was a well-known church but no hospital in the square, it is likely to have been a home birth. He was the first child and eldest son of Claude Lionel Cumberlege. A fast-rising lieutenant in the Royal Navy, Claude Lionel was commanding HMS *Locust* at the age of only twenty-eight; the *Locust* was a 30-knot destroyer built in 1896 by the Admiralty to counter the higher speeds of foreign warships. Mike's mother, Laetitia, was then aged no more than twenty. The couple are assumed to have married in 1904 or 1905, almost certainly in Gibraltar, but no marriage certificate or census details of them for the period survive.

Four years later, in 1909, Michael's sister, Diana, was born. Throughout their childhoods and well into the 1930s, the pair, often thrown together by circumstances, were close. Six decades after, in far-off Lima in Peru, the well-known author and traveller Patrick Leigh Fermor found himself at a dinner party sitting next to 'a character that might well have stepped out of [Anthony] Powell's novels—an Englishwoman married to a Peruvian and bearing the impressive moniker of Dona Diana de Dibos', Leigh Fermor recalled in his subsequent book *Three Letters from the Andes*: 'Suddenly I realized who she was: the sister of Mike Cumberlege, that amazing buccaneerish figure'.[1] The pair 'fell into each other's arms' joyfully remembering a man they both admired and missed greatly, even though Mike, by then, had been dead for more than a quarter of a century.

In his short life, Mike Cumberlege was to make a lasting impact like this on all who knew him. Before the Second World War, it was his sailing skills, contacts, determination, resourcefulness, good looks, and roguish charm that earned him a living and brought him wider renown. During the war, it was his almost reckless courage and determination and imagination. Underpinning it all was a well-developed self-identity and a lifelong love of poetry, music, and literature. A tribute by a friend in 1946 aptly described him as 'truly Elizabethan in character'.[2] By the time he was executed aged thirty-nine in squalid circumstances in Nazi Germany, he had experienced life many times over.

The Cumberlege family into which Mike was born is of Huguenot origin, with roots deep in the British Empire. Both his grandfather, Alexander Bulstrode Cumberlege, and his great grandfather, Bulstrode Whitelock Cumberlege, served in the British Army in India in the nineteenth century, the former commanding the 41st Native Infantry Regiment, Madras. In his mid-fifties, Alexander Bulstrode retired as a colonel, returned to England, and moved his family to East Sussex, near the sea. His son, Claude Lionel, was the only child of older parents and usually had to find his own amusements during the school holidays. Often, he would walk to the cliff above nearby Rottingdean and watch the ships that sailed past.

Aged about ten in 1887, he used a telescope to read the ships' names and once counted 150 vessels, mostly topsail schooners, brigs, barques, and barquentines (a sailing vessel with three or more masts), going up and down the English Channel in a single morning. This quickly led to unsanctioned (by his parents) rides around a nearby harbour on a boat called the *Skylark*, helmed by a Captain Collins. Soon he was helping Capt. Collins in his business. One day on Brighton beach, he bumped into his uncle, Jack, the brother of his mother, home for a break after a career at sea 'knocking around the world'. Uncle Jack was a born raconteur with vivid tales to tell of exotic far-off places in the South Pacific, around Cape Horn, and up and down the mysterious coast of China, likely to fire the imagination of any young boy. There and then, Claude Lionel was 'hooked for life by the sea and sails' and determined to pursue a maritime existence. However, he hesitated to broach such a sensitive topic with his Army-loving parents.

At the time, Uncle Jack, a Master Mariner, owned the *Josephine*, a brig of about 250 tons that carried granite cargoes. When he finally swallowed the anchor in his seventies, after the First World War, he had the *Josephine* towed out to sea from Honfleur in Normandy and sunk. Yet at the moment he bumped into his nephew, he was on the lookout for new business. Invited to lunch by his sister to meet potential clients, he 'spilled the beans' about young Claude's budding interest in the sea.[3] The die was cast, and a year or so later in 1889, aged twelve and a half, after an exam he 'scraped through' in fifty-fourth place out of the fifty-five boys accepted, Claude joined HMS *Britannia*, a wooden hulk moored on the river Dart in Devon that served as the main training establishment for future officers of the Royal Navy.

Claude Lionel Cumberlege passed out of the *Britannia* 'by the skin of [his] teeth' and would go on to become 'an exceptional, dashing, gallant and gifted shipmaster' to quote a family history during a colourful thirty-year career in the RN mostly spent in gunboats and destroyers. Rising to the rank of rear-admiral, he served with many of the leading naval figures of the pre-First World War era and met such personalities as Tsar Nicholas II of Russia, Kaiser Wilhelm of Germany, Emperor Franz Josef of Austria, and British royalty, including King Edward VII (a keen student of naval reform, he reported), Queen Alexandra, and their wayward grandson, the future Edward VIII, along the way. In his unpublished memoir, *Salt Horse*, written between 1931 and 1939 for his son by his second marriage, Mistral, he paints a vivid portrait of the life of a young RN officer before the First World War. He loved Malta and the Mediterranean (as did his son in years to come), frequently fell in love, learnt to play polo to a high standard in Gibraltar, and displayed an enviable ability (again like his son) to make friends wherever he went—from the captain of a tramp steamer in the Suez Canal to an Indian nobleman, the despised Irish in Berehaven, the Crown Prince of Greece, and many Cretans after his ship, the *Halcyon*, was involved in a British-led initiative to drive the Turks off the island in 1895–96.

He frequently sailed close to the wind, learning quickly how to swindle RN dockyard stores of essential equipment like paint to supply his various ships and marching his crew on one occasion straight to a pub in Devon after a three-year spell outside England. Another time, he rashly answered his commander back and was about to be disciplined when a friend told him about an opening to command the Gibraltar Torpedo Boats, a force of nine small vessels and twenty-one crew. He fired off an application direct to the Admiralty, despite his junior status, which amused the Second Sea Lord and landed him the plum job—his first command, aged twenty-five. His insubordination was overlooked. Later, he rammed one of his torpedo boats into a breakwater outside Gibraltar, faced a court of enquiry, and was exonerated. Soon after, he turned up in Tangiers on unofficial business visiting the 'uncrowned King of Morocco', the British representative Sir Harry Maclean, and 'nosing about the African shore'.

Sometime in 1904, he married Sarah Laetitia Crossley Couldwell, who was aged about twenty or twenty-one to his twenty-seven. In his voluminous memoirs stretching over 1,000 pages, he devotes a single paragraph to this event:

> But let's get back to Gibraltar. I fell in love, got married and lived happily ever afterwards. Only the 'Man with the Scythe' put an all-too early end to a union which otherwise would have been indissoluble except for the temporary vagaries and 'exigencies' normal to a Naval career.[4]

Little is known about Laetitia except for her beauty; she was to die in a Paris hospital in 1929. Being charitable, one could say that Claude's reference is highly selective. The couple were frequently apart, often for years at a time. Claude played away and had a number of irregular liaisons. He was also restless and ambitious. Good-looking and never entirely happy to abide by the Royal

Navy's voluminous rule-book (he confesses in his memoirs that he never read them), he was always seeking new career and social opportunities regardless of his growing family. In 1910, he was seduced by the wife of an industrialist while on three months' leave: 'I, who had been married for seven years and who never, never once had looked outside my wedding ring. Well, there it was, and there was nothing to be done about it.'[5] By mid-1911, aged thirty-four, with two young children to support, a pied-à-terre in London to sustain, and a private income equivalent to £33,000 a year today, he was commanding destroyers (HMS *Kale*, where he was faulted for losing confidential documents, and HMS *Fury*) based in Scotland and, in his own words, 'more than willing to take up a job anywhere in the world rather than in Home waters'.

One day, Claude got wind of a new destroyer capable of speeds up to 37 knots about to be completed at the Yarrow shipyard on the Clyde. Somehow obtaining an interview with the Second Sea Lord—an old friend—at the Admiralty, he persuaded the friend to give him the command of the new vessel, to be called HMS *Lurcher*.[6] Some twelve months later, in October 1913, the *Lurcher* was idling in the Firth of Clyde. No exercises were planned. Claude, with his notoriously low boredom threshold—'impatient with fools, lazy when not interested' ran one of his confidential reports—decided to invite Alfred (later Sir Alfred) Yarrow on board for a good lunch and a demonstration of the ship's speed and prowess. Yarrow was unable to attend but sent his son, daughter-in-law, and the chief constructor Mr Mariner instead. The afternoon went well and Yarrow later told Claude that it was the first time in the history of the firm that any member of it had been on board one of their own-built ships after she had left their hands. It was typical Claude: generous, gregarious, a bit of a show-off, and ever-restless.

Not long after this episode, he was to take an impulsive decision, which was to colour his relationship with his wife, son, and daughter for years to come. One evening, his first-lieutenant in the *Lurcher* was opening the weekly Admiralty orders when he spotted something and pushed them across the table to Cumberlege with the remark: 'Sir, this might suit you'.[7] Claude read that the Australian government was looking for an RN Commander to go out and organise its new Destroyer Flotilla: 'only Commanders with Destroyer experience need apply'. Not pausing to consider the implications, he immediately fired off an application by telegram. Others wrote letters. He got the job and so began a rewarding, near-seven-year involvement with Australia that he never regretted. Just a couple of weeks later, aged thirty-six and with no reference in his memoir to his wife or children, he boarded the liner *Orontes* of the Orient Line and made a relaxing five-week voyage through the Suez Canal and across the Indian Ocean to Fremantle and Port Adelaide. On 7 November 1913, he officially joined the fast-expanding Royal Australian Navy (RAN), which had only been formed two years earlier, on loan from the RN.

In mid-December, Claude assumed command of HMAS *Warrego*, a 700-ton destroyer. 'By temperament and personality, he was well suited to destroyer command' and particularly to the unstuffy Australian Navy according to a contemporary account of the RAN by R. S. Veale:

> He was handsome, unconventional, dashing and breezy, and his courage, initiative and lack of 'frill' inspired respect and affection among the egalitarian-minded Aussies. He expressed himself in very direct language and his letters and written reports were always precise and succinct.

He also began as he meant to go on: arriving in Melbourne, he went to a ball and spirited a willing girl back to her bedroom only to be disturbed by her parents.[8]

When war broke out in Europe eight months later, an Australian Naval and Military Expeditionary Force was quickly formed, after a request from London, with the intention of destroying German garrisons in New Britain and the Caroline Islands in the Pacific.[9] The *Warrego* took part in the first Australian military operation of the war, successfully landing assault parties at Kaba Kaul, New Britain, in August 1914 and helping to destroy a German wireless station. The very first Australian (of about 60,000) to die in the First World War, Captain Brian Pockley of the Army Medical Corps then attached to the RAN Naval Reserve, lost his life in this action tending to a wounded man. For his part, Claude was commended for decisive leadership having, against orders, despatched sixty men from the *Warrego* to reinforce a landing party held up by an ambush. In the words of the official history of the RAN 1914–18 written by A. W. Jose in the 1920s: 'The coolness and level-headedness of every man engaged, in the first fight in which Australian naval forces had ever taken part, was a noteworthy and excellent omen for the later work of the war'. The *Warrego* under Cumberlege's command later steamed safely 200 miles up the Sepik river into 'really savage New Guinea', searching for a German warship suspected of hiding away in the dense foliage on the water's edge and waiting to pounce—'the most interesting voyage I ever had,' he recalled in his memoirs.[10]

The following year, Claude was promoted to captain at the age of thirty-eight—young for the era. For the rest of the First World War, he spent most of his time with the RAN chasing German shipping shadows in the Pacific and Indian Oceans. Among his commands was the light cruiser HMAS *Brisbane*, the first man-of-war ever built in Australia. In the *Brisbane*, he averted, through some quick thinking, sabotage by striking 'Wobblies' (members of the Industrial Workers of the World revolutionary movement) who were trying to prevent the ship sailing from Sydney, patrolled across the Indian Ocean, and ventured to the Mediterranean in 1916 for a three-month refit in Malta. Here he failed to make contact with his wife (whom he had not seen since

1913) after his letters and signals to her were intercepted by RN censors who 'wanted to curtail, probably with good reason, the coming and going of non-combatants, especially women'.[11] Mike, ironically, was to run into a similar bureaucratic roadblock in Egypt in 1941.

On shore in Australia, Claude set a fast pace and filled in his free time, so family lore has it, by having an affair with the internationally-famous Australian opera diva Dame Nellie Melba.[12] If that is so, there is no mention of this in his memoirs. He was somewhere in the Red Sea on 11 November 1918 when an armistice ended the First World War—1,000 miles or more from land as he had been when war was declared in 1914. He was then ordered to Constantinople to assist in the Allied dismemberment of the Ottoman Empire. Sent on to England in April 1919, the *Brisbane* sailed to Portsmouth in England for a long refit and Claude returned to his 'native heath' and saw his family for the first time in more than five years. By then, his son was thirteen and preparing to embark on a nautical career of his own.

He did not tarry long in England, however, having accepted the position of Flag Captain and Chief of Staff in the elderly battlecruiser HMAS *Australia*, also then in UK waters. Never a happy ship, in the immediate post-war world, the *Australia* seethed with lower deck unrest over pay, leave, and discipline stirred up by what Claude called 'F.I.Fs'—'Fuck it, I've finished'—enlisted lower deck men near the end of their war service. Claude's senior on board, Commodore John Dumaresq, was his polar opposite—orthodox, a teetotaller, policy-driven, and a small man of 'unrelenting principles'. By contrast, Claude, a sun-lover and *bon viveur*, was in the habit when in port of appearing on the quarter deck of the *Australia* in a slip on his way to his galley to picnic ashore in the sun. Despite this, Dumaresq intrigued Claude and the odd couple worked well together for the next two-and-a-half years.

Finessing the crew issues in the *Australia* proved trickier. Claude took command for the return voyage to Australia. A dispute over pay on arrival in Port Said was settled with some deftness, but by the time the ship reached Fremantle in Western Australia, leave ashore had become a burning topic. This flared into a full-blown confrontation over the *Australia*'s departure time for Port Adelaide. Again, Claude resolved the situation with firm but low-key actions, including confronting the 1,000-strong crew directly after a posse of masked men entered the engine room and terrorised the stokers. The ship cast off from Fremantle an hour behind schedule. Later that day, Claude reassembled the ship's company and read it the Articles of War, but refused to call the incident a mutiny while disciplining thirty-two men in various ways. The RAN hierarchy, influenced by policy and Dumaresq, took a different view. A Court Martial was convened in June 1919 in which Claude had to prosecute: five ring leaders were charged with joining in a mutiny, three were sentenced to jail despite Claude taking the stand to testify on behalf of one of the accused, and all five were dismissed from the RAN. Before long, a heated debate took place in the Australian parliament about the affair, and the prison sentences were remitted on account of the youth of the prisoners. This led to the two senior Court Martial Flag Officers, but not Claude, submitting their resignations—the only such occurrence recorded in the history of the RAN (the resignations were withdrawn later).[13]

'Not strict enough in matters of minor discipline' ran a perceptive note on Claude's service record in July 1913, and perhaps this gives one clue to the *Australia* incident. He regarded the episode as 'no more than a sort of schoolboy escapade' caused by vanity and the mood prevailing on the lower deck at the end of a long war. Shortly after the prisoners' release, he was walking along Elizabeth Street in Sydney when he bumped into the key ringleader. 'We stepped inside [a pub] and "stopped a couple"'.[14] It was characteristic Claude, always his own man. He remained with the RAN for another three years. In May 1920, he hosted a visit to the *Australia* by the Prince of Wales, who was touring the country on behalf of King George V to thank Australians for their sacrifices during the war. Shortly after, he was appointed Flag Captain of HMAS *Melbourne*—from 1920, the flagship of the RAN—again under Dumaresq who, by then, was dying of a lung disease.

Claude's domestic arrangements in this period take some unravelling. During much of the war, Laetitia had a job, joining the Women's Royal Air Force in June 1918, aged thirty-two, in an administrative capacity at Hurst Park.[15] The next year, in August 1919, she and daughter Diana sailed to Australia in the SS *Anchises* and moved in to a married quarter in Sydney.[16] How long they remained there is not clear, but in the autumn of 1920, Diana, aged ten or eleven, entered a boarding school for girls in Sussex. Mike, meantime, after attending a prep school in Somerset, had joined the Nautical College, Pangbourne, in September 1919 aged almost fourteen and become a cadet in the Royal Naval Reserve. Nearly three years later, in July 1922, when Claude finally left the RAN, he returned to the UK, was promoted to rear-admiral, and placed on the RN retired list at his own request. In 1926, he retired formally at the age of fifty. With a brief interlude around Christmas 1918, he had not lived in England with his wife and children for more than seven years.

At the school in Sussex, Mike for the first time encountered two spinsters, known in the family as Aunt Gwen and Aunt Gladys, who were to remain influential in his life to the end. Both were 'characters' and Mike became one of four boys that Aunt Gwen, in particular, always thought of as her extended clan. In a letter about Mike to his wife, Nancy, after he had been captured by the Germans in 1943, she wrote at length about his background and character at this young age. 'He was a most lovable person, of an inquiring mind, yet upholding his dignity,' she began. Apparently, he preferred to stay with his paternal grandmother who spoilt him rather than his maternal grandparents at Littlestone 'where every day he was made to pick the sweet peas and to wear a tunic and a hat with ribbons hanging behind—"girls' clothes" he called them'. Grandmother Cumberlege, according to Aunt Gwen, was 'a splendid character and instilled much that was good in Mike'. Aged six, he once transfixed a lunch party of elderly relatives by talking knowledgeably, 'without any priggishness about the Shaftesbury Homes for poor boys'—a subject he had come across:

> Mike was always like that if he knew about something. He always expressed himself so well. At school, they said he was not clever, but I have always thought him so, especially if he was interested in his subject. He will not let go—there is much of the British bull dog in him.[17]

The choice of the Nautical College, Pangbourne, for Mike's secondary education must have been random. The school had only been founded in 1917 when his father was away on active service on the other side of the world.[18] Its roots were in the clipper era when its founder, Sir Thomas Devitt, owned a shipping line that ran twenty-nine full-rigged ships and barques on the Australia run. Always keen on improving officer training in the mercantile marine, Sir Thomas and a friend, the Liberal peer Lord Brassey, also sponsored the Ocean Training Scheme that ran from 1890 to the start of the First World War. At this point, with both vessels in the scheme requisitioned by the government, Sir Thomas decided to set up a shore establishment to offer nautical training. Eventually, he settled on a site in rural Berkshire far from the sea and high above the Thames valley, albeit with a good river frontage on the Thames. Many of the early entrants had failed to get into the Royal Naval College at Dartmouth and were using Pangbourne as a backdoor route into the RN through its RNR designation. Mike may have been one of them. Given his father's career and dominant personality, it was perhaps no surprise that he wanted to follow him to sea, but no records survive to prove this one way or the other.

In those days, education at Pangbourne was, at best, rudimentary. Each entry of cadets was grouped in a single term and class regardless of age or ability. A limited curriculum was based on practical nautical subjects such as signals, seamanship, and navigation. More academic subjects like arithmetic and physics were taught with a specifically nautical bias; the main history textbook in use was titled *The Sea Kings of Britain*, while divinity was based on the *Voyages of St. Paul*. Sport, especially rugby and boxing, soon assumed a central part in the quasi-naval routine. This began promptly at 6.30 a.m. with one of the two lower-deck instructors turning the boys out of their hammocks with shouts of 'Heave out! Lash up and stow!' Each day was dominated by bugle calls and parades.

Mike made good progress in this character-forming environment, winning the school geography prize in 1921 and shining on the rugby field. 'He is full of vigour, is not afraid of hard knocks and is a really fine tackler,' ran a report in *The Log* (a school magazine) for spring term 1921. 'In his case, it is desirable that a little more thought and intelligence be brought to bear'. Two terms later, he is described as 'the best man in the line out'. In the summer term of 1921, he was promoted to Cadet Captain (prefect), leaving the college a year later.

In the holidays, with his father abroad, Mike sometimes spent weeks at Chilgrove Manor in Sussex, the girl's school run by Aunt Gladys and Aunt Gwen. Diana was boarding here and Mike, in his smart naval uniform, quickly became the object of many schoolgirl crushes. 'He was much loved by the younger girls as he played games with them and read them stories' remembered a family acquaintance, Ben Strickland, whose mother, Barbara (then Lamb), led Mike's troupe of admirers and remained a friend of Diana's for life. Another young admirer, Pam Hoare, recalled Mike returning to Chilgrove in his teens as 'something of a heroic figure'.[19] By a quirk of fate, Mike's seven-year old son, Marcus, was sent by his widowed mother, Nancy, to these same (now aging) spinsters for a year in 1945. Aunt Gwen, sporting a huge goitre on her neck, played the piano and taught Marcus to sing the official song of the Royal Navy (and the RAN at that time): 'Heart of Oak are our ships, Jolly Tars are our men, We always are ready: Steady, boys, Steady! We'll fight and we'll conquer again and again'. She had probably taught the same words to Mike a generation earlier and he would surely have remembered them in times of adversity to come. A family story actually has him singing aloud 'Land of Hope and Glory' in the streets of Athens as the invading Germans arrived in 1941. In this case, Pangbourne seems likelier to have drummed in the words and tune to a teenager than Aunt Gwen.

Throughout his life, Mike kept in touch with his Pangbourne contemporaries, attended several of the annual Old Pangbournian Society dinners in London, and made a number of contributions to *The Log*. This practice had begun while he was still at the school. In 1921–22, in the section 'Contributions from Cadets', he penned a whimsical, slightly subversive, tongue-in-cheek piece titled 'A Polite Complaint Addressed To The Editors Of Diaries':

My grievance is that the modern diary is becoming increasingly monotonous year by year. I feel and know that we are all bored stiff with the fact that on Tuesday, the 'umpteenth' Josiah Wedgewood, painter, died and that on October the' nth' Fire Insurance Policies expire. No doubt both of these historical facts are true, but who cares? Why not, I suggest, brighten up our school diaries or are we too conservative for such a trivial move? [Mike's suggested alternatives?] Why not be sensible and fill our diaries with facts concerning the more renowned murders, more vital information and the more dramatic films? The modern young man would be enthralled.

Mike would write punchily and vividly all his life, particularly poetry. Mostly, he was self-taught, soaking up interests and experiences like a thirsty man finding water in the desert. Along with this questing spirit, his artistic side was never far from the surface. It was typified by an almost fanatical love of classical music, particularly loud tenor opera arias sung by the likes of Enrico Caruso and Beniamino Gigli, Beethoven and Mozart piano concertos conducted by Sir Thomas Beecham, and the 1930s songs of best-selling French *chansonniers* of the day such as the Corsican Tino Rossi ('*Il existe une blonde*').

By the time he was twenty-five years old, Mike spoke fluent French and passable Spanish. He had a camera with him wherever he went and took many photographs to prove it. Never one to suffer fools gladly, yet with a real gift for making lasting friendships, his robust sense of humour was notorious. From time to time, it came through in verse such as 'Ode To My Best Friend's Nose', which he wrote mockingly in the early 1930s about an unknown acquaintance. As he grew older, he also became an expert on wild flowers, pressing rare specimens between the pages of his book of Byron's verses (a particular favourite whom he loved to quote), and learning carpentry and other skills associated with boat-building. In his thirties, all things Greek—literature, culture, archaeology, history—captivated him.

Just as his father was finally returning to Europe in the summer of 1922, however, Mike was flying the nest, such as it was, and beginning his own journey through life. That July, aged almost seventeen, he left Pangbourne. To gain a nautical qualification, he decided to join the Merchant Navy as many of his school contemporaries were doing. At the start of November, he signed on as an 'indentured apprentice' with Geo. Thompson & Co. Ltd, owners of the Aberdeen Line. His total pay was £48 (£2,100 today). During the next three years, he sailed all over the world with a number of vessels, including the SS *Euripedes* (a 15,000-ton steamship that carried 1,100 passengers, mostly from Europe to Australia) and SS *Zeeland*, another medium-sized passenger steamship. In November 1925, right at the end of his apprenticeship, he is recorded in a New York Crew List as landing there in the *Zeeland*. In the crew manifest, his age is given as twenty, he is recorded as having spent four years at sea, his port of departure is entered as Antwerp, Belgium, his position is Able Seaman, his weight is 145 lb (10 stone 5 lb), and his height is 5 feet 6 inches. A few years later, his passport gives his height as 5 feet 11 inches.

This kind of monotonous, low-level, circumscribed existence, mostly spent far away from friends in the solitariness of the world's oceans doing mundane work, was never going to satisfy a young man as keen as Michael Cumberlege on sampling fully what life had to offer. In his memoirs, his father, a shrewd judge of character, expands on this theme:

> The life of a 'cadet' on board a large passenger and cargo-carrying steam ship is not too hard a one, but it is not exactly the sort of life they had expected it to be…. The greater part of their work was similar to that of an ordinary seaman and consisted largely in scrubbing decks and cleaning paintwork or hogging out boats.

According to Mike, no attempt was made to give the cadets instruction in navigation. The young chaps (there were six of them in Mike's ship) came to regard themselves as belonging to the forecastle rather than as 'young officers ... the result was that the average cadet had not much affection for his superiors and developed rather a "bolshie" outlook towards them'.[20]

At the end of 1925, after several voyages to Australia and back, he left the Aberdeen Line and 'put in some time in a Belgian fishing trawler in the North Atlantic and obtained his [2nd Mate's] certificate early this year [1926]' according to a school friend who met him and reported back to *The Log*. The friend added: 'He [Mike] is now looking forward to a year or more of adventure, going around the world in a sailing yacht, accompanied by a cinema camera'. The real situation was rather different. Mike had, indeed, put in time on a Belgian boat in 1926–27. However, it was not on a trawler but on a former Ostend pilot boat—'all oak and teak and copper [with] lovely lines'—acquired for £170 (£6,850 today) in 1924 at an auction in Ostend by his father—so like his son in his quixotic lifestyle choices and, by then, apparently separated from his wife—with a view to making it his floating home in retirement.

Mike seems to have volunteered himself as the first member of the crew. For ever after, he called his father 'Skipper'. Claude was not at all sure this enlistment was a good idea:

> I didn't think the arrangement would work as he had practically never before been under my control. Also, I was rather under the impression that the admirable training and discipline of Pangbourne Nautical College, where he had passed a couple of years, went for very little onboard the merchant vessels the young fellows [from the NCP] found themselves in on going to sea.[21]

According to his father, Mike arrived 'a perfect young Hercules at the age of about nineteen [in fact, he had turned twenty], with hands like hams, an inside knowledge of paintwork, a dislike of authority and a book on Impressionist art'. Soon after, the Admiral acquired a second crewmember, a young man called Raymond who got on 'famously' with his son 'both being thorough "bolshies" although, *au fond* [at bottom] thoroughly loyal to the ship'. The *L'Insoumise* (*The Unruly*), as Admiral Cumberlege had renamed his refitted ketch, was preparing to leave Ostend harbour when three American destroyers passed close to the boat and the Skipper ordered Mike to dip the *L'Insoumise*'s red ensign. The US vessels took no notice.

That night, Mike and Raymond dragged a huge wicker fish basket over the stern of the *L'Insoumise* and into a dinghy. Next morning, the admiral came on deck early and saw one of the destroyer's company on the forecastle and bridge of the ship gazing up at its topmast head, on which hung a dirty old basket. In his words: 'I held a dictator's court martial there and then'.

Mike's response was typical of his youthful brashness: 'Well, Dad, they either hadn't the decency to answer our salute or else they kept a damned bad look-out. So we thought we would make sure which it was'. Mike had shinned up a boat hook, hooked into a scuttle, and hoisted the huge receptacle to the masthead by signal halliards. Not content with this, he had then climbed up the rigging and lashed the basket securely so that it was impossible to lower from the deck. Afterwards, he slipped down to the deck and over the side into the dinghy where Raymond sat waiting. The admiral made the two of them stay on board for the four days the destroyers remained in port in case they were recognised, but nothing happened.

For the first voyage under the admiral's command, the plan was for the *L'Insoumise* to go from Ostend along the northern French coast to Dieppe. Here, Raymond left at his own request as life aboard 'had not come up to his expectations'. The objective was to go down the Bay of Biscay to the French–Spanish border in southwest France, but to do that more crew were needed. A vivid portrait of this trip was written in 1941 by Ella Maillart, the well-known Swiss explorer who accompanied the adventurer Peter Fleming across China in 1935, in her book *Gypsy Afloat*. Maillart had met the Skipper and daughter, Diana, on a skiing holiday in Megeve in 1926. She was trying to earn a living sailing. The admiral suddenly remembered her and signed her up to crew for him on the voyage south to Gibraltar and after that, he hinted, maybe on to the Pacific Islands. 'The climate of England and the narrow-mindedness of his compatriots were enough to send him away from home,' she wrote—a familiar theme the admiral echoes in his memoir with special reference to the rain in England and the snobbery he encountered in Henley-on-Thames where he rented a cottage in 1922.

Maillart joined the *L'Insoumise* in Newhaven and soon became chums with the teenage Diana. Mike, on board for this part of the trip, is described as 'a strong lad [who] was worth two men'. He did most of the helming, Diana took care of the shopping and catering, and Maillart helped with the sailing and also kept the ketch clean and tidy. Meantime, the admiral—'a tall, grey-haired [man] with steel-blue eyes in the middle of a sun-burnt, deeply lined face'—held court in the spacious saloon regaling anyone who would listen with stories of his time in Australia and along the coast of the former German colonies in the Pacific. As Maillart puts it: 'He was completely detached from the minor details of domestic organisation' on board. Mike left the *L'Insoumise* not long after to return to sea with the Clan Line in order to get his Second Mate's ticket. The admiral then changed course and moved *L'Insoumise* to a new temporary base at Southwick, near Shoreham.

Later that year Maillart received a second summons from Claude to join the ketch on a voyage from Plymouth to Spain. This one was carrying two rather grumpy paying guests; money was never plentiful on the *L'Insoumise*. Her job was to cook. Mike was absent, staying with his grandmother.

[Maillart shared a cabin with] the lovely Diana [and was] impressed by the calm of her smooth forehead. She had a delicate chin, cheeks like peaches and dark blue eyes under wide-set eyebrows. Her Eton crop [hairstyle] and her small upturned nose were most attractive. She is the most reserved person I have ever met. I suppose her youth must have been very lonely, as her mother was abroad all the time and her father only came home at wide intervals ... she was completely self-sufficient mentally and enjoyed being alone.[22]

In Saint-Jean-de-Luz, where the *L'Insoumise* came to rest for the summer months, the admiral seduced a young French girl called Melanie while 'dozens' of South Americans swarmed around Diana like wasps at a jampot: 'I trusted Di, aged 17, to innumerable *señors* and their high speed Bugattis. You can't drive a Bugatti at 60 miles an hour and make love, I figured'. Claude misjudged the situation and Diana fell for 'a young Spaniard—nothing to look at, but as sound as a bell' and wanted to marry him. The admiral demurred and tried to educate Diana to the facts of life over a glass or two of champagne—without success. 'I shall do exactly as I please with my own body,' she responded tartly. Maillart—'a lovely girl physically'—proved to be an awful cook and was not too good at tidying up either. The paying guests complained constantly. Eventually, in October 1927, the *L'Insoumise* moved to an anchorage on the river Adour close to Bayonne. The guests left for home and Ella Maillart was put on a train by the admiral with the immortal words: 'Farewell, Ella. I hope one of these days you will come back as my honoured guest, but never again as my cook!'

Mike was to return to the admiral, Diana, and the *L'Insoumise*, off and on, for years to come. In the spring of 1929, Claude records that 'he re-joined, a new man. A couple of years tramping right round the world had made him see things in more reason. He was charming, and such a seaman'.[23] It was decided to leave south-west France that summer and venture to Gibraltar and the Mediterranean. In a thunderstorm off the dangerous Cape Finisterre, it was Mike who saved the day when a vast topmast staysail broke loose and the *L'Insoumise* was heading for the rocks: 'Fighting like a tiger, he was able to wrap it [the sail] round and about, having been hoisted up to the topmast head in a boatswain's chair'. Reaching Portugal, Mike then made a detour in Cintra—so characteristic of his behaviour in years to come in the Aegean—in order 'to spend hours in the lovely places where Vasco de Gama, Prince Henry and Juana the Loca rest in peace'.

---

*From Tolstoy's trilogy

3

'Oh,
I Shall Buy a Sailboat'*

Four very different boats—the *Kinkajou*, the *Lady Beatrice*, the *Jolie Brise*, and the *Landfall*—book-ended Mike's existence in the 1930s, a decade during which his mother died, he married, rented a house, fathered a son, and acquired a stepmother, two stepsisters, and a stepbrother. For much of this time, he was an itinerant gun-for-hire, seeking employment and satisfaction where he could from sailing and yachts and the sea. When he turned thirty-four in October 1939, he remarked in a letter to one of his patrons that his father, by then a crusty, rather self-assured retired admiral, 'considered I might be worth knowing when I reached this salubrious state. I don't feel any more worth knowing, rather less in fact.'[1]

It was a rare moment of doubt and introspection. The Second World War had broken out in Europe and Mike was idling life away in the Cape Verde islands in growing frustration. During the 1930s, although often short of money and sometimes forced back to his father's latest home afloat for a refuge, he was never short of friends, projects, challenges, and new goals: Author Robin Bryer wrote:

> Yachts were his life, having been brought up with them. Unable to afford the sort of boats he would like to own, he had taken to skippering—largely in the Mediterranean and, chiefly, for American owners. As such, he was one of the fore-runners of the gentlemen skippers of today. In the 1920s a gentleman's son would not have become a yacht's skipper, but these were the 1930s. An attractive Englishman, with a good background, could take on what had normally been regarded as a servant's job with increasing ease, particularly when his master was American.[2]

The choice of wealthy American backers owed a lot to chance, and to the admiral's vast network of connections, but Americans also complemented Mike's can-do, call-a-spade-a-spade temperament. The link had begun at a party on the *L'Insoumise* held by the admiral in Gibraltar early in November 1929, following a couple of years during which, by the flimsy accounts that exist, Mike had travelled on a square rigger to Australia, working as he went at anything which arose to make ends meet. In Hamburg, he frequented the red-light district of St Pauli, once describing it as 'the haunt of my lost youth— the wine, the beer, the women, the songs, the shouting and, oh my god, the awful rigour!'[3]

Mike's mother, Laetitia, had died of breast cancer at the end of June that year at the age of forty-three in a Paris hospital. At the *L'Insoumise* party, Mike met a wealthy American named Leonard Outhwaite, at that point engaged in a circumnavigation of the Atlantic Ocean in his yacht *Kinkajou*. In Outhwaite's words in his 1931 book *Atlantic Circle*:

> We met the Cumberleges aboard their picturesque yacht *L'Insoumise*, a converted Belgian pilot vessel.... The upshot of visits back and forth, and a number of pleasant parties, was that Michael begged to sail with us on *Kinkajou*. So it was decided that on some convenient day we would all sail together.[4]

The first objective was to reach Dakar in Senegal, West Africa, via Madeira and the Canary Islands. Outhwaite was accompanied on this leg by two young Englishmen making a similar voyage in a smaller 40-foot yacht called *Daydream II*. One of the two, John Campbell, was later to work hand-in-glove with Mike in the caïque *Hedgehog* during the Second World War in para-naval operations in the eastern Mediterranean. 'They were very dissimilar in character,' a mutual friend, Xan Fielding, recalled after the war. 'John spoke in monosyllables; Mike's conversation was robust.'[5]

Outhwaite, a well-to-do anthropologist and staff member of the Rockefeller Foundation, had taken a year's leave of absence. To coverage in *The New York Times*, he departed New York with his wife, Georgia, who had never sailed before, for Cowes on the Isle of Wight at the end of June 1929. By the time the *Kinkajou* reached Gibraltar five months later, he had lost two captains (one to drowning in Cowes harbour), survived gales in the Bay of Biscay, and a series of crew manning problems. The *Kinkajou*, however, proved to be sturdily dependable—90 feet overall with a steel black hull, a 10-foot draught, a reliable diesel engine, two double cabins for the owners, and berths for four crew.

Mike, then twenty-four years old, occupied an anomalous position somewhere between Captain Ingpen and the owner. At first, he was responsible mostly for navigation. Off Morocco and still new to the vessel, he was 'inclined to be ill though he sets about his work with as good a grace as possible'. Between Casablanca and the Canary Islands, he was jauntily hailing Campbell and Outhwaite (who had joined the *Daydream* for a day or two) from the deck of the *Kinkajou* to say that he had sighted a whale and passed close to it as it lay sleeping. The 700 miles from Tenerife to Dakar was completed in four and a half days in warm, breezy weather. On 16 December 1929, the *Kinkajou* rounded the Cape Verde islands passing Yof and N'Gor; little can Mike have imagined that eleven years later, he would be stuck on these remote volcanic outcrops as war raged on the European continent.

The saga of the *Kinkajou*'s errant cook was one that Mike would dine out on for years to come. In Gibraltar, the British cook who had sailed from England funked the job and started back for Southampton. The yacht left for Casablanca without a cook. There, a man called Tony was recruited from a seaman's hostel. He was said to be Italian but spoke little Italian and no French, German, English, or Spanish. 'It turned out,' recalled Outhwaite in his book, 'that cooking was a mystery to him. A galley was as strange to him as a bathroom to a Berber.' He had gone along for the ride and was promptly shipped back to Gibraltar from Madeira. His replacement, Juan, was unearthed in Funchal; he had cooked before on South African Railways, spoke some English, and did an adequate job all the way to America.

Captain Ingpen left the *Kinkajou* when she reached Dakar, and for the rest of the voyage, Mike shared helming duties with Outhwaite and did all the navigation using the stars and his sextant. Dakar, over the Christmas period, involved a lively time for the young Englishman that revealed several characteristics that feature strongly in his future life—pugnacity, resourcefulness, and a willingness to take risks. First, though, on the advice of the French pilot who brought the *Kinkajou* into Dakar harbour and had noticed his sun-bleached hair, he acquired some unusual headgear—a light, white sun helmet built up of cork or pith with a visor in the back and front to protect the face and neck. Each day, he lunched at one of the sidewalk cafes in *La Place Protet* (today's Independence Square).

Outhwaite became chummy with the overworked American Consul General George Cobb, who invited him and others, including Mike, to join him for dinner on Christmas Day. On Christmas Eve, the crew, after a boozy lunch and having been paid by the owner, wanted to go ashore that evening. Outhwaite refused the request, causing much muttering. Next day, with shouting erupting among the angry crew, Outhwaite decided to stay on board and sent his wife and Mike to the Consul General's alone. Mike 'later returned with four or five men from the dinner party. I was certainly glad to see them,' he wrote. Things calmed down, and Outhwaite decided to go to the party himself and leave Mike in his dinner jacket in charge on board.

In the middle of the dinner, Mike 'turned up in informal attire, bursting with news'. One of the crew had attempted to take the *Kinkajou*'s launch ashore. Mike warned him off 'and then landed a few rights and lefts while another crew member tried to kick his shins'. In the scuffle, Mike and the seaman went overboard. The seaman was unable to swim so Mike fished him out of the harbour into the launch, sent him to bed, and tried to get aboard himself to put on some dry clothes. The crew delighted in his predicament and resisted, and 'for a time Mike was dashing about the harbour in no attire at all'. Finally, he sneaked aboard, got some fresh clothes, and, with the aid of the launch boy, came ashore. The chief offender, in his bunk nursing a black eye and sore head, was paid off the next day.

After this rumpus, the voyage to Barbados proceeded uneventfully except that the main sail was carried away in the middle of the Atlantic while Mike was helming—worn out by chafing. Undeterred, the *Kinkajou* sailed on and reached Barbados 'on the dot' thanks to Mike's impeccable navigation on 9 January 1930 after fourteen days and 2,534 miles at sea. The next excitement came a month later when the *Kinkajou* anchored off the southern part of Martinique as a major eruption of Mt Pelé took place. Outhwaite and Mike, with his camera (almost all the photos in *Atlantic Circle* are taken by him), decided to climb to the edge of the crater with a local guide. They got within a few hundred yards of the centre of the eruption before turning back: 'Our eyes swept over a scene such as comes to few men in the course of a lifetime'.

The rest of this epic adventure passed off peacefully, although the *Kinkajou* did run aground off Cat Island near Nassau in the Bahamas. Soon after, Mike was laid low with an ulcerated tooth that involved an emergency detour to a dentist in Miami, Florida. In Jacksonville, the crew was paid off, but Mike, by now a lifelong 'shipmate' of the thirty-eight-year old Outhwaite, remained on board, repainting the *Kinkajou* from stem to stern in St Augustine. He was then present when the yacht reached New York, to laudatory coverage in *The New York Times*, on 7 June 1930, after a passage of 14,000 miles just under one year since she had departed for England and seven months since Mike joined up in Gibraltar. Mr and Mrs Outhwaite divorced within a year or two and the *Kinkajou* was sold.

Mike continued to look for paid sailing opportunities where he could during the next three years, but the only clear record extant today of that period concerns his service in the Royal Naval Reserve. He had joined automatically as a Cadet RNR on going to the Nautical College, Pangbourne, in 1919. When he left Pangbourne in 1922, he voluntarily signed on as a Midshipman RNR, and for the next fifteen years, he did training spells of three or four weeks at a time most years, being promoted to Lieutenant RNR in July 1933. Much of his training was on cruisers and destroyers, but he also did two turns in HMS *Victory* in Portsmouth Harbour and four months from July–November 1933 in the battleship *Royal Sovereign*, then based in Malta. The 1933–34 period seems to have been his most demanding in the Navy as he served a total of twenty-six weeks on training stints, most of them afloat.

His reports and pay record, carefully preserved by the Admiralty, reveal a conscientious young officer with good all-round skills. The first, by a J. A. Casement, written after his time as a seventeen-year-old in the cruiser *Courageous* in 1922, concluded that he was 'above average. Good power of command; good physique. Likely to make an efficient officer. Recommended for promotion. A good type but somewhat lacking in zeal'. In 1929, still hedging his bets on a parallel track subsidised by the Board of Trade, he obtained his First Mate's certificate. Six years later, his failure to continue working for a Master's Certificate in the Merchant Navy was held against him by the Royal Navy, which, short of officers in the interwar era, was considering offering him 'Qualified Status' as a full-blown RN officer.

Whether Mike would have accepted a commission is another matter. It is true that Britain's hidebound class structure loosened in the 1930s as the Depression at the end of the 1920s ebbed. New industries emerged, commuting into cities from new-build suburbs became commonplace, and women began to edge their way into the workforce. New national organisations appeared such as the RAF, the BBC, and 'red brick' universities that actively sought a workforce with academic and technical skills rather than social connections. Yet Mike was, by birth, temperament, and upbringing, an outsider. His father by all accounts encouraged him to go it alone having stepped out of the RN straitjacket when he was seconded to the new Royal Australian Navy in 1913. The admiral, in fact, never looked back, and from the mid-1920s on preferred to live a rootless life on his boats cruising around the coast of France (sometimes with paying guests), attiring himself most days in a white dressing gown, partying hard, and, as will transpire, listening to no one but himself. He was not to come ashore until the end of the 1930s.

Still, Mike kept a foothold in the RNR for some years in the 1930s and continued to be well regarded in the Royal Navy. By the middle of the decade, he had been rated 'above average' in most areas of naval life including signals, on a torpedo course, and for his 'general ability' including his 'good French'. Indeed, on each of his last three RNR postings, he was rated 'fit for more important sea command'. Yet whether it was because of growing pressures on his time (limiting his ability to earn a living from yacht skippering), a long-standing reluctance to follow in his father's footsteps, the failure to graduate to 'proper' RN officer status at the end of the 1920s, or because of his marriage in 1936 and the decision that followed to settle in Cap d'Antibes and start a family, Mike retired from the RNR in September 1937. By then, he had made and retained numerous friends in the service who were to stand him in good stead in the war years to come and also shown his often-sceptical father that he had what it took to be useful to his country if needs be.

During the first half of 1933, he acquired his first serious boat—a smack-rigged cutter built at Looe in Cornwall in 1912 and named *Lady Beatrice*. With a length of nearly 28 feet and a draught (depth) of 5 feet, she weighed in at 7.8 gross tons and had a total sail area of 340 square feet and four sails—a mainsail, a staysail, a jib, and a topsail. It was a not-inconsiderable commitment for a young man with no regular income and cost Mike £80 for the purchase (about £5,150 today) and £275 (£18,000 today) for a conversion. This included installing a new cabin top and toilet and making other improvements, including to the engine.

Over the next three years, starting in the summer of 1933, the logs of the *Lady Beatrice* record voyages up and down the southern English coast, across the Channel, down to the Bay of Biscay, and into the Mediterranean through the French canal system. The first was a proving trip from Polperro to Plymouth harbour. Moving east, the entry for 1 August 1933 begins: 'Awaiting news of Claughton [*sic.*] who expects to come along to Shoreham. Spent the morning nursing a fat head and listening to the fishermen tell me I ought to be at sea!' At 2.40 p.m., Claughton arrived, so the pair set off in the *Lady Beatrice*, sailing about a mile offshore. A 'perfect afternoon' going west followed, but that evening, the wind died. Cold meat and beer, bread, butter, and tomatoes constituted a frugal 'dinner'.

Next day, there was still no wind and the sailors contemplated a foodless twenty-four hours drifting around aimlessly in the Channel. By the following day, still without food and still only 6 miles off the Isle of Wight, 'neither of us [was] feeling in the best of tempers'. Eventually, on day three, Mike managed to tack east and Claughton got ashore somewhere near Ventnor and bought provisions. However, the next day proved no better than the others with all wind still stubbornly absent and the sun 'broiling'. 'The question of food arises again!' runs the succinct entry in the log. As they drifted east, Mike sighted the downs at Chilgrove 'shimmering in the heat' that afternoon and recalled his holidays at the girls' school nearby. Not until noon next day (6 August) did the *Lady Beatrice* stagger into Littlehampton and complete her second voyage under Mike's command.

Many, rather more successful expeditions followed over the next three years, including trips through the French canals and down the French coast via Saint-Nazaire, La Rochelle, and Carcassonne, and as far south as Béziers and Cette (Sète) in the Mediterranean. From 1931–39, Mike belonged to the Royal Ocean Racing Club and took part in many of its competitions. He always kept meticulous work logs and every penny spent was recorded punctiliously but not any income earned. Usually, the *Lady Beatrice* wintered in Stows Yard in Shoreham—a legendary family boatbuilding business on the south coast founded in 1866 that endured to 1936. Mike was not always happy with Stows; in February 1934, for example, he notes: '*Lady B* at Stows Yard. Half full of water. Not been touched since I left. But in fine shape. Pumped out ship and commenced putting the ballast and all gear on shore'.

In Shoreham, he relied on the loyal Mrs Hawes for provisions. Entire days, regardless of the weather, would be spent on the boat doing such chores as 'scraping in the Fo'cstle', 'preparing wood', 'laying the floor', 'caulking the deck', and so on. From time to time, Stows' men were employed on heavier work such as putting in deck supports. In March 1934, he writes: 'When sweeping up found a bad place in one frame forward on Starboard side. On removing some of the concrete decided it was best to remove all the concrete so spent a very hard day with the hammer and chisel'. Shortly after, he made a three-week voyage south to Villefranche on the French–Italian border. No more work was done on the *Lady Beatrice* until September 1935 when she was 'put on the Hard' and her bottom scraped and repainted in Suter's Yard, also in Shoreham. All told, Mike spent £79.19.00 (around £5,000 today) on maintenance work on 'the little ship' in the 1933–37 years.

Early in 1934, Mike stepped up a class, in yachting terms, and began a four-year association with a renowned hybrid—the *Jolie Brise*, a gaff-rigged cutter built in Le Havre in 1913, which was the last boat to carry Royal Mail under sail and then, after a refit, won the famous Fastnet Race in 1929 and 1930. During the winter of 1933–34, she had been sold to an American, Stanley Mortimer of New York. Mortimer, then in his early thirties, was a friend of Admiral Cumberlege and cruised with him in a motor boat in the Mediterranean. One day, the boat exploded and the admiral persuaded Mortimer to change course and buy a sailing boat. Mike would help him. The *Jolie Brise*, at the end of her racing life and idling in UK waters, was selected and Mike chose to sail her to the Mediterranean, oversee an extensive refit to make her comfortable for cruising, recruit a crew, and skipper the boat from the 1934 summer cruising 'season'.

At 56 feet long, with a draught of 10 feet and a beam of nearly 16 feet, the *Jolie Brise* was (and is—today she is owned by Dauntsey's School in Dorset) a sizeable yacht. Refitting her involved a major commitment of money and time, one Mike subsequently described in an article in *Yachting Monthly* in September 1935. The main challenge was to provide accommodation— neither 'first class' nor 'third class' in Mike's words. 'In redesigning *Jolie Brise*, a medium course was followed,' he wrote.[6] The first issue was to find a firm prepared to do the work for the budget at Mike's disposal. Eventually he hit on a yard in Palma, Majorca. Language was a problem; the shipwright's tongue was Mallorquin, Mike's a colloquial Spanish, and his two crew members spoke only Breton. The work took one month longer than expected, custom duties proved to be a constant irritation, but the final price was 'considerably less than budgeted for at the commencement of the work'. Almost all the alterations were below deck except for the installation of a new cabin top and helmsman's bench that could be retracted and serve as an extra gangplank. By the end of May 1934, the *Jolie Brise* was ready for her new owner. Over the following four months, with Mike as skipper and Stanley Mortimer aboard for some of the time, the *Jolie Brise* sailed over 7,000 miles in every sort of weather. 'We were not only thankful for the change below,' concluded the *Yachting Monthly* article, 'but also for the honest workmanship of our Spanish carpenters.'

For the next three summers, the routine seems to have been much the same. The Winter Term 1935 issue of *The Log* of the Nautical College, Pangbourne, carried a lengthy piece by Mike about his experiences in the four summer months of 1935, and give a real taste of his often lyrical and descriptive writing, his ability to conjure up a sense of place and time, some of his attitudes, and his innate love of sailing. Titled 'A Sail That Made A Summer', it begins:

> Golfers always seem to talk about golf. Do motor-bus drivers only discuss the motor-bus? Or sailors the sea? Well, I was going to tell you about that summer we cut the crop at Talavera in Spain, but I shan't. I'm not a farmer! There was that day we climbed Olympus and the autumn crocuses stood almost to our knees, but then I'm not a mountaineer or a gardener, so we can't discuss that. So, I suppose we'll have to talk about the sea. And talking about the sea inevitably brings me round to *Jolie Brise*, my last ship. A fine ship she is too, and many a mile she put under her keel before I ever saw her, but not before I'd heard about her and had the ambition to sail her myself. The majority of us go to sea to 'go places' as the Americans say. But going places, and the places we went in the four summer months of this year of grace, required a ship that could move, and in J.B. move we did.
>
> I can think of nothing more perfect than the day we sailed out of the Adriatic, the sea breeze blowing into Italy, the three of us that were sailing her bare to the buff, a blazing sun and a great cloud of red canvas, the masthead spinnaker emptying itself into the balloon jib, the mainsail and topsail broad off and drawing, a steady eight knots reeling off on the log and nothing visible ahead, for the canvas hid everything. Out on the jib-boom end every once-in-a-while for a look-out, in case we should see another sail. Steadily eating up the thousand odd miles between Split and Villefranche, round the toe of Italy, and through the Straits of Messina.

Destinations are then ticked off, usually with an accompanying description such as 'Across to Capri, but no girls with golden rings on their fingers' and 'Taormina, with her flowers a blaze of colour'. It was on this voyage that Mike encountered the Corinth Canal for the first time:

> ... we were held up for three days, due to an overdose of dynamite filling the canal with debris. There were forty of us, caïques and coasters, and when the 'canal open' flag came up the forty of us made one cursing rush for the entrance to get through first, and by the grace of heaven, we were second in line.

Dozens of glamorous-sounding Mediterranean place names follow before the *Jolie Brise* reaches Falmouth where she later took part in 'the epic Brixham trawler race' around Torbay that year. In the middle of the piece, he adds a paragraph clearly designed to seduce the imaginations of his young readers in the era before mass tourism:

> Maybe this reads like a conducted tour, but we were our own masters—heave to for a swim three and four times a day, anchor in the evening in some quiet little bay and wander ashore through the pines or lie off some little village where we would buy, maybe, loaves of bread or a jar of some exotic honey. Early to bed and a start at daylight after a swim and later lashings of breakfast and coffee.

This was to be the carefree, but carefully charted, pattern of Mike's summer months at sea for the rest of the 1930s. How he saw himself at this time, somewhat ironically, is summed up in an epigram he composed: 'Roast beef with yorkshire and two veg,/ Claude Michael Bulstrode Cumberlege'. In November 1935, he attended the 11th Old Pangbournian Dinner at the Overseas Club in St James's, London. A fellow attendee wrote later: 'There is little doubt that CMBC has had more sailing experience than any other OP. He has had the idea of taking over *Jolie Brise* from her present owner. If he does this, he would like to run three fortnightly cruises in the summer holidays and suggests taking cadets [from Pangbourne]. Perhaps some OPs may be interested.' It was not to be. In the winter of 1937–38, Stanley Mortimer, a landscape painter and farmer by occupation, decided against returning to Europe as the political and military outlook on the continent worsened. The *Jolie Brise*, at the time in Southampton, was put up for sale. Mike, too, may have played a part in this decision by making himself unavailable for the 1938 season. The year before, most probably in Valetta, Malta, through a mutual friend Paul Hammond, he had begun an association with Richie Paine, the wealthy American owner of a 71-foot ketch with eighteen berths called the *Landfall*. Paine had hired him as his skipper. For both men, it was to prove a felicitous relationship.

Meantime, the Cumberlege family caravan had moved on. In 1933, Ella Maillart reappeared on the scene through a chance meeting with the admiral in Port Soller on the north coast of Majorca. In *Gypsy Afloat*, she writes that Claude Cumberlege by then had swapped the *L'Insoumise* for a five-year-old Newfoundland schooner (renamed by the admiral the *Fleur de Lys*), which was easier for a small crew to sail. This happened, according to Claude in his memoirs, in about 1929 or 1930; the new American owners promptly wrecked the *L'Insoumise* in Agay Roads off the coast of southern France and Claude helped them salvage her.

The *Fleur de Lys*, too, got into trouble. In November 1932, Mike was on board as a leading member of the crew bound from St Malo to Lisbon when several ships and steamers were lost in a violent storm in the Bay of Biscay. Twenty-one days from Lisbon, the *Fleur de Lys* was reported lost; English newspapers ran the headline 'Admiral's son feared lost'. In fact, the little craft, only about 60 tons in weight, was hove to for eighteen days under close reefed foresail and forestaysail and survived. Mike seems to have been unconcerned and took some 'amazing photos of the terrific seas ... a witness to the *sang froid* and pluck of the young man' recorded Claude approvingly in his memoir.[7] After that, and over the strenuous objections of others in the crew, Mike's navigational prowess kicked in and he steered the yacht safely to Bilbao.

Mostly, though, the admiral kept the *Fleur de Lys* in St Tropez, living on board with his young French friend Melanie and wintering in ski resorts in Haute-Savoie. In May 1930, however, a telegram sent him rushing to Paris. 'My wife [Mike's mother] had had a sudden operation in that wonderful American hospital. "Perhaps we cut too deep. Anyhow, a germ has been released, I'm afraid,"' the senior surgeon told Claude. For the next month, he lived in a spare room in the hospital. 'It was the old trouble come back, poor dear. I kept her going for a whole month, but the fever would not be allayed. At the end of June, a month later, I kissed her goodnight and she fell asleep forever in my arms. If twenty-five years previously we had loved with a love that was more than love, we parted fastest friends'.[8] No mention is made of Mike or Diana being at the bedside.

Within a couple of years of his wife's death, the admiral had remarried, and in 1933, he fathered a son he quixotically called Mistral. Ella Maillart encountered the baby on the *Fleur de Lys* that summer 'toddling about stark naked'. Diana, 'looking as charming as ever', in the meantime had married 'our friend Jose, a calm, small Spaniard who used to take us in his Bugatti through the countryside' at the Roman Catholic cathedral in Gibraltar despite the admiral's unease. The couple also had a young son. Claude's new wife, Norah (*née* Kirby), who he met by chance on a friend's boat and married in St Tropez, is described by Maillart as 'a young and cheerful person'— not a description Mike would have endorsed. The pair never got on: Mike regarded her as 'greedy'. Jose, for his part, 'looked tired and worried'. He was a landowner, living and working all year round on a 10,000-acre cash-poor estate in Castile–La Mancha but seemingly respected by his workforce. However, there was trouble brewing right across Spain and agitators were busy everywhere among the peasants. Jose, who studiously kept out of politics, knew that his workers were being fed propaganda by communist activists in the area. Yet 'he thought that with calm and diplomacy he would be able to re-establish his authority when he returned'.

It was not to be. Less than three years later, with the Spanish Civil War in full swing, the couple were forced to shelter from the mounting unrest by staying with friends in the nearby town of Talavera. It was promptly captured by the rebels, they were detected and for twenty days in a row dragged before a 'Red Tribunal' and publicly questioned and harangued. Executions were going on each night. Eventually Jose was dragged back to the tribunal at 3 a.m. one morning and summarily executed, his body thrown on a landfill site in the countryside. The justification given was that he was not political—in the highly polarised context of a civil war, therefore deemed unreliable. Diana, by now was virtually penniless and accompanied by her two-year-old daughter (the son had been sent to England the month before), scraped together the money for a rail ticket to Madrid, fled to the British Embassy, and eventually made it back to England in HMS *Devonshire*.[9]

As was his wont, the admiral, while upset at this turn of events, assessed the politics of the situation incorrectly. His instincts were always authoritarian and he certainly sympathised with Franco in Spain and even Mussolini in Italy, as his memoirs show, but, essentially, he ignored the world around him and acted as he pleased. In 1935, at the urging of Norah, he moved ashore to Spain and rented a large farmhouse in El Canuto, a mountain village 5 miles from Algeciras—'the prettiest little place in all the world' he reckoned. Within eighteen months, reality caught up as peasant unrest swept through the area and the admiral and his family had to be evacuated by the local British Consul at half an hour's notice via a dockyard tug to Gibraltar where the *Fleur de Lys* lay at anchor.

While in Gibraltar, Norah gave birth to a second son, Tarik. Claude was delighted, but within weeks had left her and hitched a ride to Malta with 'his friend' Captain John Godfrey RN, then commanding HMS *Repulse*, ostensibly to see Mike who was 'looking after an American gentleman's (Lt Cdr Paul Hammond of the US Naval Reserve) yacht laid up' there.[10] It was the *Landfall*, described in an article in the Royal Navy Sailing Association journal in the summer of 1936 as 'one of the world's finest ocean cruising yachts'. Mike had been overseeing a refit for Hammond. Back in Gibraltar, the admiral and Norah then decided the time was right that autumn for a leisurely motoring holiday through Italy to France with their two infants in tow only to be caught up in fascist demonstrations wherever they went. Reaching south-west France, they decided to rent a villa in Antibes, later buying a plot of land nearby and building themselves a home, taking possession just as war in Europe loomed.

Prior to this, Mike had married at St Peter's Church, East Marden, near Chichester, on 23 September 1936. According to Aunt Gwen, writing in 1943, this was certainly not his first romance. In the early 1930s, for example, 'the American ladies came to visit us [at Chilgrove] to find out if Mike was worthy of the hand of Miss Sally What Not—really, a very nice girl in herself, but I privately thought not nearly good enough for my lad'. That engagement, if it happened, was never announced. Nancy Wooler, ten years younger than Mike, was far more to Aunt Gwen's taste: 'You are much more suited to Mike. I always think the young men who have lots of girls and then settle down are the most constant in the end. Mike no longer has the roving eye.' He had met Nancy in 1934 at a party on Majorca and instantly been smitten. That October, he took the nineteen-year-old to dinner alone for the first time. Before long, he was writing yearningly about her and for her, notably in a 1935 poem 'Written in Loneliness':

> *I lost you sweet, I lost you through the day,*
> *So hot, so hot the pavements brazen glare,*
> *Deserted streets and silence everywhere,*
> *You were not there.*
> *No more the fountains play soft liquid tunes.*
> *Where is the green oasis of the square?*
> *Lost in a fitful mirage of thin air*
> *I lost you sweet.*
> *Now evening comes in long and slanting lines*
> *And magically people is the square*
> *With voices, voices everywhere*
> *And yours as well, I'm sure I heard it there.*

Nancy was just twenty-one when she married (Mike was almost thirty-one). Theirs was to be a total, close and loving relationship for the next four years—one that both of them recalled wistfully in many letters to each other during the war. A shared, rather starry-eyed love of Greece and the Greeks, of the sea, sailing, and boats, and latterly of gardening and flowers, buttressed by a huge circle of sociable friends all over Europe, bound them together. Money was always to be tight and they certainly lived on the edge, but always juggling, the resilient young couple made do year after year. It was a gilded, free-spirited, and enviable lifestyle.

Neither Nancy nor her elder sister, Nora, who lived with her before her marriage, had any obvious connection to East Marden so the choice of a church there, only 2 miles from Chilgrove, must have been made by Mike. Nancy's parents, Claude and Muriel Pemberton Wooler, lived in Toronto, Canada, where Claude had made money selling dishwashing products. In the crash of 1929, when business was hit hard, Claude moved the family across the Atlantic to Jersey.[11] He was reputed to have hidden cash all over his house in Canada and so been less affected by the financial meltdown than he might have been. Nancy, Nora, and John, the youngest of the three children, completed their education on Jersey. The family then went their separate ways, the senior Woolers and John residing near Antibes before moving back to Canada via Portugal in 1941. The two girls stayed elsewhere in France to be 'finished' and eventually gravitated to the Mediterranean and its expatriate environment.

Nan, as she was known, subsequently had little contact with her parents, although her mother did make the journey over the Atlantic to be with her after her grandson was born at the end of 1938 and wrote regularly to her from Canada during the war. Muriel had a most unusual background, which may have played a part in this relatively loose mother-daughter bond. Her father, Nan's grandfather, was an Anglican missionary somewhere along the St Lawrence river region in Canada in the 1880s. He had formed a liaison with an Iroquois Mohawk woman, which resulted in a daughter. Subsequently, he returned to England for a time to a parish in gritty South Yorkshire—St Wilfrid's Church, Hickleton, known for its lychgate with three human skulls set behind a grill and the encouraging words above it 'Today for me, Tomorrow for thee'.

Muriel, half Iroquois, came with him and was sent to Cheltenham Ladies College, the epitome of middle-class Victorian values, to learn to be a 'proper' Englishwoman. She remained there for two years to 1900, boarding in St Hilda's House and passing basic exams needed to become a kindergarten teacher.[12] Her father then left Yorkshire and moved to Africa on missionary work, eventually dying there. After Cheltenham, Muriel may have taught for a time. At some point, she met Claude Wooler and the couple emigrated to Canada where all her children were born. Nancy probably knew of her Iroquois origins but never spoke about them, reflecting social taboos of the time.

Mike and Nancy were to prove well matched. Both had a sense of adventure, both loved the open-air life, both were sociable to a fault, neither was hidebound by class or country, both were 'outsiders', and both were fearless sailors; Nan was often to accompany Mike on his skippering assignments throughout the Mediterranean in the second half of the 1930s. Neither seems to have been a home-lover when they married, and for two years after the wedding, the couple had no permanent base, moving from boat to boat or staying temporarily with Mike's father or friends in Cap d'Antibes.

During the interwar years, Antibes became enormously fashionable. Along with Juan-les-Pins next door, 'everyone went there' from Churchill and Valentino to Cole Porter and his Jazz Age friends, Picasso, and the Duke and Duchess of Windsor. Vacationing Americans poured in during the partying 1920s, including Ernest Hemingway and Gertrude Stein and Scott and Zelda Fitzgerald (until Zelda went mad and Scott went broke). Before long, smart hotels like the *Belles Rives*, which survives to this day, were opening their doors. 'The Cap [d'Antibes] is the rugged peninsula between Antibes and Juan-les-Pins, coated [today] in absurdly expensive real estate,' the travel writer Anthony Peregrine has explained:

> Immediately back from the sea, the Cap entices you in to keep you out. Poorly kept lanes sneak up and down between vast gates, walls and fences protecting villas on estates as extensive as small kingdoms.... There is beauty all around, sea and sunlight.[13]

In this monied, hedonistic ambience, the Cumberlege couple were seen as agreeable young hustlers. They seem to have liked Antibes as a place but only a smattering of its rootless, shifting population. 'There are very few people down here,' Mike noted gloomily in December 1938, 'and certainly nobody I ever really want to see again. I hope and hope all the time to meet someone with a touch of extra excitement in their voices.'[14] Seven months later, he added, with a flash of self-awareness: 'I know of no place which collects such a fine array of utterly useless and brainless ullages [dregs]. Nobody, naturally, can understand why Nan married me for I have a habit of being shockingly rude to people I don't like.'[15] Nor was Nancy exactly tactful, often cutting people dead at parties for the fun of it.

Around this time, Mike wrote an amusing and revelatory poem with the title 'To My Beard' to which he added (in pencil) '+ *My Darling Wife*':

> *Give me the sound of thunder*
> *Of surf on a rock strewn sea,*
> *Of my ship with her sails torn asunder,*
> *But give not, ah give not to me*
> *The voice of my wife in the morning*
> *With words that I know may be feared—*
> *Michael! You're simply disgusting,*
> *Oh Michael, there's egg on your beard.*
>
> *There's many a grim situation*
> *I've found in my long life at sea,*
> *But never I've faced a face with the face*
> *Of my wife when she's saying to me—*
> *Michael I've spoken before now,*
> *Just think of the children I've reared,*
> *The trouble, the trials, tribulations*
> *And dammit there's egg on your beard.*
>
> *Oh hold with the tale of a sailor,*
> *And if your course truly be steered*
> *And you'd marry a girl and would nail her*
> *Don't do so by growing a beard.*
> *For there's naught to my mind so distressing,*
> *No nothing so much to be feared*
> *As the voice of your love in the morning*
> *With—Look at you—egg on your beard!*

Eighteen months after marrying and with a baby on the way, the couple rented La Gardiole—'the loveliest little place'—in Cap d'Antibes for a year.

For Mike, it was a first. As he put it in a letter at the time: 'It's so funny being a householder for the first time in my life'.[16] Nan and Mike took to life in the furnished villa and its garden so much—'a very happy house'—that, in July 1939, with war in Europe only weeks away, they rented the villa (or most of it—the owner retained a couple of rooms on the ground floor) for another three years unfurnished at a cost of $180 a year (equivalent to £4,500 a year in 2017). Their plan was to lease the property out each summer for six weeks to cover their own rental costs; they would be away sailing or staying with friends. Today, Villa La Gardiole can be rented for £6,000 a week in high summer. Brochures describe it as a 'stunning property located in a perfect spot', fitted to a high standard with four bedrooms, a staff apartment, a pool, and beaches and restaurants within easy walking distance. At the end of the 1930s, the more mundane reality was rather different—a sizeable, empty, poorly decorated house with no pool or heating but a 'wonderful garden'.

In a letter sent to one of his patrons soon after signing the second lease for La Gardiole, Mike wrote: 'Nan and I have had to fix it up, get some furniture together, make curtains and in fact have a good time keeping our minds off [the threat of] war. It is amazing what one can do with a white wash brush and some paint and elbow grease'. To save money, he designed some 'simple' furniture ('knocked up' by a carpenter he knew from wood he bought). 'I've never really had such an exciting two months,' he added in a postscript in September 1939. 'I have been working like a fool to make it (the house) habitable'—painting rooms, windows and doors and producing 'a lovely "young" sitting room complete with white woolly Algerian carpet. Our bedroom is very chaste—white again—with a more-than large bed. Designed by me.'[17]

The reason for this parsimony is not hard to discover: Mike never had much money. His two main American patrons in the 1935–40 period paid him about £400 a year on average (about £24,000 today) plus board and lodging and expenses when he was at sea with them. Both thought they were getting a bargain, and one of them wondered aloud if Mike had any other means of support. If he did, it is not apparent. He owned no property at any time in his life, the admiral was still very much alive in the 1930s, and the only family inheritance he might have received would have been from his mother, who died in 1930 but does not seem to have left a will, or his grandfather. In 1940, when Mike was no longer being paid to skipper yachts (although his last American patron continued to transfer funds irregularly to him until 1943) but before he was called up by the Royal Navy, he became seriously short of money and complained vociferously to the Admiralty.

Early in 1938, Nan spent six weeks in hospital and was 'quite seriously ill'. She recovered, put on her lost weight, and became pregnant soon after. On 17 December, Mike wrote to a friend that Nan was 'marvellously well—the baby is due in three weeks'. The child actually arrived eleven days later on 28

December, a tad early. At the clinic they attended, Mike assisted throughout the three-hour delivery. Mother and child were home again within twenty-four hours. 'It was all well worth it and I feel I gave Nan more courage,' he wrote.[18] Surprisingly, the couple had previously invited house guests to stay over the Christmas–New Year period. They remained—'rather tiresome' Mike remarked laconically later. The 7.5-lb baby was named Marcus Crossley because Mike thought the name more 'European' than Mark and expected the boy to live mostly on the continent (as he has), and because Crossley was the name of his maternal grandfather. Nan must have agreed.

The years 1937–39 proved to be the one and only period of real domesticity in Mike's life. He was not really suited to a routine, static lifestyle and was always restlessly on the lookout for the next great adventure. In Antibes, he had a small boat of his own (the *Sonneta*), which he mostly moored in the harbour. Many winter days were spent 'mucking about' in her, adding features, removing others, and hoping to fit her out sufficiently well that she could be rented to visitors in the summer months. In 1938, the couple bought a baby Fiat car and Mike confessed to 'beginning to change [his] mind about cars'. Always an avid stamp collector, he also compiled several albums to go alongside a sizeable collection of black-and-white photographs and negatives.

With Nan, he attended opera and classical music concerts in Nice and Monte Carlo whenever the opportunity arose; the acclaimed pianist Vladimir Horowitz was a special favourite. He also read, widely; a letter in 1938 reports his appreciation of two books given him recently—*Listen, The Wind*, a work by Anne Morrow Lindberg that tells the story of her and her husband Charles Lindbergh's 1933 flight from Africa to South America across the Atlantic Ocean, and *Lust for Life*, a popular history of the life of Vincent Van Gogh. He also owned a Siamese cat, Bira—'clean, intelligent, not the noisy kind'. He doted on Bira for the rest of his life and took him with him on many voyages.

---

*From Mike's poem 'A Sailor's Song' written in the early 1930s

4

The Good Ship *Landfall*

In Richard Cushing Paine, an American businessman and a founding partner of the successful investment firm State Street Research & Management of Boston, USA, Michael Cumberlege struck gold. Paine's wealth and his yacht the *Landfall*, a handsome 71-fot ketch weighing 59 tons with eighteen berths, spreading 3,004 square feet of the finest tanned flax cloth, had been built to win the 1931 Transatlantic Ocean Race. Skippering her from 1936–39 gave Mike both a loyal and generous patron and year-round use of one of the best ocean-cruising yachts of the interwar era. It was a happy and successful combination that was to dominate the rest of his peacetime existence, enabling both him and Nancy to achieve the lifestyle they desired—one built around a large measure of personal freedom, the best of ocean sailing, a compatible employer, choice destinations, and endless in-depth conversation, poetry, and cultural exploration, especially in Greece. It lasted no more than three to four years until war smashed the dream in September 1939. Things would never to be the same thereafter for either of the young couple.

Ritchie Paine, as Mike knew him, had acquired the *Landfall* from her original owner, Paul Hammond. She had been designed by the innovative naval architect Francis Herreshoff and built by Abeking & Rassmussen in Bremen, Germany, specifically for the 1931 race in which she had finished second. She might have won that race had Hammond not insisted, over the designer's strenuous objections, on chopping 7 feet off her stern to improve her rating under the race rules with the result that the *Landfall* dragged her stern, slowing her down when the wind freshened.

On deck, the *Landfall* was all teak and shining brass. She steered with a huge, bus-like wheel but could also be handled from a cockpit abaft the jigger (the aft-most mast) by a 5-foot-long tiller. This culminated in a carved likeness of a nude maiden reclined on her stomach. Herreshoff added many other technical novelties such as a sail-setting track running along the bowsprit (the spar that extends forward of a yacht's prow), two-speed sail hoisting winches in brass housings, and four-wheeled 'cars' attached to the mainsail running inside a track inset in the mast. Her hull was painted a robin's egg blue with a red water line. The *Landfall's* only ugly feature came to be known as 'The Beast'—a bulky and smelly German diesel engine that was difficult to start and caused endless headaches until replaced by Mike, at some expense, in Hamburg.[1]

Although the *Landfall* could sleep eighteen, usually she cruised with five crew, the skipper, and five or six guests—family and friends. After the 1931 race, Hammond made the Baltic her home for a couple of years, bringing her down to the Mediterranean in 1934 and basing her in Malta from 1935. Here he appointed Mike as his agent to oversee a refit, afterwards allowing members of the Royal Naval Sailing Association to cruise her out of Grand Harbour during the 1936 summer. A report in a local paper that year describes one such weekend outing, quoting RNSA members as saying that in heavy seas the *Landfall's* behaviour was 'wonderful'.[2]

Mike had fallen on his feet and knew it. When Hammond was summoned to active duty by the US Naval Reserve in 1936, he could no longer continue his annual visits to Europe and sold the *Landfall* to his friend Ritchie Paine. One of the attractions for Paine—who bought the ketch sight unseen—was that the *Landfall* came complete with a qualified skipper and crew. He planned to cruise with family and friends from 1937 for two to three months each year, mostly in the Mediterranean and the Baltic. The remainder of the year, Mike was left to his own devices, with no pressure to charter the yacht out or orders to remain in port. In effect, she was his to sail and maintain as he saw fit.

According to his then teenage son, Walter, who made two cruises on the *Landfall* with Mike in 1938–39, Ritchie Paine was a somewhat taciturn man who rarely opened up to anyone, including his wife, Ellen, and children. On the *Landfall*, with Mike in charge of the yacht, he became a different person. Walter recalls the glowing tips of their cigars as they discussed poetry, books, and opera over a glass of cognac. 'Mike brought him out,' recalled Walter many years later. 'At first, Mike did most of the talking—he would discourse about anything. Then I heard my father, who was quietly intellectual and studious, joining in and talking much more than I could remember. It changed my own relationship with him. I think that Dad was surprised and delighted to find someone he could talk to about personal matters.' To stimulate the conversation, Mike also installed a library on board: '... modern books and great books and poetry. He was reading all the time. He wasn't the rough, tough sailor that he appeared to be'.[3]

On the last cruise they made together, from Naples along the Dalmatian coast to Venice in July–August 1939, one of the afterguard passengers, an American writer by the name of Don Moffat, kept a journal as he had done on two previous voyages.[4] He wrote it up later in typed form and at one point describes the usual routine when the *Landfall* was in port:

After a full breakfast, shaving and writing, getting set in various ways' ensues. At 11.00am the owner is given his bottle of Bass [ale]. Reading follows while Mike 'paces the windward deck in bow-legged British Navy fashion and tops it off with a go at the *Golden Treasury* [a nineteenth-century anthology of English songs and lyrics] or favourites from Hilaire Belloc and W. S. Gilbert.' Meantime, the crew is cleaning cabins, scrubbing decks, polishing brass and mending sails.

At midday, the owner and his guests, plus Mike, go ashore to explore. A pre-prandial drink precedes lunch at a local café. Further exploration follows and all are back on board by cocktail hour. This begins at 6.30 pm sharp. 'It is beginning to assume the proportions of a rite' [Moffat observed]. 'Jan [Kotrba, the steward] brings up a tray with shaker, glasses, ice, lemon, three bottles, peanut butter and crackers. Richard cuts the lemon peel, Mike inserts the gin, Richard the vermouth and ice. Then he picks up the shaker and paces the port deck, agitating vigorously, while we sit by like hungry cats waiting for the fish man.' A dinner of veal, fried eggplant and a novelty such as corkscrew pommes frites often came next and then dessert—frequently 'Crepe flambantes Ivan', a speciality of *Landfall*.

Afterwards, the party splits. The younger members go ashore to hunt for fun, others call home on the yacht's ship-to-shore telephone, and the rest sit on deck under the bright stars with a glass of beer, a good Havana cigar, and 'phonography' music: 'Very pleasant; bed soon after eleven'. Mike was also in charge of the young Walter's introduction to the fairer sex: 'He would take me ashore on the excuse of seeing a statue or something, and then we'd talk about women. He'd tell me how to pick one up if you didn't know the language,' Walter told the author in 2016 with a smile. 'My father would have been angry if he'd found out, but he didn't and I learnt a lot!'[5]

During those three 'seasons', the *Landfall* ranged far and wide in the Baltic, voyaged around the Aegean and its many islands and harbours, and sailed up and down the Adriatic and along the Italian and Dalmatian coasts. In 1938, for instance, Mike oversaw a refit of the *Landfall* in Malta in March, collected the Paines for an Aegean cruise in April–May, sailed from Athens to Hamburg in June, and took the Paines on a six-week cruise around the Baltic in July–August. Walter Paine's first sight of the *Landfall* and Mike had actually occurred at a dockside in Hamburg in 1938: 'I looked down at this beautiful vessel and this extraordinary man, muscular and deeply tanned, in tattered shorts and worn sandals ordering everyone around and waving his arms at a fast-approaching bumboat [boat carrying provisions], shouting "Mind my PAINT, you bloody bugger!"'[6]

This was typical of Mike's attention to detail and to the paintwork on the *Landfall*. In his letters to the owner, he spells out scrupulously each and every cent he has spent on the yacht, and why. The new engine he purchased for the

Landfall in Bremen, for example, cost £450 (£29,000 at today's prices)—'a nice clean model' he informed Ritchie Paine.[7] Two years later, in Athens, he oversaw a major refit of the yacht's electrics including installing a lamp and radio battery in the engine room, repairing the radio, fixing the lights at the saloon table, and fitting wall plugs for the gramophone in the main cabin and the deckhouse 'so we shan't need to take the battery about with us.' Not long after, he had all the beds and their covers in the after-cabin remade and the blankets drycleaned. His only real complaint was that the owner did not spend more time on board.

Moffatt began recording these trips in daily detail on the 1938 Aegean cruise. At first, the owners' relationship to Mike was formal—'Captain C.' was his moniker. By the end of the first cruise, during which Mike had presented some doggerel to the passengers 'Breakfast of Bacon and Egg' and an untitled birthday poem in honour of one of the Paines' guests ('Do you do the things you want?'), shared helming duties happily with Ritchie Paine, acted as a tour guide and fixer ashore, and sorted out clutch problems with the engine, he had won over the owner. Moffatt concluded this log: 'We had been told to expect something out of the ordinary in the Captain. We did, and the discovery was a major factor in the enjoyment we all experienced'. The next year, the Paines invited a similar group on a cruise that took in Delphi, Santorin, Khios, Istanbul, and the Bosporos. Mike had by then installed the new engine and 'been fired on by brutal and licentious soldiery while passing close to Cape Papas' in Ikaria island. Jan Kotrba was now on board—'a considerable improvement on the old steward'. Mike relaxed enough to visit friends in Istanbul and entertain them on the *Landfall* as well as producing a puzzling piece of prose whimsy, titled 'Wedgewood—A Simply Way'. Military precautions in Turkey dogged the passengers' steps when on shore and Mike seems to have spent a lot of time soft-soaping officials in the various places they visited. The cruise ended with Ritchie Paine noting with pleasure that the *Landfall* performed beautifully under full mainsail and that Mike 'despite nautical responsibilities, can enjoy a nice bottle and a light talk'.

On a leisurely voyage in the *Landfall* in May–July 1939 from Athens to Hamburg via Antibes with Nancy and baby Marcus on board, the culture-loving side to Mike's character was given full rein. The couple managed to make side visits on the way to one remote Greek temple and out-of-the-way island after another. Among other places, they took in Poros, Ieraka, Monemvasia, Cape Matapan, Kalamata, Bassae and its famed Temple of Apollo—'the most inaccessible place left in Greece, thank god!'—Mystras, Sparta, and Siracusa before making a detour to Malta.[8] Everywhere they went, they gloried together in the ruins and artefacts of a lost but treasured civilisation. Marcus, still to reach his first birthday, was cared for mostly by a nurse. In a gale at sea one day, he proved to be the only person on board who was not sick, including the Siamese cat Bira—'my lovely smiling Prince' as Mike called him.

Despite such understanding generosity on the part of the owner, there were always question marks around the relationship with the Paines. One concerned money. On the one hand, 'this whole hook-up with my father came as a blessing to Mike', remembered Walter. 'He'd get a check from my dad regularly and he'd send it back to Nan straight away for the kid. He always seemed short of money.'[9] On the other hand, the expenses Mike did submit— refitting at the start of the 1938 'season' for example, which cost £845 (about £54,000 today)—worried him. They never added up to Ritchie Paine:

> My father often wondered at the smallness of the bills. He was a businessman, he'd owned a number of boats, he was a pretty shrewd individual. The bills always seemed to be about half what the American cost would be. A 71 feet yacht is quite a thing to keep up. I think that made him a bit suspicious that Mike was getting some help. Mike never admitted it. He'd send these pathetic letters— scrawled—asking for another $100 for one of the crew to go and see his wife or something like that. Dad would dutifully send the check. He always thought he'd got a bargain in Mike.

Mike's behaviour on the cruises was another matter that gave the perceptive young Walter, if not his father, pause for thought. Often, Mike would deliberately steer the yacht to the most out-of-the-way 'tickles' and beaches and then sit sketching them in detail and recording the soundings being called out by a crewman. 'Mike was curious, but too much of a loner to have been a conventional naval officer. He would have been the perfect undercover agent because of the way he could meld with a crowd,' Walter has said:

> He dressed the part whatever it was, and he could speak the part. He would try to lose himself. Sometimes [on shore] we would wait for him for hours wondering what he was doing ashore. Mike never said a word about why he was so interested in all these little harbours and landings. And I never heard my dad ask him.[10]

An American-flagged yacht with a home port of Talinn, Estonia, on her stern was perhaps the perfect cover at that time, particularly along the fascist coasts of Italy and Albania.

There were other signs. On the 1938 Baltic cruise, Mike, according to Walter, not only sketched small harbours and took soundings but also noted which of them would be largely invisible from sea. One morning the next year, while cruising in the Aegean, by his own account, Mike put out at daylight just to have a look at the port of Monemvasia 'which I had my eye on for future possibilities.'[11] That year, too, he 'informed London' about something in Rostock that he had visited the year before on the *Landfall*'s Baltic cruise. Then, on the Adriatic cruise in August 1939, he pointed out to Dom Moffat 'new emplacements, earthworks and coast defence batteries' on the strategically-located Italian military facility on Saseno island (today known as Sazan): 'When we were within a half mile or so we heard a dull boom and Mike went about immediately. Probably it was a blank; we saw no splash. Mike told the boys to put up [put away] their cameras'.[12] Maybe it was simply a response originating from Mike's RNR training, or maybe his links with British naval intelligence were showing.

Among Mike's pre-war friends was Henry Denham, the British naval *attaché* in Stockholm. A keen sailor, Denham visited Mike and Nan in Malta in 1939 where he and Nancy also met the Royal Navy's new, and imaginative, Director of Naval Intelligence Rear-Admiral John Godfrey—the old friend of Mike's father, Admiral Cumberlege. Godfrey was to prove a staunch supporter of Mike's career in the war years just ahead. It seems entirely possible that, from the late 1930s, Mike began working informally for British naval intelligence and, in particular, made a point of scouting remote landing sites and isolated caves in the Mediterranean—places that might be suitable for rescuing agents and storing arms caches should Britain be involved in a war in the region.[13] Be that as it may, post-war accounts of British naval intelligence in the Second World War, and a lengthy biography of John Godfrey, make no mention of the use of people like Mike in these years. Yet Godfrey was to keep in close contact with Nancy Cumberlege during the 1939–42 period and after the war in a way that suggests a strong association.

Aiding Mike hugely in the smooth running of the *Landfall* was the multi-national, multi-faceted crew he assembled. They all respected him and were to prove intensely loyal—one of them, Jan Kotrba, to the point of death. Three or four occasional individuals supported a solid core of five made up of Costa Trevelas from Greece; Jan Kotrba from Czechoslovakia; the boatswain Louis Leroux, 'a skinny little monkey of a man', from Brittany, with a bristling moustache who had sailed with Mike's father from 1926 and was an expert sailmaker who Mike always maintained was best in an emergency; and two recent recruits from the Balkans: a top notch sailor called Anthony Pocina with his 'high, sharp-hooked nose and soft, sympathetic eyes', and a cook, Ivan Segavic. Ivan was 'silent and unobtrusive, small, pale and thin' and had a real flair for cooking in a confined space such as the *Landfall*'s galley.[14]

Mike kept the crew on a tight rein and designed a uniform for it: a working attire of dark blue slacks, white cotton short-sleeved shirts, and blue berets, and a Sunday-best outfit of an elegant blue jersey with 'LANDFALL' printed across the front, blue jackets, and yachting caps for shore leave. All the crew were paid in cash in American dollars, to their evident delight. In his journal, Don Moffat observed:

They are a fine, friendly and congenial lot and highly competent. They speak a *pot pourri* of European languages among themselves. Mike gives his orders in the same mixture and they seem to understand him almost before he opens his mouth. Mike's ability to remember which man speaks what language is a miracle.

Two of the crew stand out, given their future importance to Mike. The Bohemian Jan Kotrba, born in 1913, worked with Mike for six years before the Second World War. Don Moffat described him like this:

Jean's [*sic*.] friendly smile and brisk perpetual motion at the table or cleaning up about the cabins remind me of the best type of highly-trained wagon-lit attendant. He is young, good looking, slim, ambitious, and at present is waiting for war and a chance to enlist in the Czech foreign legion for a crack at the Boches [Germans]. Jean is virtue itself with drinks on the dot at the appointed hour.... He massacres all languages with unvarying cheerfulness and indifference to vocabulary and grammar.[15]

A practical man, he always had something up his sleeve if pressured. Mike was to amplify this pen portrait in 1942 when pressing Kotrba's claims to be part of his team to blow up the Corinth Canal: 'He is a very sound loyal young man with plenty of initiative and the typical Czech mechanical mentality and interest in all kinds of engines and gadgets'.

Costa Trevelas was Mike's right-hand man for years on both the *Jolie Brise* and the *Landfall*—in Mike's words, 'the invaluable Costa'. A Greek sponge diver from Ithaca, he had worked in America and spoke good English, but he only understood nautical terms in French. As a sailor, he knew the basics but no more. A strong swimmer, he was immensely powerful in his shoulders and long arms; not coincidentally, he had once wrestled for a living. He had no neck to speak of and, in Moffat's words, had 'a round head bigger at the base than at the top'. His rubbery, broad face instantly reflected his thoughts. 'I never saw such an instrument for registering emotions—perplexity, benevolence, chagrin, joy, innocence, lust,' Moffat recalled. 'He would make a fortune in Hollywood.'

Mike was a strong leader: decisive, demanding, and clear in his instructions. He expected his orders to be followed, including by the owner who once aroused his wrath when making a mistake at the steering wheel. On another occasion, Louis 'got a smack across the kisser from me' when he started a shouting match after one drink too many. But this was the exception. 'Many a night,' he informed Ellen Paine in July 1939, 'the crew would be working happily till seven in the evening.' So Mike was no xenophobe, but he did have some clear likes and dislikes.

Walking down a pavement in Hamburg, Germany, in 1938, Walter and Mike ran into a group of 'swaggering' young brownshirts who forced them into the gutter. The incident left Mike 'incandescent' with rage.[16] 'German swine. Led by a madman' as he once wrote. At Rab in Yugoslavia (Croatia) in August 1939, he encountered 'masses of fat German trippers in pyjamas'. They horrified and repulsed him, and he was not shy in saying so. He liked the French very much as individuals, but found their collective inability to sort out their politics in the 1930s frustrating. The Portuguese, he reckoned, talked too much: '... they are taught oratory at school and it becomes them naturally'.[17] Americans were 'far too exuberant [and] still in the collegiate stage with some notable exceptions' (perhaps including his employer). Once they entered the Second World War on the Allied side, Mike always found American troops 'a heartening sight'.[18] He said of South Americans: 'I consign to complete mental outer darkness'. The British upper class establishment also made him uneasy; travelling to Egypt in 1942, he found himself on a ship with two Army brigadiers as his fellow passengers. 'They were incredibly British and Blimpish, and Boring', the latter being the worst failing of all in Mike's eyes.[19]

Greece and the Greeks, as we shall see, were exempt from all criticism—'magnificent, kind, generous and so brave and proud' he wrote in 1941 to Nancy. In contrast, no derision was ever too great for the Italians or the detested Benito Mussolini. In November 1940, after Italian forces had invaded southern France, Mike declared: 'Poor Italy. I am so sad for her foolish people who hadn't the guts to be honest. What fools they have been'.[20] Mussolini's henchmen, and all their vain boasts daubed on rocks as the *Landfall* entered any Italian port in the late-1930s, were a special subject for his mockery and ire.

Towards the end of the Adriatic cruise in July 1939, all Mike's pent-up anger at contemporary Italy boiled over in an unfortunate, if revealing, incident on the final evening of the cruise in the Brioni (Brijuni) islands in the northern Adriatic, then part of Italy. In Walter's account, written years later:

The evening calls for jackets and ties, ours rumpled from the frequent formalities of the transatlantic crossing. Mike appears as we have never seen him before: pristine mess jacket, dark trousers and with a naval version of the British Union Jack tied like an ascot (cravat) around his neck. [The party enters a bistro and orders drinks. Time passes and the bistro gets noisier. Awaiting a third drink,] An angry growl erupts from Mike above the din: 'Get your filthy paws off her, you damn little swine!' Springing to his feet, he elbows his way towards the bar where a dark-haired woman is ineffectually trying to fend off advances from a pudgy little man seated next to her. Mike, with one smashing backhand, knocks the offender off his seat, blood spattering his white dinner jacket as he hits the floor.

There is a momentary stunned silence in the bistro, then 'All hell breaks loose. Shouts of "Get the Limey" mingle with female screams as Mike is set upon by a bunch of short, paunchy Italians,' Walter remembered. 'He holds his own, but suddenly someone approaches from behind him with a metal table support and brings it down on the back of his head, knocking him down to the accompaniment of loud cheers from the assembled patrons.' At this point Mike is rescued by his party and, with the crew's help, dragged back to the *Landfall* as the Garda Civil (police) arrive on the scene. Their leader steps forward and declares 'Blood has been shed' and demands 'The Americans Must Leave—please to show us your papers.'[21]

There is a perfunctory review and then the *Landfall*, helmed by Louis Leroux, quickly motors away into the bay. Mike gradually comes to, still muttering profanities about the despised 'Wops' and suffering from a severely lacerated scalp. The incident is forgotten, not least by Ritchie Paine and his friends—pillars of the Boston Establishment—who, with a reputation for sobriety to protect, want no word of it to seep out. It never does until now when all the participants bar Walter are deceased.

Just why Mike snapped like this will never be known for sure. Drink may have played a part. It was hot and humid and, after a lengthy trip and a long day at sea, he would have been tired. His almost contemptuous opinions of Italians were always close to the surface as he sailed up and down the Adriatic. He had a solicitous, almost old-school view of the way women should be treated by men, regardless of their skills and abilities in areas he respected such as sailing and photography. Maybe that evening he was suffering an overdose of British superiority. In any event, he never referred to the incident in the numerous letters he wrote to the Paines during the next three years.

On Monday 21 August 1939—less than two weeks before the start of the Second World War—on a fine, hot summer morning, the *Landfall* motored slowly into Venice and tied up behind the baroque magnificence of the Santa Maria della Salute church. It was the end of a 1,235-mile cruise and, for Mike, the end of an idyllic lifestyle. Almost until that moment, he had paid scant and dismissive heed to the war clouds gathering over Europe. As recently as late July 1939, he described rumours of war as 'mostly the work of the newspapers and their reporters'. Seven months earlier, at the end of 1938, he reckoned that 'the real danger at the moment is that France is in a mess due to the weakness of her past political life and there is no one really strong enough to put all the others in their places.... Europe is not much fun when one really worries about getting the morning paper'. As late as the second half of 1940, he believed that Marshal Pétain would be the saviour of France.

Living in southern France, often away at sea for weeks on end, and mostly mixing with an expatriate elite (including his father) that wished to keep the real world at arm's length, perhaps Mike's blinkered attitude is understandable.

When Diana's husband was shot dead by leftist revolutionaries in the Spanish Civil War in 1936–37, it must have given him pause for thought. Similarly, on his trips to the Baltic and around Italy in the 1936–39 period, he would have seen many disturbing indicators of what was to come, not to mention his own covert activities, if that is what they were. On the 1939 Adriatic cruise, shortly after the Italian annexation of Albania, the *Landfall*'s party even ran into signs of war preparations around Skradin in Yugoslavia (now Croatia). However, the bottom line must be that Mike consistently misread or ignored the political situation in Europe from the mid-1930s onwards.

In Venice, the grim reality took over. On 22 August, Mike went to the station to collect Nancy and Marcus and Captain and Mrs Fraser, who were to sail with him on the *Landfall* back to Antibes via Malta. The Americans spent the day sight-seeing. Everyone met up at cocktail hour to meet 'Mike's charming wife' before dining happily at a sidewalk restaurant near the Piazza San Marco. Don Moffat took the opportunity to read out a laudatory 'Ode to the Owner' written by a fellow guest on the *Landfall*, Francis 'Torch' Parkman, headmaster of the exclusive St Mark's School of Southborough, Massachusetts. Next morning, after Mike had lined up the crew in their best uniforms and shown the ship's accounts to Ritchie Paine, the party's seventeen suitcases were taken off the yacht. The group then passed through Italian customs and travelled by fast car to Genoa to board a ship, the *Conte di Savoia*, taking refugees to the US—only to be told the next day to disembark because the vessel had, allegedly, developed 'engine trouble'.

Italy had begun to mobilise for war and Mediterranean ports were being closed. Fortunately, the American Consul in Genoa managed to arrange a special train to Paris for 350 foreigners, including the *Landfall* party. There the group remained in a hotel for three days until a passage was secured on the *Île de France*—the last passenger ship to leave France for the USA.[22] She departed from Le Havre on the morning of 3 September, just hours before France and the United Kingdom declared war on Germany. The *Île de France* carried 1,777 passengers, 400 more than her usual number; most were Americans clamouring to leave France before the war broke out. Walter slept in a bath tub. The ship sailed in a zigzag pattern with lights extinguished. During her five-day voyage, sixteen vessels in the Atlantic were sunk by German torpedoes, mines, or gunfire. One of them, the *Athenia*, with 500 Jewish refugees and many Americans on board, was torpedoed close to the *Île de France* off southern Ireland with the loss of 117 lives—the first British-flagged ship to be destroyed by a U-boat in the Second World War.

Back in Venice, the Italians closed the harbour and seized the *Landfall*'s papers. In a letter to Ritchie Paine dated 5 September and hand-written from Antibes, Mike explained what happened next:

After long and considered thought, I made up my mind that the best plan was to leave *Landfall* in Venice. You can imagine how I felt. The British Consul told me to leave and the American Consul advised it too. So, although I had all my stores aboard and was ready to cast off, in the end we took the train. However, I am convinced that the ship will be O.K. Venice is unlikely to be bombed. And I have left Costa—the invaluable Costa—aboard; he would rather stay there than go to Greece. The American Consul knows all about *Landfall* and is going to keep an eye on her and the Agent will advance Costa up to 20 lira a day [about his wage].

In this letter, Mike added that flying the American flag in Venice should enhance the *Landfall*'s security, whereas if he had made a run for it and been caught in the Adriatic 'she would have been left to the tender mercies of anybody in some strange port'.[23] As for the crew ('all most upset'), Louis had gone back to Brittany and the Slavs were staying in Split in Yugoslavia awaiting further orders. Jan Kotrba had accompanied Mike, Nancy, and Marcus to Antibes ('what a job I had getting Jan into France'). Costa had been tasked with making an inventory of everything on board the *Landfall* and handing it to the American Consul for safekeeping. Mike ended: 'I am still your man, without pay of course, if you want me. It's a bitter blow to me, but I am one of millions who has to suffer for these German swine, led by a madman. And who knows, maybe by Spring we may be walking among the flowers at Bassae or anchored in the peace of a Greek island harbour'. Five weeks later, in a follow-up letter, he informed the Paines that, assuming he had not been called up by then, he proposed to go back to Venice, recover the *Landfall*, and sail her to Antibes 'before the New Year'. Italy was not to declare war on France and Britain until June 1940, so theoretically such an escape was possible.

In the meantime, he was stuck in Cap d'Antibes. Soon, he and Nancy had a new diversion. Early in November, Elizabeth Gwynne (later Elizabeth David, the food writer) and her lover, Charles Gibson Cowan, turned up in Antibes in their two-masted yawl the *Evelyn Hope*.[24] Elizabeth had met Mike and Nancy in Malta when holidaying there. Tiring of a rickety, aimless existence in England built around bit parts in the theatre and writing, the pair had bought the boat in 1938 and determined to sail to the south of France via rivers and canals, reaching Marseilles in September as war was breaking out in Poland. They decided to stay on in France and eventually managed to persuade the French authorities to allow them to sail the *Evelyn Hope* along the rocky coast to Antibes. Mike and Nancy introduced them to their friends, including the elderly author and traveller Norman Douglas who had arrived in Antibes in 1937 after a scandal with a young girl in Florence; Elizabeth and Douglas were to become close friends for the rest of his life (he died in 1952).

Mike had time on his hands and used some of it to instruct Gibson Cowan in the finer points of sailing. Both were good-looking men in their mid-thirties but there the similarities ended. Mike might best be described as solidly English middle class, averagely patriotic, professionally competent, outspoken, and socially self-confident. Gibson Cowan begins his memoir *Loud Report*, published in 1938 when he was only thirty-five years old, like this: 'My father was a Jew, my mother the daughter of an English mother and a Dutch father. We were lower class'. At school in the London area, he suffered from anti-Semitic bullying. Afterwards, he became involved in trades union affairs during the 1926 General Strike before drifting into the theatre and writing a play called *Eastside, Westside* that made it to the West End. In addition, he was an assertive pacifist and, according to one of Elizabeth's biographers, a conscientious objector.

Mike also plotted ways to retrieve the *Landfall* from Venice. In mid-October, he learned via his father's sailor, who had been sent to Venice to do some work with Costa, that the *Landfall* was safe and sound. The following month, he decided that Gibson Cowan should help him sail her to Antibes, despite their lack of empathy. In December, the ill-assorted pair set off by train for Venice, and another chapter in the *Landfall*'s log began, one that both Mike and Gibson Cowan subsequently recorded (in Gibson Cowan's account, Mike is known as Neil).[25]

At the French–Italian border, 'there was some difficulty about money,' Gibson Cowan wrote. 'The French refused to allow us to take out francs and the Italians to bring in lira.' They eventually entered Italy that afternoon and Gibson Cowan announced that he was relieved to be out of the war. Mike responded tartly: 'You've never been in the war'. Retorted Gibson Cowan, on paper anyway: 'Neil [*sic.*] was not particularly susceptible to atmosphere and we had a difference of opinion on a number of matters'. Relations were not improved when the pair overslept on the train and ended up in Trieste. It was cold and snowing when they arrived in Venice, and it proved impossible to get any fuel for the yacht's engine. Mike was unconcerned, worked to prepare the *Landfall* for sea by day, and settled all outstanding bills. Each evening, he repaired to Florian's in St Mark's Square for dinner under a sign reading 'It is forbidden to discuss politics'. Tony and Ivan from Yugoslavia turned up and, with Costa and Gibson Cowan, formed the yacht's crew for a 1,400-mile voyage through the Adriatic and across the Mediterranean in mid-winter—a passage that was bound to be challenging.

At first, things went well and it was calm as the yacht slipped out of Venice untroubled by the Italian authorities. On the second night, 'We got what was coming to us' when a 'full winter bora' (violent wind) made their passage to the toe of Italy a nightmare. Mike and Gibson Cowan had managed not to quarrel to that point 'probably due to the fact that we saw very little of each other, taking alternate watches, four hours on, four hours off.' The weather worsened, the sails had to come down, the engine failed, and it took five and a half days to get from Brindisi to the Strait of Messina and three attempts to navigate the strait. In the end, the *Landfall* got through stern first. Then another gale blew up; 'I was as near to murder by then as ever I've been,' Mike reported later.[26]

By this stage, all the crew had been injured in one way or the other: 'We are a sorry lot! I personally am loving it. It's a tough trip but we've had nothing serious to worry us, plenty to eat and lots to do. And the peace of being without a shred of news of the outside world'. According to Gibson Cowan's account, he had been hit by the mizzen block behind the shoulder, which Costa put back in place 'with a brutal efficiency'. Mike wrote to Ritchie Paine that Gibson Cowan was injured 'going up a shroud to clear a rope [when] he passed a spike of wire clean through his hand at the fleshy part of the thumb and first finger'. Mike himself was hurt when he took a chunk out of his hand in an accident with the main winch handle. 'It wasn't amusing,' he noted.

Christmas Day came and went with the *Landfall* still at sea; the special lunch Ivan the cook prepared did not suit Gibson Cowan who became violently ill. On deck, everyone toasted the health of the Paine family *in lieu* of the King. Off Elba, the sea died to a flat calm. At last, on New Year's Eve, conditions for sailing were perfect: 'Neil [*sic.*] was in a good humour for the first time since we had left France'. He began to sing a French song '*It était un petit navire, Il était un petit navire, Qui n'avait ja-ja-jamais navigué, Qui n'avait ja-ja-jamais navigué, Ohé! Ohé!*' The Alpes Maritimes were sighted at 3 p.m. 'Just before dusk, with a magnificent piece of exhibitionism, the only excuse for which was that he could do it, Neil [*sic.*] rode in over the surf with everything drawing and dropped anchor in the centre of the port of Antibes,' Gibson Cowan recorded. 'Everybody been watching us for the last two hours. We started a party on board right away … it went on to day break.'

Back on land, Mike discovered that Elizabeth and Nancy were not as chummy as they had been when he had left. Elizabeth had moved in to La Gardiole when the men departed for Venice about three weeks earlier. In the interim, the pair had gone to endless Christmas parties and Elizabeth reckoned that she had not been sober for ten days. She decided Nancy and her sister, Nora, were 'clothes snobs' who were jealous of her wardrobe and wasted their money drinking champagne all day in the most expensive bar on the coast.[27] She also began a burgeoning friendship with Norman Douglas, who had taken her sight-seeing and charmed her. But the situation never got out of hand and Nan, though becoming erratic in her time-keeping, was never less than kind to her. Elizabeth and Charles Gibson Cowan eventually obtained a visa to enter Italy and left Antibes on reasonable terms with the Cumberleges in the *Evelyn Hope* in May 1940. Just over a year later, at the other end of the Mediterranean in Alexandria, this was to matter.

As 1940 began, the *Landfall* was tied up in Antibes harbour alongside Mike's boat the *Sonneta*. All its gear was packed away, the vessel soon to be cleaned and polished. Tony and Ivan returned to Split in January. Costa remained in Antibes on the Paines' payroll until April 1940 as did Jan Kotrba, who was waiting to be called up by the French or Czech Army. Mike continued to keep an eye on the *Landfall* and write to Ritchie Paine about her. In April, he arranged insurance on the yacht of $30,000 (more than $500,000 in today's values) for 1940–41 through underwriters in London. Sometime near the end of 1941, the *Landfall* was sold to the Spanish Vice Consul at Nice who, soon after, is thought to have been killed in a train bombed by the RAF. When the Germans invaded southern France in November 1942, the *Landfall* was sunk by the Nazis, tied to a tug in order to block the entrance to the harbour at Antibes. 'One charge failed to explode causing her to settle sideways, spar protruding above the water,' Walter Paine recalled in 2016, quoting a letter from Francis Parkman who visited Antibes in 1945 and found the yacht in 'tough shape, masts broken, decks warped'. Her steel frame had helped to preserve her, however, and she was used to trade wine and then was leased to a film company as she appears in the 1954 movie *The Barefoot Contessa* starring Humphrey Bogart and Ava Gardner. At some point after that, she was sailed to Fort Lauderdale, Florida. Walter Paine and one of his sons, Christopher, subsequently made strenuous efforts to track her down and traced her to the Caribbean where she is thought to have been owned by wealthy Mexicans before being lost at sea.[28]

5

Going to War

About two weeks after returning to Antibes, Mike, then aged thirty-four, heard from the Admiralty that he was to be recalled to the Royal Naval Reserve as a lieutenant and would be assigned to the port of Marseilles on 'Contraband Control Duties'. Officially, he was posted on 25 January 1940 to HMS *President*, the cover given to naval officers seconded to undercover work. Before then, he had visited London to be 'fitted up' and briefed about his role: '… an unpleasant experience with the blackout and the abominable cold and I had a good dose of 'flu into the bargain'.[1]

The hand of Rear-Admiral John Godfrey, who remained Director of Naval Intelligence until the end of 1942, is apparent in his appointment. Mike knew Godfrey, spoke fluent French and colloquial Spanish, lived not far from Marseilles, knew the French coast from Italy to Spain well, and, as it turned out, was a personal friend of the officer in charge of the office, Captain Colin Lucas, who had also been recalled to duty from retirement and promoted. Lucas was to prove a friend-in-need and he had a wide hinterland—China and a fine collection of Chinese porcelain—which always made a difference to Mike. Both were paid by the British Consul General in Nice with the Foreign Office applying to HMS *President* for reimbursement. Their job was to detect and report attempts by the Nazis or their French supporters in Marseilles to smuggle arms or men through the port, to monitor suspicious ship movements, and to expose any signs of defection from the Allied side by pro-fascist elements in the French Navy or commanders in its Mediterranean fleet as Germany threatened.

It was not quite the war role Mike envisaged for himself. 'I ought to be up there [in combat in the Atlantic and North Sea] instead of sweating in a bureau,' he complained in late April, noting that men he knew were among RNR friends of his involved in sinking German battleships and cruisers. 'However, we all have our part to play.'[2] Even at this late stage, he was hoping against hope that the war would be short, and he still completely underestimated German military capabilities.

After registering with the Admiralty in early September 1939 and getting an official reply card saying 'Yours undated noted', he had kept 'pretty mum' until mid-October while he tried to sort out the *Landfall* situation. From then on, as the war at sea and in Finland escalated and Poland was overrun, he expected to be called up at any time and lived 'in a state of near tension'. Antibes emptied of foreigners, young French men drifted off to the armed forces, yet food and drink remained plentiful as autumn arrived and produce flooded the markets and those who remained continued to visit bars and bistros: 'Good old France—never been better or fatter or fuller.... God help the poor devils [Germans] if they attack the Maginot Line'.[3]

Precisely what Mike did in Marseilles during the next five months remains unclear; no copies of his reports have been found in the National Archives in Kew, but from his letters to the Paines, it is clear that he was kept busy. In one, at the start of April 1940, he wrote:

> The last few months have been one long rush of work and it has been really terrific. By the end of the day one is exhausted mentally.... I can't say much about our work but at least it is most interesting which makes up for the business of being in an office for twelve hours a day—a thing, as you can imagine, I am not used to! For the most part, we are just overwhelmed but at least we see the light and I hope we are doing our small bit to aid the general nonsense to a conclusion.[4]

It is around 120 miles by the A8 road from Marseilles to Antibes, and Mike had a car with his job, but despite this, he rarely found time to get home, even at weekends. In his first two months in Marseilles, he managed one break: '... a breath of heaven, after this forsaken city with its dust and Mistral'. Nancy, for her part, was reluctant to leave Cap d'Antibes or to upset Marcus's daily regime or to trust fully the nurse the couple employed. 'He is a delight, walks by himself and is full of fun,' proud father Mike noted as Marcus reached all of three months old. Two 'refugee' Siamese cats had reinforced the household: 'Bira treats them with an air of disdain and, when no one is looking, chases them up the nearest tree'. Despite the bitter winter, the garden at La Gardiole was 'truly wonderful' that spring; the couple took a chance that they would be in residence the following year and planted masses of flowering perennials.

In Marseilles, Mike rented a small flat on a hill overlooking the city towards Notre Dame de le Garde. In the far distance, he could see Cassis. His landlord was an absentee young Frenchman 'at the war' and the rent he paid about one-fifth the amount for a comparable hotel room. 'I am lucky.' Sometimes he went to the local opera—'*Boheme*—low taste perhaps by modern standards, but I love it'—and toyed with the idea of bringing all Ritchie Paine's records from the *Landfall* as well as his own so that he would not be without music in the evenings. Slowly, he grew to appreciate Marseilles, especially 'the odd little corners' where he could sniff out 'good Italian cooking and good honest local wine'.[5]

Soon, Mike barely spoke English except to Lucas and confessed on one occasion that he was actually finding it difficult to express himself in English because he had to think so much in French. 'Both languages are suffering in consequence.' His somewhat romantic view of the French and their colonial subjects early in the war comes through particularly in one fluent and descriptive passage he wrote in April 1940. He informed the Paines:

> [Marseilles is full of] Colourful uniforms and colourful soldiers inside of them— great snaggled-toothed Senegalese, little yellow Annamites, Tonkinoise, Zuoves, Algerians and Moroccans, not to mention British Tommies and sailors of all sorts, Polish Colonels and Czech Generals. Heaven knows what they all are. Binding it all together [is] the good old honest Poilu [French infantryman] with his pack and his naily boots and his pipe and brown burnt face. What a grand people to be fighting with and playing with! In this office, we certainly get along in fine style and are always in accord with them.[6]

By early May, the course of the war in northern France had begun to intrude. Yet Mike continued to view the conflict through rose-tinted glasses, informing Ritchie Paine on 4 May that 'everything seems to be going along quite well, thank you, in our war'. At that stage, British troops were departing Norway and it was just six days before the Germans invaded Belgium and France. Indeed, only three weeks before the Dunkirk evacuation of British and French troops, he praised British generals for having 'the courage to move our troops out of a tight spot' on the Western Front. He also passed on to Ritchie a wild rumour that British troops were shortly to move to Canada with a view to taking over the protection of the USA: '... if it's true, it's just in time'. In the same letter, he admitted that he had rather lost touch with people since the war—'I find no pleasure in writing when one is tired out after a harassing day in an office'—but announced that he was hoping to be promoted in June, not least because 'I've got some pretty hot reports lined up and with luck they will give me half a stripe.'[7] In the event, he was not promoted to lieutenant commander until he was a POW at the end of September 1943.

The *Landfall* situation still preoccupied him. In a letter to Ritchie Paine in early May, he talked of bringing the yacht to Marseilles shortly, dry-docking her to overhaul the hull and sailing gear, living aboard while the work was done, and bringing Louis Leroux down from Brittany to help. That winter, Costa Trevelas had done a 'first-rate' job stripping the motor down, scraping the iron work and painting the hull, masts, and booms, stowing sailing gear in the after cabin, and taking all the Paines' mothballed clothes and possessions on shore in a large trunk for safekeeping. On one occasion, Mike had appeared on the quay at Antibes in his British naval uniform; Costa was thrilled to see him and insisted on showing him off to his friends. Reluctantly, he had told the *Landfall* crew by then to look for other employment. Jan Kotrba had left in February for a job as a driver in the Czech Army in Exile. The duo from the Balkans, Tony and Ivan, were still in Antibes spooked by the dangers of taking a troop steamer home to Yugoslavia. In the meantime, Mike continued to pay them. Louis was idling in Brittany. Costa remained by his side.

This slightly unreal world, neither one thing nor the other, ended abruptly for Mike and Nancy on the evening of 10 June 1940 when Italy declared war on France and Britain. Not much happened until a week later when France, following the near-completion of the general evacuation of Allied troops from Dunkirk and western France, sought an armistice with Germany. As this was about to be signed four days later, the Italians launched an offensive against the French in the Alps and along the Mediterranean coast—the last major engagement of the Battle of France.

The next day, Saturday 22 June, Mike was driving to Antibes and eating his lunch at Les Foux under an immense plane tree by the side of the road when he saw Nancy in his car, licence plate BA6-1914, flash past in the opposite direction. He chased after her and 10 km later caught her up. She was taking the admiral's Russian cook urgently to a hospital in Marseilles where the cook's son had shot himself and was dying. Mike followed Nan into Marseilles but then went to his office in the early afternoon as Nan went to the hospital. At 2.19 p.m., 'the air raid sirens let loose'. Mike spent the afternoon partly in a cellar in the building and partly in a ground-floor room reassuring two old French ladies. He had no idea where Nan was. Bombs fell everywhere and then, as suddenly as it had begun, the air raid was over. Mike ventured out of his hiding place and eventually found Nan at 6 p.m.: 'We had supper under a tree, looking over the sea'.

That night, the couple slept in Mike's apartment, and at 3 a.m., there was another air raid. On Sunday morning at 6 a.m., there were more sirens but this time it was a false alarm. At 9.30 a.m., the all-clear sirens sounded, but ninety minutes later another Italian air raid began. He remembered:

> At eleven o'clock I was standing in my window looking over Marseilles, for I had a very good view, and I heard a sinister droning in the sky. I called to Nan and said 'Listen, there are bombers somewhere and they are somewhere right over us and the sirens haven't sounded.' The noise of the bombers became quite loud and then suddenly the sirens blasted out and Marseilles became like a brown partridge with her chicks when the shadow of a hawk darkens the sun. Everything came to a stop, the trams, the cars. Doors opened above and below and closed and people hurried past in the stairs. The streets all became very still, a few people running, popping into cellars. And then silence. The shrieking sirens ran down and the silence was all complete. And Marseilles lay there, as quiet as quiet, dreaming in

the sun with fleecy clouds overhead. And all the time the loud and angrier growl of aeroplane motors. Nan and I stood in our window and searched the sky but could see nothing—nothing but a summer's morning and a clock ticking and, somewhere very immediately overhead, the sinister hum of engines.

Suddenly, quick as a flash, bright as a bullet, past on the wind screaming through a white cloud, came the first plane, shining in the sun like an archangel, tilted almost vertically to the ground—a German aeroplane with enemies in it, cool and calculating, people to kill, men who had come across France from a German flying field, and almost on top of the first, a second, and after the second a third, and after the third a fourth and after the fourth a fifth. The first one went whistling past, the wire struts screaming in the wind, followed by the second, the third. Behind a row of houses immediately next to us they'd come, they'd gone.

Almost before we could formulate the thought there was the most terrific explosion. Both of us were thrown bodily back into the room. We beat it down the stairs. My knees were knocking together, so were Nan's and nothing we could do would prevent it, although neither of us was frightened. Then it was all over—not a gun was fired, not a single French chaser plane took to the sky. The Commandant in charge had given them Sunday leave because they had been up the night before. The guns weren't manned because someone had given an order. The Commandant was shot the next day. So were one or two others. But it didn't prevent two fine ships, one full of munitions, from being sunk.[8]

It was this hair-raising raid that produced a farcical situation back in Antibes, which had not been bombed by the Italian air force. Admiral Cumberlege, by then aged sixty-three and with three young children under the age of seven (a fourth, Luis, was to appear in 1941) by his second wife, Norah Kirby, had moved on shore in 1938 and built himself a house in the hills above Antibes. That afternoon, Mike recalled with some relish, the admiral as usual was in the bottom part of his pyjamas busying himself in his garden, 'when a taxi rolled up and two very definitive personages, including the local mayor dressed in funereal black with his badge of office, and top hat and white gloved hands bore down on the "Skipper"':

> The Admiral was not at all put out by his scanty costume. The Mayor delivered a magnificent speech, the gist of which was 'Courage ... I am the harbinger of bad tidings. Your son is dead. Dead? Well, I don't believe it,' Father replied. 'You couldn't kill <u>him</u> with a poleaxe!' The Mayor then showed him the telegram he had received from Marseilles. The Admiral read it and realised it referred to the cook's son. It was ambiguously worded. So they all went into the house together and had a cognac and everything was okay.[9]

The Skipper's stubbornness in the face of negative war news reached new heights the next day, Monday 24 June. Nancy had returned to Cap d'Antibes and Mike was lunching, as he usually did, at the Beach Club in Marseilles, gawping at scantily-clad girls and drinking a pre-lunch Cinzano in the sun with some friends. It was soon after noon when Captain Lucas appeared suddenly. 'I want to talk to you. Alone,' he said to Mike. 'We've got to be ready to leave France in five hours.' Mike thought of Nancy and Marcus and Bira the cat and his garden and said to himself 'What's the point of getting into a panic?' He returned to his office in the British Consulate and stayed there until 11.30 p.m. that night, 'laying plans, making bonfires and arranging to go to Nice to warn the Consul General'. He set off 'with a moon, and the whole of Provence asleep' just before midnight, but ran out of petrol at 1 a.m. at Frejus and ground to a halt in the market square:

> Dawn came very slowly on the shoulders of three bakers covered with flour [who] went into a very small bistro followed by me and a woman brewing the first coffee. At five, a place opened for selling petrol and at 6.30am I arrived at La Gardiole. Such a lovely morning with all the flowers in the garden and the sea as still as a lake.

Having woken Nancy and told her she must pack up the house and pay all the bills and go back to Marseilles with him, Mike went to see his father, who by then had lived in France onshore and offshore for the past eighteen years, to inform him that the news was rather bad and he should prepare himself for worse. The admiral pulled a blanket over his head and responded, 'You're a damn fool. How could you know anyway?' He said he would make his own arrangements and 'to hell with everybody'. Mike replied that he might not see him again and was telling him the news 'for what it was worth'. He then moved on to Nice, visited Costa Trevelas on the *Landfall* in Antibes harbour, and was back at La Gardiole by 7 p.m. for dinner: '… such a good dinner with some of the last *Landfall* wine'.

The admiral turned up at La Gardiole later that evening and Mike 'gave him a good talking to, but he wouldn't believe the news' (of the imminent French surrender) and Mike was not allowed to say all he knew. Early next morning, Nancy and Mike packed two cars, bid farewell to his father (by now worried; he had heard on the radio that the Germans were at Dijon) and stepmother (once described by Mike as 'an old cat'), offered the Skipper the use of his flat in Marseilles ('he was still being difficult' so refused), and set off for Marseilles at 9 a.m. It was very hot; the two small cars were stuffed with all sorts of things and one of them refused to start. While having a quick stop for lunch, Italian warplanes flew overhead and dropped bombs nearby but also lost eight of their twelve aircraft as the French air force by now was reacting. Then a fan belt on one of the cars broke and had to be fixed.

The couple finally reached Marseilles, normally a fast three to four-hour drive, at 4.30 p.m. Three notes were pinned to the door of his flat, all marked urgent. He read one: 'Come immediately to such and such a ship at such and such a dock. We sail P.M. Monday'. It was already Monday afternoon—in fact, 5 p.m. Monday. Not pausing to enter the flat, Mike and Nancy tore down to the docks but there was no sign of the ship. Mentally preparing to drive to Spain, Mike then spied a 'dirty little ship, very ancient, just like those that come fussing into Patras or the Piraeus with a Greek name.... Suddenly I saw Captain Lucas and the Consul General sitting on deck on a suitcase and other officers, all in civilian clothes.' Lucas urged Mike to take off his uniform quickly and throw it in the sea. Mike, with the sort of nonchalance Sir Francis Drake might have envied, said: 'I'm very sorry but I refuse to be hurried and I'll be damned if I throw my uniform into the sea!'

Nancy was then informed that she had too many suitcases and also that it was not permitted to bring Marcus's French housekeeper Arlette on board. Mike looked around, realised it would be at least an hour before the ship sailed, and rushed off to Marseilles railway station with Arlette where he gave her all his cash and bid her a tearful farewell. He then went to his flat, packed another suitcase with some of his clothes, abandoned his car outside a garage, and took a taxi back to the ship. When he got there, he was furious to discover that the Consul General was surrounded by several of his steamer trunks and his car had been loaded on board along with his furniture and two other cars.

The ship was filthy; it was in use at the time as a Jewish emigrant vessel plying between Constanza and Haifa. Mike was concerned enough about its safety to search the dock during the night for an extra lifeboat complete with oars, sails, and life belts and to get it loaded on board. He stayed up all night at the ship's telephone. Not until 4 a.m. did the orders to sail arrive. Hugging the coast, the vessel reached Gibraltar safely the next day. There the Cumberleges sent a telegram to the Paines saying that they were safe, changed ship, and, with 2,000 others—'all the riff-raff of the Riviera'—set off for England through the increasingly dangerous Bay of Biscay. They finally got to dry land on 28–29 June.

The whole episode had roused Mike's fighting spirit: 'I was dreadfully rude to everyone. They certainly deserved it'. Another word he used to describe the chaotic and panicked British departure from Marseilles was 'disgusting'. He added, sorrowfully, to the Paines: 'I lost everything in France except my wife, my child and my beautiful [cat] Bee Orchid Bira'. Even now, the admiral hung on in Vichy France until, along with other British citizens still in southern France, he was given a week to leave in July. 'After much trial, tribulation and considerable expense through not taking my advice,' in Mike's more-in-sorrow-than-in-anger account, he reached England in September after a difficult trek with his wife and young children via southern France through Spain and Portugal. The family moved into Diana's house in Sussex and the admiral joined the Home Guard.

Back in Cap d'Antibes, Arlette and Costa Trevelas were left holding the fort—the villa La Gardiole and the yacht *Landfall*. It was not a smooth relationship. In an eight-page handwritten letter to Nancy at the start of May 1941, Arlette unreeled her many grievances with Costa.[10] He was not handing over money from the Paines that she felt she was owed. He was taking women on board the *Landfall*. He had removed precious yachting objects from the villa. Mike's one-year old Simca 5 car, which had been abandoned in a park in Marseilles, had been sold for a song to a man who promised to sell it back to Mike if he ever returned to France; the money involved was now in the possession of Mike's friend Renée.

Meantime, Mike's landlord in Marseilles was refusing to allow Arlette into his flat there to remove his possessions unless she settled an outstanding gas bill. At the villa, Madame Aubain, the somewhat devious mother of Antoine Mounier, the owner of La Gardiole, who had some time back fallen out with Nancy, had intruded into the garden—Mike's pride and joy—and claimed some of the land as her own to grow vegetables. Still, the Cumberleges' possessions in the house were intact, the roses were in bloom again, Arlette had secured a part-time job with a Romanian couple, and the property had not been requisitioned. How Nancy responded is a mystery; there was little she could do.

Diana, by then Peruvian by marriage, remained in Biarritz until mid-October 1940. In a letter to Nancy in March 1941, written from her new home in Lima, she described what happened following the Nazi invasion of south-west France. First, Jorge Dibos Valdeavellano, her husband, managed to shepherd the admiral and his brood across 'that ghastly frontier' into Spain. Then, just a few hours later, the Germans arrived:

> The remaining, very few Englishmen in the area were put into concentration camps and the women made to report daily to the *comandante*. We had 294 German soldiers living in the garden. Their officers lived in the house, their stinking, colossal swastika flag was hung from our bedroom window and every morning and evening the whole company paraded in front of it. They had all their horses and full camping equipment with them, they washed all their clothes and hung them to dry all over the rose bushes and terraces in spite of 75 acres of land which wasn't actual garden, they took the children's nursery over and turned it into an office and they made themselves loathsomely objectionable in every way.

Diana and Jorge stayed until they could get away in mid-October through Spain to Portugal and then via New York to Peru.

In London, the French-speaking Mike was immediately given a diplomatically-sensitive job by the Admiralty: liaison officer to General de Gaulle and the Free French contingent then forming in the British capital. Although he had leave owing, he preferred to keep working. At first, Nancy stayed in a rented flat in London with Marcus. In August, a month before the Luftwaffe Blitz on London began, the Paines (who continued to advance money to Mike) also offered to take the baby for the duration of the war. The Cumberleges declined the generous offer in part because, as Mike wrote, 'my family fortunes for the moment are bound up in England.'[11] Soon after, Marcus was despatched to Somerset to stay for a time with the two 'Aunts', Gladys and Gwen, on a guarded estate in the heart of Exmoor—'as safe as any little boy can be in England today'—together with half a dozen other children from the Big Smoke.

During the following six weeks, Mike worked as 'never before' trying to keep the humiliated French on side: 'The consequence has been one of the happiest few weeks of my life'. It was not, however, easy work. 'The first volunteers to join de Gaulle were a motley band who resembled medieval knights pledging themselves to a baron who had put himself forward to the rank of Constable of the kingdom,' Jonathan Fenby argues in his biography *The General.* 'De Gaulle demanded unquestioning allegiance as a matter of course. With him, it was take it or leave it.' Visitors to his gloomy suite of offices in St Stephen's House on the Victoria Embankment found him 'inexpressibly remote, intensely reserved, apparently lacking in humour or concern for others', in Fenby's judgement.[12] For his part, Mike found de Gaulle 'colourless, though honest. He is in a very difficult position. Britain, post-Dunkirk, is not really able to do much to help him and, if it hadn't been for Churchill, I think we should have thrown the French completely by the board.' With his faulty political antenna, Mike seems to have harboured hopes for Vichy France and Marshal Pétain: '... a pathetic old man, but he could yet prove the saving of France'. He also noted shrewdly that de Gaulle did not help himself: 'The trouble was that the first clause on his [de Gaulle's] contract with Britain was that he should never fire on Frenchmen when, of course, they fired on him. It put him on the spot'.

According to several of his subsequent letters, Mike worked such long hours supporting the Free French at this time that he had to give up letter writing: 'It has been inspiring and I was very lucky'. One day he accompanied two of the leading Free French adherents, Vice-Admiral Emile Muselier and Capt. Georges Thierry D'Argenlieu, on a day trip to Chichester to show them the cathedral made of stone from Caen. Muselier, 'a headstrong voluble character' according to Fenby and an 'unbearable busybody' according to de Gaulle, had been appointed by de Gaulle Commander of the Free French Navy and effectively number two in the movement. Later, he was to feature in a bungled and unauthorised British attempt to divide and rule the Free French. As a result, he lost de Gaulle's confidence and was forced out of the leadership group in March 1942. D'Argenlieu, a naval officer, stuck it out with the general, became head of Free French naval forces in 1943, and entered Paris with de Gaulle in August 1944. 'It has been inspiring to work with General de Gaulle's staff and the Free French and I was very lucky,' Mike reflected later. 'But I was taken away.'

Before that happened, Mike found himself at the centre of a diplomatic incident. One day at the end of July, he went to see Muselier 'with a view to coming to an amicable arrangement with reference to the policing of the [French] merchant seamen at Crystal Palace waiting to be repatriated' as he put it in a subsequent memorandum.[13] In the process, wittingly or unwittingly, he ran into a storm of French bitterness and resentment. Muselier rejected Mike's proposal that a 'commandant' be appointed who, while an 'ally' of General de Gaulle, was 'independent' of the Free French Forces. Muselier erupted and became extremely angry and then widened the discussion to lay into all French officers and men who had decided to join the Royal Navy rather than the FFF. 'I ignore completely all officers and men serving with the British,' he told Mike. 'For me, they don't exist. If I see such an officer in French uniform I shall order him to remove it.'

Following this outburst, Viscount Halifax, the Foreign Secretary, sent de Gaulle a memorandum through the Admiralty saying that Muselier 'has completely departed from the principles which have been the basis of our understanding'.[14] Muselier's views were 'intemperate ... most unfortunate ... and harmful to discipline'. He urged de Gaulle to rein in Muselier and said that if this was not achieved, future naval coordination between British and French forces would be 'impossible'. Ironically, only two months later, with de Gaulle having stabilised his leadership and the British having received some old American destroyers, the Royal Navy decided that no French officers or men would be allowed to serve in the RN and all those already in the RN would be 'encouraged' to join the FF Navy.

Mike was thousands of miles away by then. Only three days after the Muselier meeting, he embarked early in August on a Royal Mail liner for Portugal and the Cape Verde islands in the central Atlantic, 350 miles west of the African coast. The posting had been sudden; it turned out that his predecessor had met with an accident. It proved to be a dull nine-day voyage, although Mike enlivened it by searching for enemy submarines. On board with him were 'four empire builders, a sprinkling of Czech Jews and pale Polacks'. The food was edible and the rest did him good. Mostly, it was overcast, but eventually the sun came out. By the end of the voyage, it was hot and he became stiff from countless games of deck tennis: 'How the English love to play games. We bound about in joyful abandon. My behind aches, I can hardly bend down to pick up the quoit and yet I bound on'. Already he was missing Nancy and Marcus: 'I love Marcus—he is delightfully astonished and wondering about everything'.[15]

On Cape Verde, he had been assigned (probably sponsored by the Director of Naval Intelligence, his old friend John Godfrey) to the UK Consulate on Sao

Vicente as 'Consular Shipping Adviser' for the Naval Control Service (NCS). This was a shadowy, Grimsby-based organisation set up by Britain early in the war to provide the Admiralty with information about all vessels entering and leaving ports on the UK coast and the movements of enemy aircraft and convoys along the coast as well as to route merchant vessels out of UK waters on the safest passage available on their way to join Allied convoys. It possessed several armed patrol trawlers and other small craft, and its senior officers were all Royal Navy or RNR captains and commanders recalled from retirement. Having a representative in faraway Sao Vicente was certainly a first.

Mike, however, had rather different duties to those previously associated with the NCS. His appointment had been touched off by concern in the Admiralty that the Nazis might seize islands in the Atlantic to serve as bases for submarine attacks on Allied shipping in the north Atlantic and elsewhere. In Führer Directive No. 18, issued in November 1940, Hitler actually outlined a detailed plan to capture Gibraltar, the Canary Islands, and the Cape Verde islands. Portugal, which owned the Cape Verde archipelago, had declared its neutrality in 1939. The plan relied on support from Franco in Spain, which was not forthcoming. Soon after, early in 1941, Hitler's attention turned east and the idea was forgotten. The British, too, had been preparing a plan to invade the islands and assembled a Royal Marine brigade in Freetown, Sierra Leone, for the purpose. One of Mike's tasks was to prepare the ground for this force by scouting out landing sites and cultivating Portuguese support. Another was to keep track of all shipping arriving in the islands. A third was to assess the strength of sympathy locally for the Axis side.

On paper, it sounded like an exciting assignment for a young RNR officer making his way in naval intelligence. In practice, the next five months proved to be the most unrewarding of Mike's entire life. He did not use his military rank and all mail to him via the British Consulate on Sao Vicente had to be addressed to 'Mr. Cumberlege' or 'Michael Cumberlege Esq.' He discovered that he need pay no income tax while based in Cape Verde and, at first, thought it was a 'nice part of the world' for a wartime posting. Fairly soon, he decided that the local residents were 'unamusing and earnest and withal unintelligent', the work was 'of the most tiresome kind', ships called in too irregularly, the only air links were unreliable via Portugal and Italy, and news and mail from England arrived erratically if at all. From late August to the end of October, he heard nothing from Nancy: '... not a single solitary stray letter'. Inevitably, this caused marital problems. One of Mike's letters home was actually posted in South America by a young Czech refugee who got to know Mike in Sao Vicente before he moved on. Letters to the Paines in the United States went via Bermuda where one of the censors, H. Cotton Minchin, was a good friend of Mike's and another of his sister, Diana.

Within a couple of months of arriving in Cape Verde, he was fed up: 'I have slowly and surely deteriorated into a sullen, morose and utterly impossible person'.[16] Eleven letters that he wrote to Nancy in the August–October period survive. They paint a picture of a young, active man keen to get into the war and becoming rapidly disillusioned by his job—'utterly moronic and tiresome'—and his colleagues: '... snobs and little Empire builders.... My work really starts after dinner and goes on to any old time'.[17] The basic lack of interest in London in what he was doing added to his frustration, particularly once it became clear that the threat of invasion from Vichy French or German forces had receded, as did the claustrophobic character of a small community where 'my every move is watched and there is nothing unknown.'[18]

News from Nancy arrived intermittently, if at all; one batch of her letters was on a ship torpedoed in the Atlantic by the Germans, another batch was returned to her unopened towards the end of 1941, ten months after Mike had left the islands. This did not help mutual understanding, and throughout the 1940–43 period, Nancy, mostly resident with Marcus in London and Sussex, had difficulty imagining war, the dislocation and constraints that inevitably went with it, and Mike's role in the conflict. The secret nature of his work and, once he left the Cape Verde islands, his constant movement from one place to another, often with no postal or telegram address, did not help either. Nor did Nancy's mercurial emotional temperament, one minute wildly up the next wildly down, often in the same letter.

In his first couple of months on Sao Vincente, Mike's best friends turned out to be four visiting Portuguese naval officers from the British-built sloop *Bartholmeu Diaz*. Another diversion was the unexpected arrival of the *Capitana*, a yacht once owned by his American patron and friend Paul Hammond (who had sold the *Landfall* to the Paines), which had been used to retrace the Atlantic voyages of Christopher Columbus in 1939 and was then *en route* back to America for a new owner.[19] An endless round of expatriate parties and receptions was hard to avoid and the fact that most of the work Mike did (writing and collating intelligence-related reports, and 'quietly nosing around' as he put it on one occasion[20]) involved staying in his office added to his frustrations.

At one point, so intense did his boredom become, that he even played a round of 'GOLF' (written in capital letters) and a game of tennis ('not a success'[21]) with a fellow RNR officer. His reading list at the time included *The Rover* by Joseph Conrad which he reread to remind himself of Provence, the satirical Byron poem *Don Juan*, and a 'magnificent book' (a present from a friend), *The Life of Greece*, by Will Durant. Soon he was agitating to be more involved in the war effort and Nancy was enjoined to 'go and see' two well-placed friends: Stephen Roskill, then working on the Naval Staff at the Admiralty, and John Godfrey, 'to keep all my lines open for me.'[22]

Money, as ever, concerned him, but in his usual devil-may-care way. He calculated on arrival in Sao Vincente that he would be able to bank £41 a month in London (later increased to £45 a month or £2,700 in today's money) through a combination of his naval pay and continuing transfers from Ritchie Paine who also generously agreed to pay the rent on the villa in Cap d'Antibes. But he faced a large UK income tax liability going back several years and also owed both the naval outfitters Gieves and his bank substantial amounts. In early September, Nancy, by then living with Marcus in London in a rented house in Godfrey Street, Chelsea, was earnestly requested to 'try to get our finances out of the red' as Mike looked forward to the repayment of a war loan bond in December. By the new year (1941), 'we should be in the clear,' he wrote optimistically.[23]

At the end of October, to lighten his mood, he moved in with the UK Consul Captain James Sands: '... a sweet old man, Irish and intelligent. It is a great joy to me'. The Consul, a retired Royal Navy engineer from Armagh aged seventy, had held the honorary rank since 1926. In 1943, he was to play an important role in the seizure by the Allies of several Italian tankers in the islands. He possessed the best house in Sao Vicente sited on a promontory by the ocean, superb for viewing sunrises and sunsets and gazing across the horizon for a ship. The pair usually took early morning swims in the sea together before drinking cups of strong fresh local coffee roasted on a bit of old tin over a charcoal fire on the terrace of the house: 'Then I read for a bit, have a shave, dress, and bicycle into town at 8.30. So my day begins'.

The Portuguese proved non-committal politically and militarily but generally friendly. Mike got to know the Governor, Amadeu Gomes de Figueiredo, and wrote a vivid pen portrait of him in action to Ellen Paine after a reception at the Consulate:

> He [the Governor] made a magnificent speech. The Portuguese are taught oratory at school and it becomes them naturally. He was delightful from the opening pose, the foot slightly forward, the index finger of the right hand pointing to a spot on the ground slightly in advance, the head back and the eye fixed on the infinite. And then the gradual awakening of his speech, at first moderate, then gradually taking impulse from impulse, crescendo Corazon, beautiful words and silence.[24]

Far more Germans and Italians than British, however, lived on the islands, and walking the streets could involve some tricky moments: 'We pass one another at every turn but look glassily ahead. What a world and what a life!' Early in 1942, a report sent to London, most likely based on work by Mike, analysed potential Nazi support on the islands. It identified Mindello, a port in the northern part of Sao Vicente, as the headquarters of a quasi-military Nazi unit based on a cable company; Porto Grande as the only port on the islands with adequate harbour facilities for an invasion force; and three out-and-out Nazi sympathisers. Thirty German sailors had been shipwrecked on the islands in

April 1940 but had left by the end of the year after attempting to spread Nazi propaganda. A list of known German sympathisers was included. By 1943, the United States had entered the war. This swung local opinion decisively against the Germans and Italians.

To counter the tedium, and no doubt to seek new military information about the islands, Mike took to long-distance, rough walking—'real hard slogging, the only satisfaction to be found here'—and cleaning up mountain tracks as he went. This, he claimed, was 'a pleasant and extremely crazy pastime which produces a very copious and satisfying thirst'.[25] One walk in mid-November produced another of Mike's lyrical moments:

> Yesterday's walk was new to me and more interesting than usual. I climbed up a rock-strewn valley to a kind of pass (as I thought) between two peaks. All was hot and still, but as I approached the pass and the rocks became more twisted and wild-looking, I heard the roaring of the wind. It was blowing very hard but I was in the lee. The effect was really frightening in that desolation. There was a thunderous amount of noise and I expected to find a huge pit leading to bottomless perdition and penal fire. I approached, climbing cautiously, until suddenly I was enveloped in the wind. It was blowing me over the pass like a cork in a cataract. Suddenly, below me, instead of vistas of land there was a vertical drop straight down into the sea whose shattering on the rocks below was adding to the shriek of the wind. It took me some while to pluck up my courage to continue climbing because it was easy to imagine devilish winds suddenly snatching one up and whisking one into the surf and rollers below. I climbed to the top of the peak and made a square altar, or cairn, from the strange slabs of stone I found there.[26]

In December 1940, some excitement arose after English merchant sailors tore down the Nazi escutcheon from the front of the German Consulate. The group was rounded up and imprisoned. Mike then got everyone released and deported. Just before Christmas, he was at his wits end:

> I am completely fed up with this ghastly place. It has nothing to commend it and on the whole the people are a menace. They don't even have the attractive faculty of scoundrels but are merely nondescript. There is nothing to relieve the monotony except reading and walking and one can't do this all the time. Even the [local] drink is unattractive. I have tried to justify my existence but without much success.

Relief, however, was at hand. Early in 1941, he was informed that he was being recalled to London for unspecified duties. His phoney war was over.

6

Into Battle

On arrival in London sometime in February 1941, Mike spent a few days on leave with Nancy and Marcus before meeting the Director of Naval Intelligence Rear-Admiral John Godfrey in the Admiralty and being informed that he was to be appointed to command the grandly-named Allied 'para-naval force' in the Aegean and eastern Mediterranean. The task was to run covert missions into the area under the auspices of the Special Operations Executive. Given his pre-war sailing background and extensive knowledge of the coasts and inlets in this part of the world, it was a clever appointment. The SOE Middle East section in Cairo, informed of Cumberlege's selection, responded that at that moment this 'force' consisted of one vessel, the *Dolphin II*, and she was away on a mission to Crete.[1] Nevertheless, on 6 February, Godfrey formally appointed Cumberlege to HMS *President* for special duties with MO4 (as SOE was then known in the Middle East). The appointment was typical of Godfrey's unorthodox approach to his job.

In his biography of John Godfrey, *Very Special Admiral*, Patrick Beesly writes:

The paradoxes and contradictions of John Godfrey's career were only equalled by the quirks and complexities of his character; ambitious, extremely able, physically and mentally resilient, he was shy and suffered from an inferiority complex; liberal minded, forward looking and capable of many acts of personal kindness and thoughtfulness, he was also ruthless and sometimes selfish; inspiring general admiration, much loyalty and often affection, he could equally arouse antagonism, jealousy, even dislike; a charming host and a good listener, he did not suffer fools gladly and made little attempt to conceal his contempt for colleagues of lesser mental calibre; an excellent chooser of men, fiercely loyal to his subordinates, he was sometimes naive about his superiors; a superb organiser of the devious and unscrupulous art of Intelligence, he was a man of great moral courage, who refused to depart from the very high standards he set himself ...a man with a marked talent for securing help from important and influential people for any project he had in hand, he was unable or unwilling to use that talent for his own personal advantage.[2]

Mike seems to have left Nancy and the UK by air, initially for Gibraltar, around 18 February. It would be stretching the point to imply he set off optimistically or in a gung-ho spirit. In an introspective letter from 'a miserable little room' in the Bristol Hotel that he scrawled in pencil to Nancy on the 20th (the only one of his letters home that remains from 1941), he mentions that he was travelling to Egypt 'in exalted but extremely boring company' with a senior civil servant who 'knows the name of every Cabinet Minister's under-secretary and [their] under-secretary for the last five hundred years, combined with the theories of Karl Marx etc. He is also <u>extremely</u> well read'. Mike happened to be reading *Sentimental Education*, Gustave Flaubert's story of a young lawyer in the 1848 French Revolution and one of the most influential novels of the nineteenth century, but this had not impressed his blinkered companion. With the Blitz on London in full swing at the time, he added: 'I believe that at last we are at war. We weren't before but now I have a feeling that the war is on us. There is going to be much suffering and many years will pass before we can have the old comforts of peace'. Shortly after, Nancy moved out of London to live with her father-in-law and his brood in uncomfortable proximity in a house owned by Diana in the village of Ifield in Sussex.

In Alexandria, Mike, who on his appointment had been denied promotion to lieutenant commander by hidebound RN red tape, met several of those who were to work with him closely over the next couple of years. Principal among them was his nominal boss Lt Cdr Francis Pool, a rotund forty-seven-year old RNR officer who oversaw all the SOE's naval operations in the eastern Mediterranean. At the time, Pool, reflecting a directive from Winston Churchill (actively opposed by the Foreign Office), was exploring ways to make use of members of the paramilitary Jewish Haganah on naval sabotage missions. The Haganah was happy to cooperate, seeing this as a way to enhance its fledgling maritime prowess with a view to expediting Jewish emigration to Palestine at a later time. One of Pool's instructors in Haifa was a thirty-four-year old classical scholar called Nicholas Hammond, soon to become a staunch friend and colleague of Mike's in Crete. Also present was Mike's thirty-five-year old cousin, Major Cle Cumberlege, with whom he had always been close. Cle had managed to detach himself from routine staff duties with the Royal Regiment of Artillery in the deserts of North Africa to work with Mike. It was Cle who introduced Mike to Jewish members of the Haganah who had already been trained in naval operations by the SOE—a group Mike mostly came to respect but, in the dismissive tones of the time, captioned 'My three Jew boys' on a photograph with the island of Hydra in the background that he took of the group and later sent to Nancy.

It was not until the start of April, however, with German forces about to invade Greece that Mike actually caught up with the *Dolphin II*, by then in Piraeus, and assumed command. The vessel turned out to be a ketch of 40 tons, built in Haifa, with no sails and equipped with a diesel engine. She was armed with two Lewis machine guns, two Bren guns, and a 2-pounder—one gun at the bow and the two machine guns on either side of the bridge. Cle was put in charge of the *Dolphin II*'s armoury and Ernest Saunders, a 'cheerful' Able Seaman with seventeen years' lower deck RN experience most recently on the aircraft carrier HMS *Eagle*, made responsible for three additional Palestinian Jews as well as for the others who had already been trained in Egypt.

Reaching Piraeus, Mike immediately took the *Dolphin II* on a week-long 'shake-down' and reconnaissance tour of the Dodecanese islands and Rhodes in particular, ahead of a proposed amphibious landing. Intelligence was gathered about local sentiments and coastal conditions, gun practice held in isolated places and the novice crew put through its paces at sea. Shortly after, on returning to Piraeus, the port was devastated by an air raid as the German invasion began. One of the Palestinian Jews, Yoel Golomb, who had been trained by Cle in Egypt, subsequently wrote an account of what happened.[3] According to him, his group had arrived in Athens and three members had been sent to a small vessel anchored in a bay outside Piraeus rather than to the *Dolphin II*. The air raid took place and a bomb hit a ship loaded with ammunition in Piraeus harbour. A huge explosion followed. Several vessels were sunk and houses close to the dockside destroyed. The *Dolphin II*, with her crew on board at the time, survived. She had been moored alongside the ammunition ship but the debris flew over her and everyone on board: 'It was a miracle that none of them was hurt'.

The vessel then set off on a two-week reconnaissance tour to Crete. A photo in Mike's collection shows a stop at Monemvasia, a small island off the east coast of the Peloponnese famous for its fortress, where he 'had *meze* [a snack] with the locals'. There was also a stop at Cape Skyli where Mike would land in 1943 on Operation Locksmith. This trip proved to be 'uneventful'. Golomb, though, claims that throughout this period the Jewish sailors' relations with the British officers (Mike and Cle) 'were not good. They were aristocratic and regarded us as "natives". We did all the work on the ship.' Another Jewish member of the crew, Jacob Agayev, made even more pointed complaints about their treatment in interviews with *Maariv* newspaper before he died in 1991. As he put it: 'I cannot help feeling that the English wanted to get rid of us Jews and gave us the most daring operations. It seemed [as though] they could not care particularly if we did not return to the land of the living'.[4]

Contradictions abound in these accounts. Golomb, for example, claims that Mike ran to the bridge during the Piraeus attack, knocking him down on the way while Yitzchak Spector, another of the Jewish crew, manned the machine gun on the starboard side of the *Dolphin II*, fired at the lead plane, hit it, and kept on firing at a second plane, which he also hit. He makes no mention of Cle Cumberlege, who presumably was in charge of the 'artillery' on board. SOE war dairies confirm that a two-engined bomber was shot down in this raid but disagree with Golomb's account over dates and the sequence of events. Moreover, as Golomb himself makes clear in another part of his account, he was not actually on the *Dolphin II* when the Piraeus attack took place.

Agayev goes on to claim that he was later 'abandoned' on Crete by the British and only got back to Palestine thanks to his own ingenuity. That may well be so in the chaos that followed the German parachute invasion of the island, yet Mike and Cle's allegedly uncaring attitude towards their Jewish crewmembers while operating together under highly dangerous wartime conditions seems very unlikely given Mike's meticulous attention to detail when at sea, his ever-scrupulous attitude to all those who sailed with him throughout his life, and the *Dolphin II*'s dependence on her crew to survive. However, it could well be that Mike was less than sensitive to the understandably complex and touchy Palestinian Jewish feelings about the British during the war. Almost certainly, too, he was trying to discover which of the Jewish men he had been given was up to the job of clandestine naval operations in the Aegean. Golomb departed the *Dolphin II* soon after the Dodecanese voyage and was fortunate to escape Athens as the Germans arrived, eventually reaching Crete and getting off the island on the last ship to leave before the end of the Allied evacuation. Two of his colleagues, Shmuel Ben Shaprut and Shlomo Kostika ('Sam' and 'Johnny' to the Englishmen), remained on the *Dolphin II* for a while longer before they were replaced by Greek sailors. They all reached a camp in Tel Aviv via Egypt by the end of May.

If Mike was concerned about all this, he never mentioned it. Instead, he immediately moved on to the next objective he was given: the destruction of the narrow (70-foot), four-mile long Corinth Canal, built in the 1880s, which he had several times transited in his pre-war sailing days. By this stage, Nancy had written Mike twenty letters, but his replies do not survive (one, written from Lisbon *en route* to Cairo, took eight weeks to reach her). In her correspondence, Nancy, who was now in Sussex, describes being in 'a horrid uninteresting world of children's diets and golf handicaps'.[5] Her furniture had arrived from London but she loathed Norah, Mike's step-mother—'the old dragon ... an awful woman'—who fussed constantly about money and passed on disturbing news of the *Landfall* crew (Costa claimed he was destitute and refused to hand over funds from the Paines to Arlette, the maid at La Gardiole, while the two Croats had made it to the USA but were penniless). Early in February, a letter to Nancy from Ritchie Paine indicated that he planned to sell the *Landfall* if he could.[6] A nearby RAF mess, where Nancy worked part-time in the canteen, provided some diversions as did gardening. John Godfrey once came down to Sussex on a visit bearing a box of chocolates and later sent her a reassuring note about Mike. Increasingly, though, as spring began, it was the deteriorating war situation in the Balkans and Greece that dominated her thoughts. She understood that Mike must be 'happy and proud' to be helping the Greeks—'lovely, kind people'—but worried every day about his safety. As the Germans reached Athens at the start of April she wrote: 'I hate them [the Germans]—I'm quite speechless with loathing and disgust'.[7]

It was now that Mike's years of covert sketching came into play. Blocking the Corinth Canal, which offered German and Italian forces a shortcut to move supplies in safety to eastern Greece, Turkey, and North Africa, had been investigated by the Admiralty earlier in the war and was favoured in principle by Admiral Andrew Cunningham, the Commander-in-Chief Mediterranean. Yet as long as Greece remained an active ally and resisted the demolition of its infrastructure, the British could not act. For much of this period, planning for such an action was left in the hands of the UK Naval *attaché* in Athens, Rear-Admiral Charles Turle. He paid little attention to the matter and never regarded it as a priority. Soon, he was swamped by more urgent demands such as ensuring that the Greek Navy did not fall into Axis hands. However, a plan using caïques had been hatched by the SOE office in Athens. With the *Dolphin II*'s arrival on the scene, and the military situation in Greece reaching a critical point, Turle adopted it and put the operation in Mike's hands. Very quickly, he acquired one 1,500-lb mine from an RN corvette and eight depth charges. Later these explosives were supplemented by magnetic limpets with seven-day delay fuses and a 'largish rowing boat' that Mike purchased in Corinth and named the *Corinthus*. The Greeks were not informed about the operation, which had to be carried out in secret at the last possible moment to allow retreating Allied forces use of a bridge that crossed the waterway.

On 21 April, the *Dolphin II* set off for the canal, stopping at a small fishing village called Epidavro where Mike, Cle, and Saunders 'were given a wonderful welcome and a meal' before anchoring for the night in a small bay close to the canal.[8] On 22 April, the ketch made a dummy run through the canal, feigning an engine defect to account for the delay, and while the *Corinthus* was loaded with the depth charges, the banks of the canal were checked for weak spots and friendly relations established with the Greek guards and canal officials still in place. A spot about 400 yards east of a rail bridge near the eastern bank of the canal was chosen for the explosives, in part because a big rock fall in 1938 had left a large crack in the canal wall that, it was hoped, would collapse when hit by the detonations. Exactly who was on board with Mike has never been clear, but the core crew certainly included his cousin Cle, AB Ernest Saunders, and 'two Palestinians', most likely Shlomo Kostika and Shmuel Ben Shaprut.

With everything primed for action, Mike 'hitchhiked', in his word, the 50 miles to Athens on 23 April to request permission to proceed with the operation. This was given that afternoon by Turle and by Tom Baillie-Grohman, the rear-admiral responsible for the naval evacuation of Allied forces from Greece. Mike returned to the *Dolphin II*. At 6.30 a.m. the next day, the canal opened. Allowing four other craft to move ahead, the ketch followed, towing the *Corinthus*. Passing the bridge as the sentry on it 'conveniently strolled off' as Mike put it in his subsequent report, he gave the order to Cle to scuttle the *Corinthus* and its depth charges at 6.55 a.m.[9] As the boat sank and the tow line was cut, Mike released the magnetic mine 'with hardly a splash' and substituted a dinghy for the sunken rowing boat in case its absence behind the *Dolphin II* was noted. The mine and depth charges were timed to go off on 1 May. Displaying notable coolness, Mike then disembarked from the ketch to pay the canal dues: 'The port officers were very helpful. I explained that I had been recalled to Athens. They were quite unsuspicious and were more concerned with the war'. The *Dolphin II* made her way to Athens where Saunders' diary recorded that she was 'fired on' and Mike laconically stated that they received 'a hostile reception from the natives'; the Germans were on the outskirts of the city and captured the Corinth Canal forty-eight hours later. Having messaged Baillie-Grohman that the explosives had been laid, Mike moved on to Nauplia (Nafplio) to assist the headlong Allied evacuation of the Peloponnese.

Events in Greece now moved so fast that it was not until mid-May that Cumberlege heard any news about the canal operation. A businessman he met in Crete at the time informed him that the canal operation had been successful and the waterway was blocked. Unfortunately, this was incorrect. Neither the mine nor the depth charges seem to have exploded. Within a month, the canal was in full operation under Italian control. Recriminations began shortly after. Admiral Cunningham blamed Turle for his reticence and lack of preparation. So did John Godfrey in London. Turle cited the pressure of events and his other priorities; his wartime career as naval *attaché* was terminated although he was given other naval posts later. Cunningham came under criticism in the Admiralty for his failure to prioritise the operation earlier. The one person not criticised was Mike Cumberlege. He had carried out his work 'boldly and efficiently within the terms of his instructions', declared Godfrey at the end of July. He added that Mike was 'an officer exceptionally well qualified for work of this nature [due to] his unrivalled knowledge of the Aegean, his seamanlike qualities especially in small sailing ships, and his natural aptitude for just such tasks as the one which is here reported upon'.[10] Godfrey proposed that Mike be promoted to lieutenant commander. The recommendation was not acted on by the hidebound Admiralty for another two years.

In Nauplia, the *Dolphin II* encountered a Dunkirk-style evacuation emergency in the making. Thousands of retreating Allied troops were crowding into the port and other harbours and onto neighbouring beaches seeking a way out as German troops advanced relentlessly. Mike and his crew rolled up their sleeves and did what they could. Over two days, 25–27 April, the *Dolphin II* ferried some 1,250 troops to various ships from the beaches at Nauplia and nearby Monemvasia, often under fire from enemy aircraft. Still in the thick of things on the 28th, 'as we were coming into Mona Vasia [*sic.*] we were attacked by dive bombers who bombed and machine gunned us, hitting our masts and rigging,' recorded Saunders in his diary. 'We put into a small bay and went ashore for the day. We sailed at dusk, calling at a harbour where we took some more chaps off to ships.' Later that night, the *Dolphin II* headed for Crete, arriving at Souda Bay on 30 April.

The month of May 1941 in Crete that followed must rank as the most dramatic of Mike Cumberlege's action-packed life. All his ingenuity, doggedness, courage, leadership skills, and admiration for the Cretans and their history and culture came together in support of the desperate and ultimately hopeless Allied struggle to halt the German advance on the island. All around him, collapsing lines of communication, non-existent transport, broken Allied units, German and Italian air attacks, and shifting loyalties on the ground made his task more hazardous by the day. He insisted on remaining on Crete to the last possible moment before making his own escape. Most of the time, he was acting on his own initiative; the *Dolphin II* was not equipped with radio and orders frequently never arrived or were lost or ignored or overtaken by events. His personal account of these weeks did not survive, maybe lost in the warehouse fire in Cairo that destroyed SOE Middle East records in 1942. But, in addition to the Saunders' diary, Nicholas Hammond, who joined the *Dolphin II* at Canae (Chania) in Crete, wrote a vivid account of this period in a contribution in 1982 to the journal *Balkan Studies*: 'Memories Of A British Officer Serving In Special Operations Executive In Greece 1941'.[11] And other British 'irregulars' such as Paddy Leigh Fermor and Xan Fielding, who both knew Mike, later wrote about this period. So much is known or can be pieced together.

After a day or two in Canae, during which a gale blew up and waves of German dive bombers attacked shipping in Souda Bay, once embarrassingly catching Hammond in open water in a dinghy as he was ferrying explosives from a dump, the *Dolphin II* moved on to scout remote beaches like Loutro and Sphakia on the south coast that might be used in future to land stores. In Sphakia, Mike managed to buy a box of eggs and a crate of fish for the crew. 'Mike also had in mind the value of such a reconnaissance for a return to Crete if it was lost to the enemy,' noted Hammond several times in his account. The *Dolphin II* then sailed to the little Venetian harbour of Heraklion on a quiet, sunlit summer's evening where, during a week-long stop, her troublesome engine was overhauled, the two Jewish members of crew departed, and two new recruits signed up. One, a tough, adventurous Rhodesian named James

'Jumbo' Steele, a private in the Black Watch, was a first-class machine gunner. He was also to act as the ship's engineer. He remained with Mike to the end of his life. The other, Kyriakos Kiriakides, was a veteran sponge diver from the Dodecanese with a sense of humour. He was to prove useful to Mike in many ways, not least by diving for fish to eat. While the crew changes were going on, Cle and Hammond crossed the island and scouted four northern beaches— again with a view to landing stores and agents in the future—and contacted some local partisans being trained for guerrilla warfare by an acquaintance of Mike's, John Pendlebury.

On paper, Pendlebury, a renowned pre-war archaeologist, was the British vice-consul on Crete. Unorthodox, charming, trustworthy, and popular with the locals, he sported a swordstick and had acquired the sobriquet of the 'uncrowned King of Crete'. How Mike knew him is unclear; possibly the couple had met pre-war at Knossos where Pendlebury had undertaken excavations. Now, with war upon them, the two shared a sense of daring and a burning desire to take the fight to the enemy to help save Crete from fascist rule. As Hammond later wrote in a privately published biography of Pendlebury:

> Both were men of vigorous speech and independent ideas, with great force of character and abundant humour; and both possessed that clear-headed audacity which undertakes the apparently more dangerous course after a detached study of the advantages and disadvantages. They possessed, too, the simplicity of motive in facing or inviting danger, something much more spontaneous and automatic than the ordinary man's sense of duty, a rare quality which I only met once again during the war.[12]

In addition, they admired each other and Mike made Pendlebury an honorary crew member of the *Dolphin II*. With Cle and Hammond, Mike and John 'had some happy evenings' together in Heraklion. Pendlebury was keen to plan a raid on the nearby island of Kasos, then controlled by Italy, in order to capture some prisoners from whom information about enemy plans for Crete might be gleaned. Mike was only too happy to volunteer the *Dolphin II* to take part in this cheeky provocation.

Mike's time in Crete was often interspersed, too, by unexpected encounters that illustrate his great gift for friendship. While anchored off Canae, to give one example, Mike and 'a blond Sergeant Major called Alfred Simpson' were collecting military stores from dumps around Souda Bay when they came across the Vergos family. Mike had run into some of the members in the Greek capital. Strongly pro-British, the family had had to flee Athens as the Germans advanced and had managed to reach Crete, ending up forlorn and hungry on a small island in the bay. Costas Vergos, then an eleven-year old boy, recalled years later being impressed by Mike's 'kindness and his *skoulariki* [ear-ring].... Alfred cooked bully beef, sausages and baked beans for us and Cumberlege carried two small beds and some blankets ashore on his back for us'.[13] A month or so later, Mike was to lunch with the Vergos family in Alexandria, his hand still in plaster after his escape from Crete.

Another time he was journeying across the Askypho plain and came across a local fable, which he delighted in relaying to all and sundry. It went like this:

> An ancient bearded bandit of Askypho was arguing with a Cretan from another village. After much talk he became tired of talk. 'Listen,' he said 'now you will agree with me, politically speaking, the world is Europe?' 'Yes, that is true.' 'Well, you must then agree that Europe is Greece?' 'Yes, that also.' 'And without question that Greece is Crete?' 'Oh, undoubtedly.' 'Well, then you must finally agree that Crete is Askypho?' 'Yes, that certainly is the case.' 'Well, I am Askypho so now shut up!'

Out of the blue, another distraction cropped up. Accounts vary as to exactly what happened, but the gist of the story is that one day early in May, Elizabeth Gwynne (David) and her partner Charles Gibson-Cowan were on the quayside in Heraklion during a bombing raid, having escaped from the Germans by the skin of their teeth from the island of Syros where Charles had been teaching English.[14] Here they bumped into Mike briefly, who knew both from their stay in Cap d'Antibes. By then, the couple had nothing. All their possessions had either been abandoned in the flight from Syros or seized by the Italians who had interned them in the summer of 1940. Fleeing Syros in a fishing boat at the last moment with a failing motor and torn sails, their pilot panicked and got lost. Charles had seized the tiller and steered due south to Crete, no doubt making some use of the navigational instruction he had received from Mike two years before. The 300-mile journey had taken them four days. On encountering them, Cumberlege seems to have handed over some food and cash and aided their departure from Sphakia beach to Egypt a dozen or so days later on one of the civilian convoys organised around then.

The situation in Heraklion and Souda Bay quickly deteriorated as German fighter-bombers increasingly ruled the skies, especially at dusk. The *Dolphin II*, anchored for her refit in the inner harbour in Heraklion, was extremely vulnerable and the men on board often had to dash ashore to shelters or to machine-gun posts on the quayside. 'In between raids, life was blissful,' reckoned Hammond. 'We bathed in the blue waters of the harbour, breakfasted on fresh fish killed by the German bombs and made friends with the Cretans over a glass of wine or a dish of *yiaourti*.' Most evenings, the crew went ashore for a meal. On 17 May, the *Dolphin II* put to sea at night, having been instructed by the Naval Officer in Charge in Heraklion to assess the chances of salvaging a cargo of weapons and ammunition from an Allied supply ship that had been torpedoed at sea and managed to make the harbour at Hierapetra on the south coast. On getting there, it became evident that the wreck was under German observation from planes flying overhead. Mike waited until nightfall. Kyriakou then dived down to examine the hull but quickly concluded that only specialist equipment from Souda Bay could do the job.

On 20 May, the *Dolphin II* headed for Kasos to rendezvous with Pendlebury. Enemy air activity the next day, when German parachutists began to invade Crete, was intense and Cumberlege realised that the raid on Kasos would have to be delayed. He was never able to reach John Pendlebury to inform him of the situation. Pendlebury had decided to remain on Crete after any invasion in order to lead and inspire resistance; he 'felt himself a Cretan' in Hammond's words. On the 21st, he was wounded and captured by the Germans in a firefight a mile or so outside Canae Gate. He was not in uniform and next day was put up against a wall and summarily executed as a sniper or resistance fighter.

Mike was unaware of the parachute invasion or the fighting around Canae. After leaving Hierapetra, he had sailed along the coast to Sudero, near Matala, scouting landing sites, one of which he was to use himself later in 1941. The *Dolphin II* then began to develop engine trouble, calling in at Sitia before returning to Heraklion. As the vessel approached the harbour, it was hit by machine-gun fire. The crew 'began to suspect that things were seriously wrong on shore' as Hammond put it forty years later. Steering well away from the firing, Cle and Hammond clambered ashore and spotted a Nazi flag flying on a power station half a mile from the Venetian-era fortress of Koules that guards the port. Several dead British servicemen lay on the ground in the inner harbour. There was nothing to be done except leave as quickly as possible for a deserted island opposite Heraklion.

Mike, typically unhappy at this tactical retreat, decided to take the fight to the Germans that night by firing from the *Dolphin II* at a shore battery, but the ketch's engine would not start. Eventually it did, and the *Dolphin II* limped towards Souda Bay to report on what had been seen in Heraklion. Fired at several times on the way to Souda, and buzzed by a Heinkel, the engine finally gave out at the entrance to the bay. Hammond and Kyriakou towed the *Dolphin II* in to a small island in the bay by rowing ahead in the dinghy. Jumbo Steele and Mike then spent the next day trying to revive the engine while the rest of the crew sheltered for the next three nights in what Saunders described as 'a very fine cave'.

By 27 May, it had become clear that the group would only get off Crete if it could find a replacement for the *Dolphin II*. Mike had reported earlier that day to the NIOC in Heraklion and discovered that no caïque was available.

However, one was spotted to the west in Souda Bay, a small, red, wooden-hulled vessel with a sail called the *Athanasios Miaoulis*—named after a famous admiral of the Greek War of Independence. She was owned by 'Old Johnny' Strati. He agreed to join the *Dolphin II* crew—Mike, Cle, Hammond, Saunders, Steele, and Kyriakou—provided he could bring along three other Greeks. Among them was Efstratios Bournakis, a twenty-one-year old seaman who had ferried a party of British service personnel to Crete before being sunk in his caïque by a German air attack. Bournakis had actually crossed the Corinth Canal the month before and informed Mike that he had seen a collapsed bridge but it turned out this was the result of a defensive action by retreating Allied engineers.

All the gear, food, and water on the *Dolphin II* was transferred that afternoon to the *Athanasios Miaoulis*. A desperate group of Allied soldiers was persuaded not to seize the now unseaworthy *Dolphin II*, and explosives were laid in her and in the old fort nearby, timed to explode at 6 a.m. the next day. At midnight, Mike gave the order to sail and the disparate ten-man party set off for the Bay of Sollum on the North African coast 400 miles to the south. At that stage, Mike had no idea if Allied forces still held any part of what is now Libya. Rumours had reached Crete that the Axis powers, who had retaken Benghazi in April, had advanced further east along the coast but there were no up-to-date facts. Yet Libya was closer to Souda Bay than Cyprus or Alexandria or Haifa, and the route directly across the Mediterranean was almost certainly safer than zigzagging through the Aegean. Enemy planes circled constantly overhead between 28 and 30 May, a German motor boat bore down on them but was shaken off by a sudden change of course, and progress proved to be very slow, with the party travelling mostly at night and sheltering during the day in coves and small bays until the open sea was reached. Mike, to the annoyance of the others, insisted on scouting the whole coast of the island of Dia—the party's first overnight stop only 7 miles from Souda Bay. 'His argument was that should one return some day to a German-occupied Crete, one would need some local knowledge,' explains Hammond in his *Memories*.

As this risky venture around Dia was ending, seventy-nine German troop carriers roared overhead: 'After that, even Mike agreed that we had better hide up in a crack in the cliffs. We stayed there till dark, bathing and sleeping'. At dusk, the *Athanasios Miaoulis* set off again, this time for the deserted Yanisades islets to the north-east and, as it happened, right into the centre of an invading Italian amphibious force. Mike was navigating with a box compass and the vessel perforce edged ahead and was not detected. The engine's top speed proved to be 2 knots, and that was only for a few hours at a time as the cylinder head was cracked and had to be plugged with pieces of cotton waste every half hour.

Close to the Yanisades, the caïque was approached by a British destroyer supporting the Allied evacuation from Heraklion. 'Mike signalled with a lamp saying who we were' but was ignored. That day, 29 May, the party laid up in a cove in the Yanisades. Walking across the island in the afternoon, Mike spotted a German motorboat lying off an outer island and was immediately keen to attack it. The group agreed to try, using its three machine guns, but Mike uncharacteristically had second thoughts. Instead, that night, the caïque 'lumbered', in Hammond's words, through the dangerous Kasos Strait on the way to the south coast of Crete, hoping to make contact with the Pendlebury group there and set up a resistance cell.

Next morning, 30 May, as Saunders tersely describes it in his *Diary of a British Sailor 1941*, they 'put into a very small bay below a white-washed monastery on the side of a cliff'. This monastery was 7 miles from the nearest road on Koufonisso, a near-deserted islet opposite the island of Kyphonisi. The monks proved to be friendly, but German troops were nearby and the *Athanasios Miaoulis* party clearly could not linger for long. This led to unusual disagreement among the crew. Mike wished to sail to Sphakia, three days away, to help with the Allied evacuation, arguing that it was the crew's duty. Cle, 'a quiet, reserved man [who] refused to be drawn into a quarrel', disagreed: 'Mike, being hot-tempered, said things which he later regretted'. Saunders became depressed and increasingly pessimistic about the group's chances of escape, while Jumbo Steele was annoyed with his skipper for allowing such open divisions to surface. Hammond was asked by Mike to decide. He voted for Egypt 'with the condition that, if we got through, we should try to return with a better vessel to Crete. Mike was disappointed but showed no resentment'. At once, he set course for the Bay of Sollum: 'As in all matters of the sea, we had the greatest faith in his judgement'.

Nicholas Hammond was the only witness to the events that followed who recorded impressions that survive. It seems best to let him speak for himself:

Dawn of May 31st found us well out to sea on a calm, hot day and we were all rather tired and sleepy after a series of night watches. At 9 o'clock or so, when the heat was oppressive, I noticed a plane very high above us and gave the alarm (we had no look-out on duty). Cle and Jumbo, our best machine gunners, took a Bren each in the bows, Mike took the tiller and a Lewis machine gun. The four Greeks got into the engine cabin and Saunders, Kyriakou and I got into the hold from which we could see a patch of sky through the hatch. Forward of the hold there was a smaller hold full of explosives and detonators.

We heard the plane coming in low and received the full force of her guns. Saunders was hit by two bullets which entered the back of his shoulders. He lost consciousness but was evidently in pain. I tried to make him comfortable and put blankets on him, while the plane came round again and gave us another series of bursts to which Cle and Jumbo replied from the bows. After that attack, Mike came to the hatch to say that Cle had been killed outright. He asked me to stay with Saunders who was twisting and turning in pain. Mike rested his Lewis [gun] on the winch by the main hatch. Then the third attack began. When it was over, I came on deck to find Mike wounded in the elbow by an incendiary bullet but Jumbo was O.K.

The plane was flying away towards Crete, low down and with smoke pouring from one engine. Jumbo had had a narrow escape both times. When Cle was killed, Jumbo had seen the plane jerk as it pulled out of a dive to come head-on towards the caïque. That jerk had put the hail of machine gun bullets on one side of the bows, and Jumbo had been grazed on the head by a bullet. In the last attack, Jumbo had hit the plane as it pulled out of its dive. Of the Greeks, one boy had been grazed by a bullet on the side of his head and was deaf in one ear. Mike had a bullet through his elbow-joint which was very painful later. Saunders was still twisting and turning, and I gave him some morphia. He died soon afterwards. Mike was sobbing and we were all near to tears. We wrapped Cle and Saunders in a Union Jack which we had brought from the Dolphin and I read an impromptu service in English and Greek before we slid them into the sea. The phrases of the 102nd Psalm went straight to our hearts.

'Hear my prayer, Lord, let my cry for help come to you. Do not hide your face from me when I am in distress. Turn your ear to me; when I call, answer me quickly. For my days vanish like smoke; my bones burn like glowing embers'.

Mike recited the poem 'Say Not The Struggle', written in 1849 by Arthur Hugh Clough:

> *Say not the struggle nought availeth*
> *The labour and the wounds are vain,*
> *The enemy faints not, nor faileth,*
> *And as things have been they remain.*
> *If hopes were dupes, fears may be liars;*
> *It may be, in yon smoke concealed,*
> *Your comrades chase e'en now the fliers,*
> *And, but for you, possess the field.*
> *For while the tired waves, vainly breaking*
> *Seem here no painful inch to gain,*
> *Far back through creeks and inlets making,*
> *Comes silent, flooding in, the main.*
> *And not by eastern windows only,*
> *When daylight comes, comes in the light,*
> *In front the sun climbs slow, how slowly,*
> *But westward, look, the land is bright.*

The aircraft turned out to have been a Messerschmitt 110 fighter-bomber. It seems unlikely it survived. Several bullets it fired had passed through the explosives in the bows of the *Athanasios Miaoulis* but failed to detonate them. By the evening of the next day, 1 June, Mike had become delirious with his wound; Hammond had to take over some of the steering. Low-lying land was spotted at dusk. The next day, the caïque reached the Bay of Sollum and then headed east for Mersa Matruh. Just before dawn on 3 June, two Italian bombers flew over the *Athanasios Maioulis* but ignored her. Nearing Mersa Matruh, an RAF bomber passed by and the crew waved happily. Someone on shore began signalling to the caïque and Mike came on deck to interpret; they were asking the name of the vessel. Then the *Athanasios Miaoulis* sailed into the harbour. The naval officer in charge on the quayside, known to both Mike and Hammond, did not recognise them and thought they were Greek fisherman with their dirty clothes and beards.

The Greeks remained with the caïque while Mike had his wounds dressed at a field hospital. After a day's rest, Mike, Hammond, and Jumbo Steele sailed to Alexandria in a three-masted brig. On arrival, they were feted by the Royal Navy as the latest arrivals from Crete. Admiral James Sommerville, one of the Navy's ablest commanders and fresh from the successful chase and sinking of the German battleship *Bismarck* only ten days earlier, invited them to lunch. Mike and Hammond discussed ways of returning to Crete and still hoped to make contact with John Pendlebury and his men and deliver supplies. Mike favoured the use of a fast motorboat and 'hide-up' bases on the small islands off Crete, but although his arm was mending, he realised it would take time before he was fit for such a foray. Meanwhile, he accompanied Hammond to Cairo to report to the SOE office. A few months later, the *Athanasios Miaoulis* was taken over by the SOE and used for special operations in the eastern Mediterranean.[15]

Back in England, Nancy received word of Mike via her sister, Nora, who worked in the same building in the Admiralty as John Godfrey, on 14 May, the day before the DNI left on an important hush-hush visit to Washington DC. Mike, she was informed, had 'got out' of Greece safely and 'done wonderful work there'. Somewhat indiscreetly, Godfrey had added some details of the attack on Corinth Canal. 'I am so proud—I knew you'd do something good and brave. How did you get away? The devil looks after his own and you are safe and sound,' Nancy wrote to Mike on 19 May not having heard from him for seven weeks. Mike received this letter and others only on his return to Alexandria. Three days later, Nancy guessed correctly that Mike had gone on to Crete. The news from there, she wrote, was 'very upsetting. I am in a daze trying to see things in their real light. How different we must be once this [war] is over.' At the end of May or the start of June, she wrote again to Mike. The evening before, she had dined with John Godfrey in London, and the next day, he had called her to inform her that Mike had a new job similar to his previous one and was in line for promotion and some leave in England. She added:

> John [Godfrey] was thrilled with all you've done.... He said that he worried about you the whole time he was in America. He is sweet about you, Mike, and I think he loves us both dearly.... He also said that if your letters were as good as I said they were, he would publish them in some official paper they have going. What do you think, if I edited them?[16]

Late in June, by which time she knew that Mike had been wounded and Cle was dead (his death had been announced in the newspapers), she had started to use Godfrey's office to get letters to Mike. Mike's father, who had been in hospital for an operation, was predictably dismissive about Mike's wound—'He probably stubbed his toe' he informed Nancy—but actually worried 'terribly and tries not to let me see.'[17]

Cle's father, Mike's uncle, had been in touch to ask her to ask Mike to send him details of his son's death. For weeks, Mike could not bring himself to write. At last, in late June, Nancy received a long letter (it does not survive) informing her of 'what really happened', which she forwarded to Cle's father. Nancy reacted immediately with one of her own: 'I'm so glad you were in Greece and thrilled what you say about the Greeks'. Later she wrote to Cle's mother, who still had not been told by her husband about Cle's death, giving details of the action. In a letter in July to the Paines, she described Mike's relationship with his cousin: 'Mike adored his cousin Cleco [*sic*]. He was such a sweet person, an only child and would have made a wonderful career for himself. He was on Wavell's staff all through the Libyan battles and gave it up to go on this special job with Mike'.[18]

Nick Hammond later got in touch with Cle's parents and wrote: 'His [Cle's] goodness and his honesty were of that timeless quality which makes me feel that I had known him not for three weeks but for years'. One of the Greek sailors on board the *Athanasios Miaoulis* had described Cle to Hammond as 'Timios, a man precious in the sense that honour is precious'. It turned out that just before Cle was hit, he had given his steel helmet to one of the young Greeks who was near him in the bows. Hammond also contacted Ernest Saunders' parents, writing: 'We all loved him for his humour and his willingness to help in any work and his kindness of heart. He was a fine man and a fine seaman'.[19]

In Egypt, Mike sank into despondency for a time—'terribly lonely and sad and upset' in Nancy's words. He and Cle had been sharing a flat in Cairo. Now he hated the place and was determined to move to Alexandria and return to Crete as soon as he could.

7

Hitting Back

It would be some months before Mike got back on an even keel. While the wound to his elbow healed relatively quickly, the scars to his mind and emotions took longer to recover. It was not until mid-September that he felt able to write to Cle's mother, his Aunt Leila, to describe the circumstances of Cle's death. For months, he found it difficult to be left alone. In North Africa, the war fluctuated dramatically and the mood in the Egyptian capital shifted wildly from week to week. Bereft of his cousin, unhappy and somewhat forlorn, the usually carefree Mike arranged to move to Alexandria, which was nearer to the sea and Crete and his core para-naval activities, much more cosmopolitan and socially diverse and more stimulating. In his book *Justine*, Lawrence Durrell, who arrived there in the spring of 1941 and probably met Mike, described the city, once the centre of the Hellenistic world, as a community of 'five races, five languages, a dozen creeds: five fleets turning through their greasy reflections behind the harbour bar'. Durrell also reckoned that the women of Alexandria were 'certainly the loveliest and most world-weary in the world'.

By mid-1941, Mike had been away from Nancy and Marcus for nearly a year with only a single very brief interregnum in London. For three months without a break, he had been risking his neck day by day in one highly dangerous exploit after another. Relaxation through reading or writing poetry or going to concerts or sailing for pleasure with the wind in his face and the sun on his back—all core staples of his pre-war existence—had become distant memories. In one letter around this time, he confessed that he found it hard to write anything to anyone apart from (censored) letters home to Nancy, and she began to notice as the year wore on that his communications had become more and more infrequent and pro-forma. In Cairo, Mike had very quickly tired of a bachelor existence built around meals in the mess, pointless parties, endless war talk, and a variety of sporting activities such as golf and polo, which he disliked. Like Durrell, the loss of Greece had been an 'amputation' for him and he mourned deeply and, gradually, developed a strong desire to hit back. At heart an untamed free spirit, he admitted to enjoying 'the fun' as he termed his daring-do para-naval life but also yearned for a return to his pre-war normalcy.

Basing in Alexandria offered a way out of this cul-de-sac, or at least a partial one, since the war was not going end anytime soon. Following the German invasion of Greece in April, 50,000 Allied troops had escaped to Egypt but up to 10,000 had had to be abandoned there and become POWs. More than 1,000 Greek refugees ended up on Alexandria's beaches. On Crete, as many as 5,000 Allied 'stragglers' had been left behind in the hurried evacuation from the island, which had cost the Royal Navy more than twenty ships lost or badly damaged and 2,000 casualties. In the desert, a German general, Edwin Rommel, had arrived in Libya and vowed to invade Egypt from the west. An Axis naval offensive against Alexandria and the Suez Canal in support of such a push seemed possible at any time. This perilous situation may or may not have played a part in Mike moving to Alexandria. Yet despite the threatening circumstances, he deliberately sought out the offbeat and the distinct there—people and places in the city with a back story to tell or an interest to offer or an insight to explore together. The disparate expatriate community was shifting constantly—by this stage, the large Greek community was strongly anti-fascist. However, not everyone, as he discovered, recoiled from the Italian or German embrace.

The heart of Alexandria at this time, after the best part of sixty years' colonial occupation, was 'The Square' as the British knew the Place Mohammed Ali—a central space surrounded by the Bourse, the Anglican cathedral, and the main courts. Well-known cafes within walking distance of The Square, such as Pastroudis and Baudrot with its atmospheric 'American bar', served as informal meeting places, as did the Hotel Cecil overlooking the Eastern Harbour and the ornate Majestic Hotel adjacent to the French Gardens. Several clubs for off-duty service personnel in the area were devoted to R&R with dancing at weekends. Most evenings there was cabaret for officers-only at the Excelsior; somewhat racier was the Phaleron near the Hotel Cecil, where Greek hostesses doubled as call girls.

A favourite bookshop, for expatriates and for Mike, was the Cité du Livre on the rue Fuad. Foreign films were shown frequently and advertised widely in many languages. For a meal, Santa Lucia restaurant was the place or Petit Coin de France off the Rue Cherif Pasha. The contrast with the meagre rations and daily hardships of existence on the ever-changing front line in the desert to the west was total. A *fin de siecle* devil-may-care mood suffused much of the city. 'Any girl who was at all presentable could go out every night if she wished,' noted Elizabeth Gwynne, who reached Alexandria in mid-May.[1] Swimming and tennis could be enjoyed at the Sporting Club run strictly on British club lines. However, members of the yacht club on the edge of the Western Harbour were now confined to duties as part of a volunteer inland patrol.

Jews were well represented in this vibrant, if ever-shifting community. One of them, Baron Georges de Menasce, was a close associate of Chaim Weizmann, the head of the World Zionist Organisation, and went on to raise funds for an organisation facilitating Jewish immigration to Palestine. De Menasce lived in what Michael Haag, in his vivid portrait of the city, *Alexandria,* describes as a 'great rambling house on the Rue Rassafa in Moharrem Bay'. Georges was a collector of beautiful things—and beautiful people. He soon became a firm friend of Mike's. A skilled pianist, his Tuesday and Sunday afternoon concerts played from behind a curtain had become an Alexandrian institution and may well have been the *entrée* through which Mike met him. Another possible intermediary was Elizabeth Gwynne who had met de Menasce on a visit to Egypt in 1936.

Elizabeth, with her paramour Charles Gibson-Cowan in tow, had reached Egypt from Crete in early June thankful for the help they had received from Mike and unsure what to do. Soon after, she informed Gibson-Cowan that their relationship was over. Stranded in Cairo without means of support, she found a job as a cypher clerk with British naval intelligence in Alexandria. Looking for a place to live, she ran into Mike in the street. 'He asked me to keep house for him in an absurdly grandiose apartment he had got hold of—there was even a bar made entirely of mirror glass,' Elizabeth recalled.[2] The flat was in the rue des Pharaons in a building 'then and now of expensive and enormous apartments, eight rooms or more' noted Haag in 2004. A cook called Anastasia had been recruited to look after Mike, but she got into trouble with the military police for handling stolen goods from an Australian depot. Mike replaced her with his resourceful sponge diver from Siri, Kyriakou Viagtses, who before long was organising life in the apartment.

Elizabeth Gwynne was at a crossroads. A socially rebellious, upper-class, attractive, rather shy and insecure twenty-seven-year-old, at this stage she had a history of minor acting parts, poor decision-making, and unhappy relationships. The most recent concluded with her realising—following her disastrous and misguided adventures in Italy and Greece—that the perennial outsider and chancer Gibson-Cowan had been a major mistake. He departed to skipper a schooner on a perilous voyage north from Mombasa in Kenya along the African coast and up the Red Sea to Alexandria. He survived, but when he got back, Elizabeth refused to see him. 'I never want to feel a scrap of emotion for the rest of my life … I will never return to the kind of existence I led before the war … I have learnt to make up my mind for myself, and not be influenced by emotions,' she told her sister, Pris.[3]

Her relationship with Mike, whom she had met for the first time in Malta in the mid-1930s, had always been arms-length rather than close. In some ways, she almost resented his marriage and lifestyle and how he seemed to her to fall on his feet in life: '… the sort of person who would get into and out of anywhere and everywhere'. Mike, by 1941, was nearly thirty-six, and his wife was far away. 'He

Above left: Laetitia Cumberlege, Mike's mother, in the early 1920s.

Above right: Mike as a child, taken in 1910 aged five.

Capt. Claude Cumberlege (to the left of the prince of Wales, centre) on HMAS *Australia* with Commodore Dumaresq on the right of the prince.

In the 1st XV at Pangbourne (*back row, fourth left*) in 1921.

Above left: Mike Cumberlege as a young man in the early 1920s.

Above right: Mike at sea in the Royal Naval Reserve in 1923.

Above left: Sister Diana taken from Ella Maillart's book.

Above right: Len Outhwaite's yacht *Kinkajou* at Cowes, 1929.

In the Bahamas with the Outhwaites—Mike is back right.

Left: Diana Cumberlege, Mike's sister, in a studio image taken in the 1930s.

Below left: Jolie Brise on the slip in Palma de Mallorca while undergoing an extensive refit under Mike's direction.

Below right: Taken in 1935-36. Mike Cumberlege, the professional sailor.

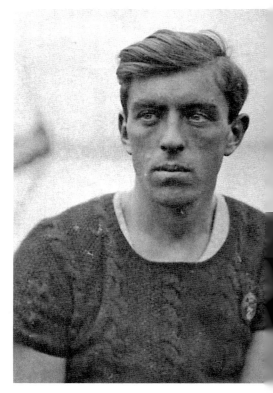

Mike and Nancy on their wedding day in Sussex in 1936.

The only known photo of Mike's boat *Sonneta*.

Left: Nancy Cumberlege.

Below left: On *Landfall* in 1937— Mike taken by Nancy.

Below right: On *Landfall* in 1937— Nancy taken by Mike.

Above left: La Gardiole, the house that Mike and Nancy rented in Cap d'Antibes in 1938.

Above right: 'Prince' Bira, the cat Mike loved and took to sea with him.

Right: Jan Kotrba on *Landfall* in 1938 when he was the steward.

Above left: A fateful passage. Mike going through the Corinth Canal on *Landfall* in 1938.

Above right: Mike at sea—with his distinctive gold earring clearly visible.

Below: In his element. Mike at the helm of *Landfall* in 1939.

A damaged watercolour of *Landfall* kept by Nancy Cumberlege.

Mike with the Paines and two friends sailing in the Adriatic.

Above: Ritchie and Ellen Paine on their Adriatic cruise in August 1939.

Left: The photo of Mike that Nancy kept in her wallet. It was taken in a café in Croatia in 1939.

Above left: Charles Gibson Cowan. (*Mrs Aileen Gibson Cowan*)

Above right: Mike's cousin Cle who lost his life escaping from Crete with Mike in 1941.

Map of Crete. (*www.crete.org.uk/map-of-crete.html*)

CSM 'Jumbo' Steele training Jewish saboteurs at Haifa, April 1941.

Jewish members of the *Dolphin 11* crew in April 1941.

Above: The wreck of the *Clan Cumming*, a British merchant vessel blown up and photographed by Mike in Piraeus on 14 April 1941.

Right: The escape of the *Athanassios Miaoulis* from Crete, May 1941. Mike is slumped in the middle of the photo.

Above: Elizabeth Gwynne (David) at work in Cairo.

Left: Renne Catzefils with her future husband Robin Fedden at the pyramids sometime in 1941.

The famous *Baudrot* café in Alexandria. (*Martin Haag*)

Fitting out *Escampador* in an Alexandria yard for a new rôle in October 1941.

Escampador was small enough to hide under the lee of many remote cliffs and caves in Crete.

Above left: Mike's going-ashore kit for his forays in Crete.

Above right: Looking a bit wild and unshaven, Mike *en route* to Crete sometime in 1941.

Escampador and *Hedgehog* on their first clandestine trip to Crete, October 1941. Mike is on the back left in *Escampador* typing a report for Cdr Pool.

The crew of *Hedgehog* (ltor): Little Strati, Lt Beckinsale, 'Jumbo' Steele, Crook, John Campbell.

Mike's invaluable Cretan companions—Capt. Boreas (*left*) and Capt. 'Satan'.

The abbot of Preveli with the monks of Tres Eklesias, taken by Mike in December 1941.

'Jumbo' Steele (*left*) with Shepperd on Crete in 1941.

'Jumbo' Steele loading a donkey with ammunition for the Cretan resistance and Mike's cigars.

A photo Mike took of his nerve-wracking encounter at sea with HMS *Talisman*.

Above left: The Maridaki cove where Mike wanted to hide with *Dolphin 11* after the German invasion of Crete in May 1941.

Above right: Kyriakou Viagtses, a former sponge diver and Mike's loyal friend.

Escampador hidden in a cave in Crete.

Capt. Boreas (a.k.a. Stefano Delavasilis) at the helm of the *caique* in which he escaped from Crete.

Above: Returning from Crete November 1941. Papa Strati at the helm. The man with the white cover on his head is wanted for murder.

Below: Escapees from Crete in November 1941 including some Allied 'stragglers'.

Escampador off Crete carrying two tons of stores for the resistance, November 1941. Viagtses is on the right.

Mike, Nancy and her sister Nora in London in 1942. (*Daily Mail*)

Rear Admiral John Godfrey, director of naval intelligence, in his office.

The courtyard of the Averoff prison in Athens during the Second World War. (*wikivisually.com*)

Above: Seidler oversees torture in Mauthausen.

Below: The Jimmy James map of Sachsenhausen.

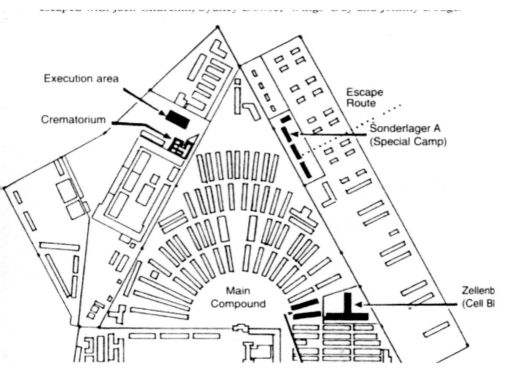

Ordinary prison garb of the sort worn by the Operation Locksmith team in Sachsenhausen. (*www.myguideberlin.com*)

Above left: Taras Bulba-Borovets, photographed in 1941. (*commons.wikimedia.org*)

Above right: Anton Kaindl, the camp commandant at Sachsenhausen 1942-45. (*en.wikipedia.org*)

Above: The brutal Zellenbau guard Kurt Eccarius after his arrest in 1945. (*collections.ushmm.org*)

Below left: Lt-Col. Jack Churchill before his capture. (*memeaddicts.com; machote: nivel chuck norris*)

Below right: Gp-Capt. Harry 'Wings' Day. (*post-war image Wikipedia*)

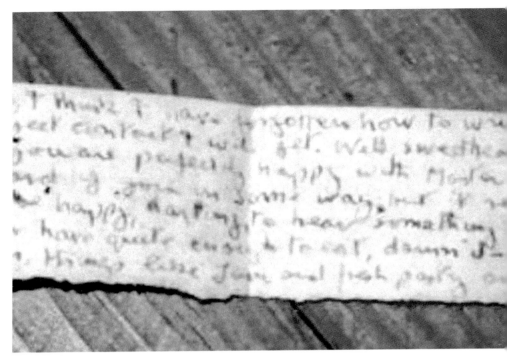

Mike's last note to Nancy 30 January 1945.

All that remained of the Zellenbau in the 1950s.

Right: A cell in the Zellenbau in 1945.
(*geo-reisecommunity.de*)

Below: The memorial plaque to Mike and nineteen other Allied servicemen murdered in Sachsenhausen during the Second World War.
(*en.wikipedia.com*)

Commonwealth forces, many still unknown, who were interned in Sachsenhausen and perished here or elsewhere at the hands of their captors:

In Erinnerung an die tapferen Mitglieder der britischen und Commonwealth Streitkräfte, viele noch heute unbekannt, die im KZ Sachsenhausen gefangen gehalten und hier oder an anderen Orten getötet wurden:

Pte Cyril Abram
Capt Graeme Black DSO MC
OS Neville Burgess RN
LSgt William Chudley
Sgt Jack Cox
Lt Cdr Claude Cumberledge RNVR
Pte Eric Curtis
Sub Lt John Godwin RNVR
Capt W. Grover-Williams Fr CdG
Sgt Thomas Handley MM

PO Harold Hiscock RN
Capt Joseph Houghton MC
Cpl Jan Kotbra
Pte Reginald Makeham
OS Keith Mayor RN
PO Alfred Roe RN
CSM Miller Smith
CSM James Steele MM
Maj Francis Suttill DSO
OS Andrew West RN

"Greater love hath no man than this, that a man lay down his life for his friends"

The BCIS team searching for the missing gold near Cape Skyli after the war. (*National Archives*)

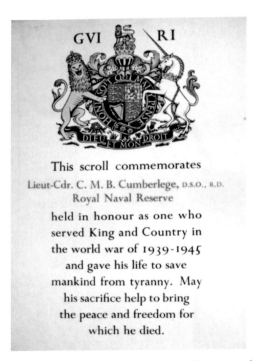

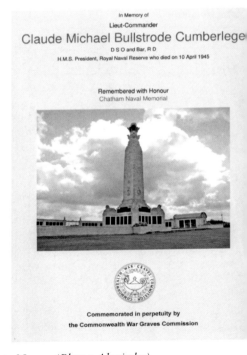

Above left: A commemorative scroll presented to Nancy. (*Platon Alexiades*)

Above right: The Chatham Naval Memorial.

Right: The famous memorial sculpture to the victims of mass murder in Sachsenhausen at the Père Lachais cemetery, Paris.

Below: Some of Mike's papers found in a suitcase in Bruges.

Marcus Cumberlege at his desk in Bruges in the 2000s.

Granddaughter Eunice Cumberlege in 2016 with Walter Paine, then aged 93.

was bookish, great fun, fantastically good-looking—and he had this small, close-fitting gold earring in one ear which made him look very dashing,' the author Patrick Leigh Fermor remembered in conversation with the biographer Artemis Cooper years later. Neither Elizabeth nor Mike were looking for complications. Mike, it is true, craved company in the aftermath of the death of his cousin, and soon the flat came to resemble a hotel with people dropping in, staying temporarily, and leaving their possessions to be collected later. Informal gatherings took place almost nightly when Mike was around, with Kyriakou often saving the day.

Some weeks after they began sharing the flat in June, Elizabeth declared confidently to her sister that it was a relief to be able to live without 'sex rearing its ugly head'.[4] For his part, Mike failed to inform Nancy that he had even seen Elizabeth in Alexandria until it came out twice by chance early in September. First, a stranger she met at a cocktail party in London who had no idea who she was informed her that he had heard that Mike Cumberlege was living with a woman in Alexandria, only to be taken to task by Nancy who informed him in no uncertain terms of her identity. Soon after, she dined with John Godfrey, Norah, and Henry Denham in London. Denham was the UK Naval *Attaché* in Stockholm and a pre-war friend. He knew Pris and mentioned that he had heard from her that Elizabeth and Gibson-Cowan had been staying at Mike's flat: 'So you see how <u>very</u> careful you will have to be my darling,' she warned him subsequently. 'Isn't it awful that you can't escape my clutches?'[5]

It was during the summer that Elizabeth introduced Mike to a young friend of hers called Renée Catzeflis. The daughter of Italian-Greek parents from Alexandria, Renée had been educated in France and was a strong-willed beauty with numerous admirers. One of them was the English writer and traveller Robin Fedden, then lecturing in Cairo. In September, Fedden visited Renée and Elizabeth and met Mike. 'His arrival was the signal for a series of parties and picnics,' Elizabeth wrote. 'Robin and Mike started by getting on very well but it didn't last and with Renée doing a butterfly dance between the two of them the situation was rather delicate.'[6] Mike, it appears, was having an affair with the flirtatious Renée, which must have lasted several months and coincides with a period when his letters to Nancy dried up. Those who knew him, like the young Walter Paine, were not too surprised when the word reached them of the affair: 'He cut a romantic figure among the ladies—sensitivity combined with rugged charm'—always an alluring combination.[7]

The real truth about the relationship was not to reach Nancy until the end of October. Well before then, she had confronted Mike about his living arrangements in a succession of pointed letters. A mercurial, emotional character always prone to depression and sudden ups and downs, the situation she imagined in Alexandria sent her into overdrive. The first reference to Elizabeth appears in a letter dated 21 September: 'There's only one thing I want to know. Is Lizzie staying with you in the flat? Not that I mind, but I think it's a rather stupid thing to do if she is—from all <u>our</u> points of view. However, it's up to you'. Her suspicions had not been allayed by the recent return, unopened, of thirty loving letters she had written to Mike when he was living in Cape Verde. Meantime, the atmosphere in the house she shared with her father-in-law and his tribe in Sussex had become hard to bear. Norah, the admiral's wife, had disgraced herself (not for the first time) at a local party, 'Prince' Bira, the cat Mike and she doted on, had disappeared, and the admiral had begun to question the parentage of his latest offspring.

At the start of October, increasingly showing the strain of ten months apart from her husband, Nancy received a letter from Mike informing her of his flat-sharing set-up. She replied the same day. Claiming that Elizabeth 'smelled', she continued:

> I am glad you told me she is living in the flat with you. I might say, I <u>absolutely</u> believe your explanation. But I would just like to put on record that I think it is probably one of the unkindest and most unfeeling things you could think of to do.... I do resent having to assume a quite <u>unnatural</u> tolerance ... which I possess not <u>one</u> iota.... What a good laugh you will both have over this, but oddly enough I <u>mean</u> it.... I just know myself that you <u>couldn't</u> [sleep] with Lizzie, but I hate what everybody else must think.

She went on:

> It's very strange, for a man and woman to live alone together in a flat in an unnatural relationship. Perhaps you never thought of that, my fine <u>insensitive</u> husband. Nag, nag, nag, you'll say!! Please do something about this right away, or I shall take retaliatory action.... You're a horrid, unkind stupid husband and I love you very very much.[8]

By the time he received this letter a couple of weeks later, Mike was feeling guilty. He suggested that Nancy join him in Cairo. As he must have known, this was a non-starter in the wartime conditions of the day, and Nancy was duly turned down when she applied for a travel permit. Before then, she had weighed in again on the subject of Elizabeth who, she seemed to think, Mike was supporting financially: 'You must get Lizzie out of the flat before I set foot in the country. <u>I won't have her there</u> and I mean it. I hate the sound of it [flat-sharing] and think you're a brute to do it to me.... Why did you have to do it? It was very foolish of you'. For the first time, she mentioned Renée Catzeflis by name in reaction to something Mike had written in passing. 'Who is Renée?' adding ambiguously, 'I'm trying hard to forgive you your silliness.'[9]

At the end of October, Mike left Egypt on the first of his perilous sorties into occupied Crete. Nancy was left hanging with no word from Alexandria.

'I'm not a bit brave or any of the things I ought to be,' she acknowledged. Absorbed by her mistrust of Elizabeth, only now was the truth about Mike's relationship with Renée Catzeflis dawning on her. On 28 October, she received an apparently confessional letter from Mike that he had written before setting off for Crete. Her reaction was to pour out her heart:

> Was it exciting Mike? With R I mean. Don't tell me, but oh darling, it's funny. I knew, I guessed it in spite of your very loving letters. But you told me in such a funny way ... it hurts so much. I just want to know if you told her, if you told her you liked her 'in our kind of way'—your quotation. Oh God, I don't know what I want to know.... You say 'it won't go any further than that' because 'you won't be there.' Strangely cold comfort. I don't want that kind of comfort. Don't make me more unhappy.[10]

Mike's contrite letter does not survive. Nancy later described it as 'probably the loveliest ever written to me ... I know it almost by heart.' Still, it aroused her curiosity and she posed a series of personal questions to Mike about Renée—about her hair and figure and so on. Mike had admitted to going swimming with Renée, but Nancy was certain there was more to the relationship than that. 'Does she feel the same?' she inquired dangerously. 'Did you or didn't you?' A few days later, she regretted these questions, writing 'I've let myself be very silly.' But the hurt went deep. Elizabeth and Mike continued to flat-share until mid-December, but added another person to the menagerie—John Campbell, now one of Mike's key para-naval colleagues in arms and the same young man who had sailed alongside Len Outhwaite and Mike in his own boat during the Atlantic crossing in the *Kinkajou* twelve years before. Sometime in December, Mike and Elizabeth decided it was time to split. The cost of maintaining the flat had risen a lot, Mike was often away on secret missions, and, by then, so many people were dropping in to use the apartment as a base that it had come to resemble an airport terminal. They went their separate ways, but remained friends. Renée was to marry Robin Fedden in Cairo in October 1942.

The war meantime ground on. On his arrival in Egypt at the start of June, Mike had gone to Cairo to give a full briefing on events in Crete to his SOE superiors. The urgent need was to rebuild the para-naval 'fleet' of caïques after the loss of the *Dolphin II* and two smaller vessels in the Aegean and to recruit and train competent people to join the force. Mike was put to work in Alexandria and Tobruk and Haifa interviewing the crews and passengers of escaping caïques for useful information and searching out any vessels that might be used to transfer arms, stores, and men to the resistance groups springing up in Crete and in mainland Greece. Another objective was to find a way to rescue 'stragglers'—those servicemen left behind in the region by the precipitous Allied retreat—and valued Greek sympathisers from some of the occupied islands. Mike was also asked to draw up a plan for striking back at the enemy, particularly in Crete.

The first successful Royal Navy attempts to collect stragglers in July and August had involved the use of submarines and proved time-consuming and not very effective. With the tide of war in the central Mediterranean swinging the Allied way during the second half of 1941, demands on the RN's limited resources in the area were growing and it was becoming less possible to detach submarines and destroyers with any regularity for such operations. Some Greek caïques, however, had managed to make their way to Turkey and Egypt and Mike realised that they might form the backbone of a worthwhile raiding and rescuing unit. He was prescient. By the end of the war in Europe, fourteen such vessels were operational, SOE craft had covered 300,000 sea miles, 1,700 tons of stores and 164 agents had been landed, some 550 Allied stragglers had been evacuated, and forty-six enemy ships and 190 enemy personnel captured. All told, according to an official report compiled in June 1945, over 300 operations had been carried out at sea by SOE in the Eastern Mediterranean from the start of 1942. The Executive had eventually employed 112 British officers and other ranks in these activities. The overall cost was put at £2.46 million (over £100 million today): 'The only casualty was a 6-ton caïque'.[11]

One such boat was a small 30-foot caïque that reached Alexandria carrying fourteen men, including several Greeks and four British officers who had eluded capture, in August 1941. On the way south, her engine broke down in bad weather in the Kasos Straits and the vessel ran out of fuel, food, and water 60 miles north of Alexandria. One of the soldiers on board cleverly constructed a still, which gathered 3 gallons of water, and by burning the hatch boards, the group limped on for another five days before being sighted and rescued by an Allied destroyer. Most of the 'passengers' were taken on board the warship while the rest, with a new supply of fuel, took the vessel into harbour. This caïque eventually was known as the *Escampador*, or 'The Scamp' to Mike. Originally, he told Nancy on one occasion, she had been called the *El Soliador*, which means 'The Dreamer'. Escaping to Alexandria, those on board had renamed her the *Elpice* ('Hope'). Her 'owner' proved to be a young Greek living in Athens, anxious to escape the German occupation. He had hired the boat for a month and filled her with fuel and provisions. After some trouble with the police, the party had slipped safely out of Piraeus.

Mike quickly spotted the potential of the vessel. After interrogating all those on the boat, he took the three Greeks into his employ and set about organising a conversion, overseen by a Mr Fort in the Khedeuval Mail Company's shipyard in Alexandria. The old engine was replaced with a 35-hp National Diesel, giving a fully loaded top speed of 6 knots—'a fine little engine which did 2,000 miles running without a single stop before being fully serviced' Mike wrote later. She was, he reckoned, 'a very graceful and beautifully-built little craft'. The *Escampador* became Mike's home from home for the months ahead. Her size and manoeuvrability allowed him to hide for days on end in small coves or on remote beaches almost at will. She was never detected, easily camouflaged under fish netting, and rather larger than she looked. On Mike's first Cretan reconnaissance in October 1941, 'she actually brought home a total of 19 men a distance of about 400 miles' in Mike's proud words.[12]

The other key components of the para-naval force in this early 1941–42 period were two rusty old boats known as the *Hedgehog* and the *Porcupine*. The *Hedgehog* was larger than the *Escampador* at about 60 tons weight and had a length of 48 feet, a maximum speed of 6.5 knots, and a small sail. She had been known as the *Peled* (Jewish for pellet or nugget) before the war and was part of the Palestinian Fisheries fleet until Mike unleashed his considerable powers of persuasion on Madame Strumpf, her 'manageress'. On the back of a photograph he took, he described the *Hedgehog* as 'almost as broad as she is long and as slow as a church'. Both required some adaptation into armed vessels able to carry heavy loads, and concrete ballast had to be added fore and aft to each craft, slowing them. Early in October, the transformations were completed and the crews ready for a trial run. The two caïques sailed up the coast to Abu Kir Bay armed with Breda, Lewis, and Bren guns and looking for kite (bird) targets to shoot.

To skipper the *Hedgehog*, Mike had recruited his Irish friend John (J. H. P.) Campbell. The writer Xan Fielding, who knew both men through his time working for SOE in Crete, described them like this: 'John and Mike both had the same rather specialized interests. They had known each other for years, and before the war had sailed all over the world together, each in his own small yacht. As so often happens in a friendship as close as theirs, the two were vastly dissimilar in character and appearance'.[13] Campbell spoke in monosyllables, while Cumberlege's staple conversation tended to be robust and pointed. Fielding reckoned that Mike knew the Cretan coastline better than any man alive and had 'a corsair's flair' for finding unknown beaches and hidden coves. The military historian Anthony Beevor has called the pair 'sailors of extraordinary skill and courage'. The couple hand-picked their crews from a pool of Greek and British volunteers and trained the men themselves. Campbell remained with the para-naval force to the start of 1945 when he was asked to form a similar unit in the rather different waters of the far flung Far East. He, too, was awarded the DSO.

While this was going on, Mike submitted a paper to SOE's guerrilla warfare section in Cairo outlining a plan to strike back at the enemy in Crete.[14] Its first objective, he wrote, would be 'to sabotage enemy shipping, tugs and caïques at Souda [Bay], Heraklion and Sitia by the use of limpets'. It listed five other possible tasks, including helping to build up the capabilities of Cretans so that they would 'be ready to take their part in the liberation' of the island, collecting information and arranging locations where munitions might be dropped by air and stored in safety. Lastly, 'generally to keep the Cretan morale at concert pitch but avoiding any overt acts so that when the time comes they [Cretans] will be able to carry out extensive sabotage of communications, attack airport personnel and act as guides to the main bodies of troops'. Four appendices added details on what each person taking part would need, 'toys' (weapons), rations, and 'codes' using the Allied broadcasting service in Egypt. The proposals were supported by Mike's immediate superior Cdr Pool. SOE Middle East then gave the ideas a generally positive response and facilitated Cumberlege's mission in various ways.

On 27 October, Mike led his first foray to Crete, using the *Escampador* and the *Hedgehog*. The *Hedgehog* crew included Jumbo Steele and Stanley Beckinsale, a British Army officer who was to remain with Campbell to 1945. On board the *Escampador*, which the *Hedgehog* towed to Crete for this recce, were Costa Orfanides, a ship's fireman who spoke eight languages and was 'a delightful character' who helped Mike on several rescue missions; the ever-loyal Viagtses, now proudly wearing a British naval uniform; and Captain Boreas. Boreas (also known as Stefano Delavasili) had escaped from Crete in September 1941, bringing sixteen men with him, by patching up a craft that had been lying neglected on a beach for years. The inch-wide seams had had to be caulked, a telegraph pole cut down for a mast, and an improvised sail devised. Using a scout's compass and a child's map of the Mediterranean, Boreas made it to within 10 miles of Mersa Matruh, where he was picked up by a British destroyer. Cumberlege recruited him without hesitation once he reached Alexandria after he said he was prepared to return to Crete. The caïques also carried captured Italian rifles and boots for the Cretan guerrillas.

While at sea, they had an unnerving encounter with a patrolling British submarine HMS *Talisman*—'one of our nastier moments' according to Mike. The *Talisman* was returning to Alexandria from a patrol off the Libyan coast when it ran into the *Hedgehog* (with the *Escampador* in tow) late at night. After a challenge, which was answered correctly, the caïques continued on their way and the submarine commander, Lt Cdr Michael Willmott, ordered his crew to secrecy. In his log, Willmott described one of the two occupants in the *Escampador* as 'a most suspicious-looking character'. This was probably Captain Boreas. The other person was Mike, and if he had known it, the submarine commander was a fellow Old Pangbournian who had arrived at the Nautical College in 1922, the year he left. In 1942, Willmott won the DSO after undertaking five successful patrols in the Mediterranean in the *Talisman* but died later in the year when the submarine struck a mine off Sicily.

Shortly after the *Talisman* encounter, the *Hedgehog* and the *Escampador* ran into a gale, but reached the south Cretan coast safely. Mike's objective was the isolated beach at Maridaki, a tiny hamlet 40 miles south of Heraklion, which had no direct road to two nearby villages: '... an ideal spot with running water, shady trees including oranges and a small monastery. A truly sylvan glade with fierce rocks rising to the mountains behind. Where I had wished to hide after the collapse of Crete,' Mike scribbled in pencil on the back of one of his photos. He had first visited the St Nikitas monastery before the collapse of Crete and believed it to be unvisited by the German occupiers. It had, in fact, been entered by a German patrol only the week before the caïques arrived. Nevertheless Mike was able to make contact with an Allied SOE unit on the island, unload weaponry and supplies on a chilly, wet morning, collect an important report from the SOE group on the state of the Cretan resistance, and pick up seventeen refugees, including nine British 'stragglers'. This group also included a notorious murderer facing justice, two Palestinian Arabs, and three Cypriots, as well as one of Mike's more colourful volunteers. This was Papastrati, a veteran Cretan blackmailer and thief who had been part of a Greek boat party that wiped out a small Italian garrison near Samos. He had escaped with Mike on the *Athanasios Miaoulis* and now returned with him to Crete to act as a guide. He was later captured by the Germans and ended up in a concentration camp because, in Mike's words, 'he couldn't keep his mouth shut'. By 2 November, after some serious seasickness among the passengers, the two caïques were back safely in Alexandria, proving that such sorties were both possible and worthwhile.

A second 'recce' to Crete set off three weeks later, again involving the *Escampador* and the *Hedgehog*. This time, the *Escampador* carried 2 tons of stores for the Cretan resistance. Reaching the island on 25 November, a rendezvous was made with a large party of Allied 'stragglers', including twenty-eight New Zealanders.[15] Campbell left with a total of eighty-six escapees and four Greek refugees the next day and reached Alexandria safely on 28 November. Mike decided to remain behind to explore the 50-mile stretch of coast between Cape Lithinon (the most southerly part of Crete) and Tsoutsouros Bay, close to the Maridaki beach. With him were Jumbo Steele, Kyriakou Viagtses, Costa Orfanides, and two other Cretans. Eluding German patrols by taking the *Escampador* into remote bays or hiding in caves, Mike was able to visit a number of villages inland, seeking word of any Allied soldiers still at large.

It was possibly during this visit, or one around Christmas, that he got into a fist fight with a German. In a letter to Nancy at the start of January 1942, he wrote:

> My own little effort nearly finished me off, the result of the experience being that three fellows are in hospital and a couple more are attending the doctor. My own hands are still poisoned but very much better. They have taken a hell of a time to begin to look right and even now I have some marks.[16]

He had problems, too, with his teeth 'having inadvertently smacked myself in the face with a recoiling anti-tank gun' and damaged the nerves in three teeth. In another letter around this time, he admitted that he had 'got a lot of virus off somebody's three teeth on my knuckles. It has been painful'. He also met with Monty Woodhouse, who was on Crete assisting with the evacuation of Allied troops; Woodhouse thanked him profusely in a scribbled note that survives for the 'fine collection of stores' that he had just delivered: 'They will be invaluable'.

On 13 December, shortly before returning to Alexandria, he met the SOE's Lt Jack Smith-Hughes and his group who had been landed on Crete in early October to establish a link with the Cretan resistance. The meeting took place at the Preveli monstery and the Abbot of Preveli, Agathangelos Lagouvardos, and some of the monks of Tris Ekklesies were also present. Located at the top of a mountain, mostly hidden away, with nothing but cliffs and the sea below it, the monastery was well chosen as a base for clandestine activities. The Abbot was staunchly pro-British and had met Mike during his time on the island in May and later helped a number of Australian soldiers to escape. By way of retaliation, when the Germans found out about this collaboration, they blew up the Lower Monastery building, removed or destroyed everything inside other buildings, and placed a permanent guard on the beach below. The Abbot, who carried a gun, was forced underground (he joined the Greek Army in the Middle East and became a priest). Many of the monks were arrested and tortured. Mike was eventually instrumental in getting an OBE for the Abbot— '... to his intense joy ... I have a lovely picture of him and Mike with the medal' Nancy wrote in 1946. After a couple of days at Preveli, the *Escampador* left Crete on 15 December and was back in Alexandria hours before a daring Italian human torpedo raid crippled two Allied battleships in the harbour.

Almost certainly, just before Christmas 1941, the *Escampador* and the *Hedgehog* made a brief third visit to Crete despite the worsening sea and weather conditions. The *Hedgehog* was damaged and had to turn back, stranding some 100 Allied 'stragglers' who had been gathered by Woodhouse. The *Escampador*, Mike implied in a letter the following year, had nearly sunk. Before long, though, he was planning another sortie. In a letter to Nancy at the end of the year, he wrote: 'I am once more off again.... All my life, which is so exciting and very worthwhile to me, must remain hidden from you ... [but] our work has been crowned with no uncertain measure of success'.[17] Captions written by Mike on the back of the many photographs he took of his covert missions shows a hideout at Chercolo, near Sudsero, that offered 'protection in all winds' with a date of 1942 on it. This seems doubtful as there is no record of a trip by the *Escampador* at this time. By 11 January, Mike was staying with John Campbell—'a nice flat but not as nice as mine was by half'—and admitted to taking Elizabeth Gwynne out to supper on New Year's Day 'because she had apparently spent the day in bed in tears'.

The *Escampador* was not to survive the war, being lost in stormy conditions a year later while taking part in another covert action. Mike's exploits in Crete, however, now earned him a DSO 'for daring and enterprise'. Nancy saw the announcement in *The Times* on 22 January and was over the moon: 'I hope you understand how very pleased and proud I am and how much it means to me'. Three days later, she added: 'I have been told that for a Lieut RNR to get the DSO_is *quelque chose* indeed. I know you deserve it.... John G wrote to say how delighted he was and that he <u>knew</u>, heavily underlined, just how thoroughly you had earned it'. Congratulations rained in, including one from Captain Sands and his 'absolutely neglected and forgotten, unloved and unsung crowd' on Cape Verde. Mike himself was schizophrenic. As he put it to Nancy:

> In many ways Cle and I did far better things, perhaps far more dangerous and in many ways more valuable. But I should like you to let Uncle Cle and Aunt Leila know that it is only Cle, and the spirit of Cle, that has given me the drive and desire to do what in the last six months I have done.... My medal is as much shared by him as if he himself had been with me.... I didn't go out to win medals; I couldn't be bothered. But I am glad for you and Marcus.

Mike was also awarded the Greek War Cross later in the year by the exiled King of Greece, as was John Campbell. This led to an archetypal red tape row inside the British civil service. The Admiralty claimed to the Treasury that it had not been 'consulted' about the Greek honours and had not talked to a Treasury committee 'about accepting them'. The Treasury was requested to ask the King of Greece to desist from making such awards without first seeking the agreement of the British government. The King subsequently agreed to this stipulation. For whatever reason, the Admiralty in London was being disingenuous. It had been informed of the award by the C-in-C Mediterranean Station before this exchange took place and stated at the time: 'Their Lordships have concurred in the acceptance and wearing of the decorations and medals listed' including Cumberlege's.[18] Campbell later designed a ribbon for the Greek decoration, which he wore when on the *Hedgehog*. Mike followed suit.

The official Greek recognition of Mike's efforts in Greece was mirrored by the grateful messages he was sent in this period by the many Greeks he had helped. He was proud of these messages, usually received on a postcard, and made sure that Nancy saw them. Typically, a card from a George Koutiniakis to Mike went: 'To the courageous son of immortal England, Michael Cumberlege, who is an honour to her name by his heroic activities for the common fight for Democracy. [I send] this picture, historical to me, and dedicate it as a small example of my exceptional esteem and love for his great love towards my enslaved country'. Another, from his loyal supporter Kyria Viagtses, goes:

'Dedicated to my dear and brotherly friend and fellow combatant Michael Cumberlege, as a souvenir of my stay in Alexandria as a refugee having been condemned to death and prescribed by the Hun for having fought for the honour and glory of my country and our allies'.

In his book, *The Nazi Occupation of Crete*, G. C. Kiriakopolous writes: 'Michael Cumberlege left a deep impression on the Cretan guerrillas with whom he had come into contact.... They admired his buccaneerish air, his humour and his Hollywood-like good looks. Most of all, they smiled at the single gold earring he wore which was so symbolic of his piratical nature'. The son of George Vergos, Costas Vergos, got in touch with the author in 2015 and wrote that he first met Mike as a boy on a small marina in Piraeus at the end of April 1941 and again in Alexandria when Mike's arm was in plaster. He was 'a great man'.

In turn, Mike reciprocated these warm sentiments, praising and encouraging Greek spirits and people whenever and wherever he could. He was clear-headed, noting in a 1942 memo that Greek villagers and police, while generally 'friendly, interested and helpful', had a tendency to be 'too talkative'. But, he added: 'Most are only waiting for a sign to get together and revolt.... They will go to extremes' for the Allies. On several occasions he intervened to protest about the British neglect of some of the Greek refugees that he had rescued, such as Georges Koutendakis and the Petrakogeorgios family. They had been promised the status of 'honoured guests', but were dumped in Palestine with no financial help.

As 1942 began, however, all was not well with Mike. He began to feel ill in the middle of January; his last letter to Nancy from this period is dated 11 January. She heard nothing after that until 4 February, when a telegram from the Admiralty informed her that he was unwell. John Godfrey investigated and telephoned the following day to tell her that Mike had paratyphoid. He would keep in regular contact with Nancy for the next couple of weeks and dined with her alone on 10 February when she 'cried on his shoulder'. Recovery would take at least a couple of months in hospital and not be straightforward. 'You feel like hell,' Nancy recalled as her sister had once had the same illness. In reality, matters proved to be rather worse than this. Not until 19 March was the Admiralty able to inform Nancy that Mike was off the danger list. Soon after, he was able to write to Nancy and informed her that he had very nearly died, not once but twice 'with an interval between'. He could remember little of the medical drama, but admitted that for five days prior to collapsing, he had been 'living on double whiskies and brandy while he shuttled from Alexandria to Cairo and Haifa by plane and car and train.... An impossible existence, a kind of dream'.[20] When he saw a doctor, influenza had been diagnosed.

In hospital, where he characteristically 'raised the biggest stink' about the treatment he was given once he was well enough to do so, he was visited by all and sundry and had to change wards to get some rest. Among the friends to arrive at his bedside was the Abbot of Preveli—'we have an eternal invitation to live in his monasteries'—and other Cretans 'with mountain faces and bloody great German automatics hidden in the back of their pants, taken in the dust and heat of individual and unequal battles'. Once Mike was able to leave hospital in April, he was offered a bed and nursing in three homes in Alexandria and chose the one proposed by Georges de Menasce, as did Elizabeth Gwynne after an operation on her foot later the same year.

Throughout this saga, the Director of Naval Intelligence (DNI), John Godfrey, had kept a close eye on Mike's health. It was another manifestation of the warm regard he had long felt for both Cumberleges. The ties went back to the mid-1930s. Stephen Roskill, the leading naval historian, has recalled how, in 1936 as a junior officer, he and his wife dined on the *Jolie Brise* with Mike and Nancy in the Grand Harbour in Malta. 'After the meal, Mike suddenly said "Let's go and visit John Godfrey"' then Captain of the battleship *Repulse*. 'I was a little alarmed because most Post Captains of those times did not take kindly to visits by uninvited and unknown junior officers. However, Mike persisted and so I found myself in the presence of a very impressive, slightly daunting but obviously highly intelligent officer'.[21] Mike's easy relationship with Godfrey, reckoned Roskill, 'demonstrated his [Godfrey's] liking for unorthodox and original characters'.

Five years on from that 1936 meeting, with Mike now putting his life on the line on a regular basis, Godfrey made it his business, despite his new eminence, to support Mike by constantly recommending him for promotion despite repeated rebuffs from others in the Admiralty and by trying to ensure he was paid correctly and had the resources he needed. He delighted in taking the good-looking Nancy out to dinner in London with or without others, sharing some secrets with her and even visiting her in Sussex. He was also happy to allow his staff to act as unofficial postmen forwarding her letters to Mike. One of Godfrey's predecessors, 'Blinker' Hall, the DNI during the First World War, had informed Godfrey when he took the job in 1939 that 'boldness always pays', personal contacts and assessments were critical as DNI, and devolved decision-making mattered when it came to successful intelligence gathering and subversive warfare. In Mike Cumberlege, John Campbell, and other unconventional young sailors like them who were largely unimpressed by rank or seniority or naval protocol, he found the perfect adjutants.

Eventually, on 17 May, Mike had recovered sufficiently to travel to England for further convalescence, to be followed by consultations with SOE and the Admiralty in London. His pay, though, was to be cut as he would no longer be considered 'on active service'. Nancy was 'desolate' about this cheese-paring decision, but joyful beyond words at the prospect of seeing Mike again. She still harboured worries about Renée Catzeflis and, while asking Mike to 'forgive [her] horrible October letters', continued to berate him for the original flat-sharing arrangement—'an extremely stupid, hurting thing to do'.

On his way to London on an interminable journey by air across Africa—his only companions were two brigadiers 'incredibly British and blimpish and boring'—Mike took the opportunity, while at a stopover in 'the damp heat of the Gold Coast', to sit down and pen what turned out to be his last letter to Ritchie and Ellen Paine.[22] His ever-generous American benefactors had sent Nancy $1,000 (about £8,000 today) in January, as well as food parcels throughout 1941. In December, Ellen had informed Nancy that a man from Marseilles was going to Antibes to collect the *Landfall* blankets and sheets and coats that the Paines had left behind in 1939 in order to give them to internment camp inmates held in Vichy France. Ivan, the cook on the *Landfall*, meantime had reached California where, she wrote, 'he was happy fishing'. Arlette, the maid at La Gardiole, remained at odds with Costa Trevelas who still refused to hand her money she was owed. Costa, so Arlette had previously told Nancy, was now taking women on board the yacht.

Apologising for his long silence, Mike began:

> I can't think why I don't write. I've written to no one, only Nan excepted, and even that I find difficult to do. Now I am in a period of transition and just in case of accidents I should like you to know that I think of you often and that you often have been part of my conversation and, more important, in my/our schemes for the future.... I haven't changed. I have had a year full of intense excitement, full of new faces, full of work and undertakings which seem, some of them, almost legendary.

Acknowledging that paratyphoid had left him weak and unable to make much physical effort, he was pleased to be going home both to refresh and 'to give me more courage to carry on.' He went on:

> Three times in the year I have been <u>near to death</u>—no four times—perhaps others I don't remember. But four times so close that it's only really by the grace of God and the prayers of friends that I have stayed to tell the tale. The first time was off Crete when I was wounded, let us say by fire. The second time was when I was 'straddled' by two 500lbs bombs and my hotel [in Port Tewfik] collapsed on me—let us say by air. The third time was in a very small boat, my darling little *Escampador*, when I got caught in a dreadful storm—let us says by water. And the fourth time was my illness when my chances were very slim indeed—the Devil's reprisal for my taking liberties with him!

Yet survive he had.

Operation Locksmith

Mike Cumberlege reached London on about 20 May 1942. Officially, he was convalescing and taking some leave before consulting with SOE HQ. Nancy by then had just moved back to the capital having finally had enough of her mother-in-law in Sussex, whom she had come to loathe. She rented a house in Chelsea in the same road, Godfrey Street, in which she had lived two years before. The 1940–41 Blitz had ended, and although German air raids still took place, life in London was a lot safer than it had been.

In the Mediterranean and North Africa, however, the war had taken a distinct turn for the worse. The British Eighth Army was in full retreat, Tobruk and Mersa Matruh fell in June, besieged Malta was on its knees, and submarines from the Tenth Flotilla had fallen back to Alexandria and Haifa. On 1 July, Axis forces reached El Alamein, but their supply lines by then were more than 300 miles long and stretched to near-breaking point. A shaky front stabilised. Once again, the importance of the Corinth Canal as a shortcut for German and Italian supply ships heading for North Africa became starkly evident to Allied planners. On 22 July, the Admiralty requested that Cumberlege, who was still in London, produce a new plan for blocking the canal.

Prior to this, Mike had found himself, against his better judgement, drawn into what became known as the Atkinson affair. The origins of this murky business, which stirred up bad blood between SOE and MI9 Mediterranean, the Military Intelligence department based in Cairo responsible for communications with POWs and organising escapes, are hard to unravel. Mike had been happy to help MI9, if requested, by providing a vessel for its operations and by vouching for any Cretans MI9 wished to employ to sail her, but MI9 had circumvented him and set up a rescue mission by itself to the island of Paros. One of its goals was to extract John Atkinson, a wounded British officer from the Royal Army Service Corps. A rescue was achieved and the caïque carrying him reached Alexandria early in October 1941.

Atkinson was immediately recruited by MI9 to aid future escapes of Allied servicemen from occupied Greece and took part in one such evacuation successfully the next month. He then approached SOE and volunteered to work for it, provided MI9 was not informed. The day after Christmas 1941, a submarine took him and his team to Antiparos but failed to return to pick them up. Atkinson was then wounded and the group captured after a firefight with Italian forces on the island. Several attempts were made by SOE to free Atkinson from the hospital in Athens where he was held, but they failed. Accused at an Italian military tribunal of the murder of an Italian officer, he and six Greek resistance fighters were executed in February 1943. All kinds of reasons for this debacle existed and Mike was reluctant to get involved in a row between the Admiralty, SOE, and MI9 over where responsibility lay. Pressed in London to produce a written report, he finally did so in July and was highly critical of the judgement of both Atkinson and the officer in charge of the mission, Major Anthony Simonds—the man from MI9 who had originally gone behind his back. The subsequent official inquiry proved to be inconclusive 'pending further information'.[1]

At the end of August, with fighting at El Alamein still going on, the RAF made an effort to block the Corinth Canal by bombing it but caused little lasting damage. Thoughts then turned to other means. According to an unmarked file kept against all orders at home in London by Mike, and subsequently retained by Nancy, he had begun devising a new plan to block the canal on 20 July.[2] By 2 August, his ideas were ready to be examined by colleagues in the Navy, and on 10 August, a refined plan was forwarded formally to the Admiralty. Technical discussions ensued over the rest of the month until 26 August, when Mike informed SOE in Cairo of the progress being made. By mid-September, SOE and the Admiralty in London, the C-in-C Mediterranean Admiral Andrew Cunningham, and the C-in-C Levant Vice-Admiral Henry Harwood had all aligned behind the Cumberlege plan.

Mike's concept essentially involved having a special mine of 45 lb made by the Admiralty's Mining School in Havant of which 25 lb would be high explosives. The sixteen-page report he typed at the start of August is both cogent and technical, covering the physical state of the canal, the use of local agents, the role of limpet and magnetic mines, personnel needed, landing sites, and supplies. An idea going the rounds in the Admiralty of staging a collision at the canal's entrance to block passage is dismissed—'all the earmarks of improbability' (Mike was never one to mince his words). Instead, he plumps for a mine-based strategy. A mine laid on the canal's floor, he argued, would be detonated by the magnetic field of a ship passing over it at a distance of less than 5 feet. Since the Corinth Canal was around 27 feet in depth, this meant that a vessel with a draught of at least 21 feet was required. Five such mines would be needed. In addition, five counter-mines weighing 65 lb each would be added to the explosive cocktail, all timed to go off in tandem to the magnetic mines in order to cause maximum damage. The vessel used to lay these mines would need to sink in such a way that it could not be raised quickly or easily, so blocking the canal for long enough for the RAF to complete its destruction. John Godfrey, still DNI at the Admiralty, but increasingly at odds with the naval establishment, is thought to have helped to push the plan through the Admiralty in early September. On 15 September, he was promoted and dismissed from his post the same day. Three weeks later, he was sent far away to Asia to command the Royal Indian Navy.

Mike's meticulous attention to detail and growing skill in navigating the obstacle course of Admiralty and SOE red tape shines through in his planning. He began by persuading the head of the SOE Balkan Section Lt-Col. J. S. A. Pearson to get behind his ideas. At the end of August, he visited the Navy's specialist mine unit at Havant for expert input. Efforts then began to recruit the four or five men he wished to accompany him on the mission; sometime in August, it had become known as Operation Locksmith. Numerous related topics such as water depths in the canal, soil quality and type on the banks, barbed wire coils on either side of the canal, nearby roads, and the state of a sunken warship at one end of the waterway were all researched closely. So were food supplies, clothing, passes, money, and back up supplies like dinghies and wire cutters.

Little appeared to be left to chance. Five Browning 'American-type' machine guns and two .32 Colt Automatic pistols, for example, were ordered well in advance and delivered to 64 Baker Street, the SOE headquarters building in central London. A special forty-eight-hour ration tin—cylindrical, light, and easy to carry—was designed by Mike. A meeting with the chief instructor of the War Office Battle School led to an order for 'Special Equipment' suitable for winter conditions in the Aegean, including Norwegian cooking sets, Artic sleeping bags, cold weather boots, weather-resistant rucksacks, and mountain rations. Another meeting settled on the best type of radio transmitter for the operation—one fitted inside a suitcase and weighing 43 lb—and Mike was given detailed instructions on the best way to contact Alexandria. By 20 October, he was able to give a precise estimate of the weight of Locksmith supplies that would have to be airlifted to Cairo: 2,858 lb or about 1.4 tons. Meantime, under insistent prodding from Cdr Pool, his line manager in Cairo, he was doing his utmost to procure a replacement engine and much-needed spare parts for the *Porcupine*, the best caïque in his para-naval force, and wrestling with Admiralty bureaucracy, which refused to agree this, was a priority.

Two particular aspects of the planning for Operation Locksmith concerned Mike from the outset: selecting the best location for a disembarkation from a submarine and choosing the best team. Cumberlege had initially suggested landing at the nearly-deserted island of Kyra in the Eastern Peloponnese, close enough to the canal and also to Nea Epidavros where he had local contacts. Later, following concerns about submarine safety, the focus switched to the Cape Skyli promontory. Mike had surveyed this area in April 1941 and had often sailed between the Kelevini Islands before the war. In a report he wrote, he described the proposed landing area as 'treeless and consists of broken limestone covered with bushes and heather. The small bay ... is sometimes used as a harbour of refuge for caïques temporarily weather-bound. There are no buildings and no communications to the point. There are quite fair hideouts among the rocks'. Testimony about recent conditions from an escaped Allied serviceman and a local courier added weight to Mike's revised preference. Cape Skyli was chosen.

In late-September, having unofficially sounded out several potential colleagues, Mike identified five men he wanted to accompany him on Operation Locksmith: Capt. Michael Lowe of the Royal Engineers, an expert in sabotage who had worked with SOE previously; Capt. Victor Attias, a Free French officer and fluent Italian speaker who would be the radio operator; Warrant Officer Antonios Fakaros, a Greek naval petty officer and friend of Mike's who had taken part in a special operation in Crete and had local contacts; Sgt Jumbo Steele, the Rhodesian member of the Black Watch who had escaped with Mike from Crete and later returned there on two missions with him ('a highly competent engineer and handyman in general'); and Jan Kotrba, the Czech steward on the *Landfall* who spoke five languages and was working at a driving school run by the Czech Army in Exile in England. For unknown reasons, neither Lowe nor Attias was able to take part. Attias was replaced as radio operator by Sgt Thomas Handley, a Yorkshireman who, unlike the others, Mike did not know. At the start of October, Kotrba was released from the Czech Army for six months. Two weeks later, he was sent to the SOE's training school at Airsaig House near Lochaber in Scotland to take part in a sabotage course with some Norwegian resistance fighters.

At the end of October, Mike also found time to attend a fascinating meeting to discuss another topic of importance to the mission—Folding Boats, or 'folbots' in the slang of the day. These were intended to be tough, lightweight boats suitable for covert landing operations rather than assault craft for commando raids. They had to be suitable to hide on or near a beach in enemy country yet also be durable and able to ferry agents ashore and return them to a parent ship offshore. The existing folbots were too flimsy and unseaworthy and had not come up to Mike's exacting standards. On his return to England, he had visited the Foldboat Section HQ and found that no improvements to the existing model were planned, although a new type of canoe, known as Cockle Mk 2, was being added.

On 28 October, Mike wrote a highly detailed, knowledgeable six-page memo about these craft.[3] The next morning, an 'unofficial' meeting convened at the Combined Operations headquarters at Richmond Terrace in London to discuss 'small boats'. Around the table were three men all destined to be remembered for their Second World War exploits: Cdr Robert Ryder VC who had led the Saint-Nazaire Raid in March 1942; Major 'Blondie' Hasler who was to win a DSO for his leadership of the daring December 1942 raid on Axis shipping in the Gironde (the so-called 'Cockleshell Heroes'); and Lt Mike Cumberlege DSO. Ryder represented the RN outlook and wished to collect various points of view so that a new basic small craft might be built. Hasler represented the Royal Marines Small Boat Section and focused on the need to devise a craft suitable for individual assault operations that might be carried in a submarine. The Cockle Mk 2, he said, was not perfect, but it could be assembled and supplied inside a submarine, had a very low silhouette, and could cover considerable distances in tidal waters. Mike argued in favour of an all-purpose boat capable of carrying a sizeable body of men, and a smaller boat able to carry three men under operational conditions. The group decided, no doubt under the prodding of Maj. Collins of Combined Operations HQ, who was also present, that 'it would be in the interests of all if each would modify his views so that a reasonable craft suitable for all the services might be evolved'.

The following week, Mike met an officer in the Air Ministry to make final arrangements to take the Locksmith team and stores to Cairo. He was told that he could bring cargo weighing up to 3,000 lb and that the aircraft would leave on 7 November. Several delays ensued and not until the morning of 19 November did the Locksmith team take off from RAF Lyneham for Egypt via Gibraltar after 'intense' arguments. To accommodate three last-minute and unwelcome VIPs on the plane—an air vice-marshal, a major-general, and a Foreign Office official—Mike had had to ditch three wireless sets and much other important materiel weighing 1,050 lb—the first entirely avoidable setback in a trail of misfortune that was to dog the operation.[4] A second issue began to emerge as the team reached Cairo on 21 November and learnt that, following the success of the pivotal Third Battle of El Alamein at the start of the month and the onset of Operation Torch, Vichy French forces had laid down their arms in Algeria and Morocco. As a result, the destruction of the Corinth Canal was fast slipping down Allied naval priorities in the Mediterranean. As long as Edwin Rommel remained in North Africa attempting to regroup German forces, there would always be reason to think another Axis comeback might follow. But it never did, and Rommel left for Germany early in March 1943.

At the time Mike reached Cairo, the implications of these seismic events in the desert were still being absorbed. Moreover, regardless of the situation in North Africa, the Corinth Canal remained an important supply shortcut for the Germans and Italians as long as Axis forces held sway in Crete and the Aegean. So the Cumberlege plan went ahead, but other issues began to emerge. Another operation to block the waterway involving the Greek Resistance in Athens had been in the planning stage since September. It fell apart in December 1942–January 1943 due to internal divisions, poor security, logistical problems with explosives, and the reckless behaviour of its leader. The fallout was to involve the execution of John Atkinson and his Greek helpers in February and an immediate tightening of Italian defences in the Greek capital and around the canal. That, in turn, was to make it harder for resistance partisans to support Locksmith as intended.

Mike had been sad to leave Nancy but grateful to have been back in England for six months. His strength had returned, he had made a lot of important new contacts, he had been happy to see the three-year-old Marcus 'at this darling age; he is a smart little boy', and he looked forward to a time after the war when the family could be reunited at La Gardiole. 'You know why more cannot be written,' he remarked in a letter to Nancy sent from an hotel on Northumberland Avenue in central London as he waited to fly out to the Middle East. On arriving in Egypt, he had hoped to launch Locksmith almost immediately, but delays finding a suitable RN submarine to deliver the party ashore and also in producing an up-to-date intelligence assessment of the proposed landing site on Cape Skyli meant that the team kicked its heels for the next seven weeks, mostly in Alexandria and Beirut. Mike amused himself by writing twenty-one letters to Nancy, all of which survive.[5]

At the beginning of December, Jumbo Steele joined the party (he had earlier been listed as a deserter but reappeared and any charges against him seem to have been dropped), and 'at last [they had] all the necessary'. Mike's pay, however, had been cut as he had not been considered on active service since May. He responded by avoiding most of his old friends and 'living a spartan life full of work'. Five days later, he added: 'Life is very difficult in so many ways—really because I have loads to do and so little money to spend. It's appalling my pay has been cut by nearly £400 a year while I risk my life'. One evening, in the company of his close friend John Campbell, also back in Alexandria and doing 'excellent work', he had let his hair down and cursed the 'inefficiency' of Middle East projects. By 8 December, he was again expecting to leave shortly. As he put it cryptically: 'The day after tomorrow the Halibut doth spread her fragile wings not to see the Fleshpots again for some long time I imagine'. Once more, it was not to be. A reconnaissance trip to Cape Skyli by the submarine HMS *Taku* ended with her revealing her position and having to escape from a German submarine chaser. Antonios Fakaros, the only Greek-speaking member of the party, had meanwhile been rejected as the fifth person in the team by Mike's superiors. It was another 'own goal' that was to handicap the operation severely. Mike, nevertheless, still sounded undeterred. 'I have a fine little gang and couldn't wish for better,' he wrote.

On 11 December, the team moved to Lebanon with a new plan to use a Royal Hellenic Navy vessel *Papanicolis*. Further delays followed due to engine problems with the ageing submarine. Mike decided to join the local naval mess: '… with many people I know. I'm living in a small suitcase with half a shirt but it doesn't matter'. His thoughts had begun to wander to the post-war world: 'I want to come back to the old life. Won't it be strange? And how shall we live with nothing to live on?' By chance, he had bumped into the owner of La Gardiole, Antoine Mounier, who was serving in the Free French Forces in Beirut, and learnt that Antoine was proposing to pull down the villa in Cap d'Antibes after the war (he did not). Ritchie Paine also loomed in his musings as a potential employer even though, by then, Mike must have known that the *Landfall* had been sold. One bright spot concerned his pay, or more precisely his pension, which, he had been informed in Cairo, would be tied to the rank of lieutenant commander from the start of 1943, even though he had yet to be formally promoted.

To keep the team up to the mark, Mike then devised a series of physical trials. In mid-month, he organised a 4-mile paddling exercise in two canoes that ended up at 1 a.m. 'in the beam of the largest searchlight in Europe [*sic*.]. Very disconcerting'. The day before, he had put the team through a 14-mile hike. Just before Christmas, Jumbo, Jan, and Mike hiked to Krak des Chevaliers, a Crusader castle on the Lebanese–Syrian border. This, surely, must be the only undercover operation in the Second World War that, as a prelude, involved a cultural tour of one of the Middle East's most iconic sites. It also produced one of Mike's most descriptive bits of writing:

What a time we've been having. It's such a long story, I hardly know where to begin. I think, as usual, I shall begin in the middle. The winter is lovely in this part of the world. That is, it isn't brown and skinned but green and fresh with winter grasses and mauve crocuses, frailest of autumn flowers, and yellow ones like stars, wide open to the pale, yellow sun, and mauve anemones in places. And hills and plains and further hills and further plains and then the great mountain dreaming and gleaming with snow and the cedars crawling up their sides, vaguely possible as black specks in the far away distance.

Over the brow of the next hill you will see Talaat el Hosn. Two towers and a wall of golden yellow against a far-away green hillside—this was the Krak des Chevaliers about which we had dreamed so much, a tiny blot on an immense landscape. So we walked, and we walked and we walked. The castle disappeared behind sloping hills and reappeared again, small and far away. We arrived at an appalling village with a wild feel and a drum beating out an Arab fiesta. And above it was the Krak which still seemed disappointing if correct—a toy castle. We went into the gateway of the Chevaliers and having paid a sum and denuded ourselves of forty Syrian children chanting 'Backsheesh, focking English bastards,' we disappeared into a vast tunnel.

At last we became of IT. It is immense. I have never been in anything which so immediately takes one into itself and then loses one. It was mentally and morally immense. It grew on one. There are other, bigger castles and probably better castles but never a castle like this one. It's difficult to explain its vastness. Much is in proportion, there are no cathedral-like corridors stretching upward, the great central dining room is about a football field and a half long, the table at which the Chevaliers themselves sat is 29 yards round. The lovely green grassy rectangle by the chapel, the towers, the tower of the Fils de Roy, the frescoes and so forth. The sixteen wells, the three lines of galleries in the outer walls instead of the usual one, and this that and the other.

In the silences of the late evening Abdul Kerim Fayad Dandashi, a bloody old Arab tyrant, took us to his bosom and for the whole time we were there took complete charge of us and fed us and instructed us and bedded us in his guest farmhouse and treated us like honoured guests. He is simply perfect—68, tall, aquiline, merry, stern, dignified, friendly, four wives, twenty-one children and whole villages of aunts and uncles and cousins. His home is beautifully run.

We had arrived at the fortress at dusk. We'd been turned off the [train] at Tel Kalakh and the view was bleak—not a tree, not a curve in the ground, only a cold and dismal wind and a helpfully expectant moon. We suggested to the station master that we might borrow a few convenient logs and he said 'What for?' So we said that we wanted to walk to Talaat by moonlight and sleep in a field but there didn't seem much wood to make a fire. So he said 'I should say not, but you see that house in the distance? Well, go there and the man will help you.' So we did. We crept into and up various steep stairs, saw a vague light and a round charcoal brazier through a window, and a lot of hooded, hook-nosed men. I knocked timidly on the door and all rose to their feet. In one minute we were dragged in, hands shaken, chairs produced, the charcoal stirred. So we can into the bosom of Abdul Kerim Fayad Dandashi.

First, we had coffee—you know, that bitter coffee, three drops in a tiny handless bowl. We said we could really do with a cup of tea and then must be on our way and that if they could let us have hot water we could arrange the tea which we had with us. So they said 'We don't understand—do you wish tea now or after supper, or do you wish your tea before and after supper?' Well, the result of it was that we realised we were completely trapped. I've seldom spent a happier evening. The three of us and the old man sat at a table groaning with food whilst five sons stood around fixing us up with every little want. We ate until the old man couldn't force any more on us. Then the other members of the family were let in. We ended up by being hauled into a spotlessly clean room with mattresses laid out, clean linen and lovely quilts to lie under. The old man tucked us in whilst seven sons and two daughters watched us undress and go to bed.

Just before I turned in the old man took me to a window and, with a sweeping gesture of his arm, showed me the sleeping moonlit countryside, still and lovely in the night. We slept well. And stayed two nights with him and had many discussions which ranged back and forth and touched on the lovely women he had seen in Paris and a graphic representation of the cleansing ritual prescribed by Mohammed before sleeping with one of them![6]

The delays dragged on over the Christmas–New Year period, enabling Mike to purchase a model boat for Marcus and hand it to 'Skipper Pool' for safekeeping while on a brief visit to Cairo. Here, on Christmas Eve, Georges de Menasce, his wealthy Alexandrian friend, gave him a 'beautiful silver chain key chain specially made for [him]'. Christmas Day 1942 was spent marooned at an airfield when his plane back to Haifa broke down. On 30 December, he waxed lyrical again about a 'perfect dinner' he had enjoyed two nights before: 'terrine, bécasse [woodcock] flambé and curly salad with croutons of bread rubbed in garlic, coffee and a cigar'. Earlier that day, he had been to a tiny village above Beirut to watch two ancient silversmiths ply their craft: 'It was quite fascinating'. On New Year's Day, he dined alone at the landmark St Georges Hotel on the Beirut waterfront, sitting near a Turkish princess: '… we made eyes at one another'. The next day, he took his team out to dinner at an officers'-only club—a restriction that Mike ignored to the others' delight. Another delay ensued at this point 'due to a minor and aggravating accident'. So he and a friend, 'Fluffy' Baker, walked through the Adonis river gorge—'a hell of an undertaking' that involved going down a 3,000-foot cliff to the river, crossing an icy-cold waist-high flow four times, and tramping through a vast landslide dodging huge boulders: 'We became very frightened—thousands of tons [of rocks] were just waiting to come down'. It was an epic walk that lasted six and a half hours: 'I loved every minute of it. It was beautiful and wild—a real haunt of Pan'.

To kill time at his temporary base, Mike learnt by heart his favourite poem—'The Loss of Eurydice' by Gerald Manley Hopkins, all thirty verses about a shipwreck off the Isle of Wight in 1878: 'My trouble is that I cannot sit about doing stupid things. I must be up to some nonsense or another. I haven't the temperament to do dull jobs'. Admitting that he was 'looking forward to everything', he warned Nancy not to expect to hear from him for a time: 'I look forward to the future with great confidence, without fear and in good heart. If my machines [presumably the mines] are kind to me, I have no fear. I can't say any fairer words than that'. A couple of days later on 12 January 1943, he penned what proved to be his last lengthy communication with Nancy: 'I am either the daring young man on the flying trapeze or the man waiting to make his first parachute jump. Or perhaps I am just me'. Asking Nancy to give the Paines 'my love' and to pass on messages 'to our many friends', including Aunts Gwen and Gladys, the Skipper (his father), and his Uncle Cle and Aunt Leila, he ends: 'I shall do my best to be careful. Your own kind loving Michele'.

On the night of 12 January, Operation Locksmith finally got underway and the submarine *Papanicolis* arrived without incident off Cape Skyli early next morning. A suitable landing area was chosen at Buofi Cove, an almost deserted inlet on the mainland. Mike and his team paddled ashore, taking 2 tons of stores with them. An almost minute-by-minute description of the events that followed between 13 January to 1 April exists in a brilliantly-researched book, *Target Corinth Canal 1940-1944*, by Platon Alexiades. Most of the detail that follows is based on this work and also on two post-war enquiries, one conducted by an official Greek commission, the other by the BCIS (Balkan Counter-Intelligence Section).[7]

After landing, the Locksmith party made contact with a frightened fisherman who lived in a small, secluded house close to the beach, and stayed nearby for four days. The 2 tons of stores were not easily camouflaged and, within days a German caïque may have arrived at Boufi Cove seeking evidence of a British landing. The team meantime had built a small hut at Tselevinia, close to Buofi Cove, installed one of its two radio transmitters, and begun signalling Cairo. Within days, Mike had radioed that the group had been betrayed by 'a fisherman' and that its 'position causes some uneasiness'. Seeking local support, Mike encountered a landowner and civilian policeman, Dimitros Sambanis, who proved helpful and had a wife who spoke some English. Eventually, Sambanis found a small motorboat for the team to use. Follow-up developments in Athens associated with the earlier aborted Greek resistance effort to block the Corinth Canal now intruded and the plan for a large caïque to be found and delivered by partisans to the Locksmith party for the journey through the waterway had to be revised, causing further anxious delay. Shortly after, one of SOE's key radio operatives in the Greek capital was caught transmitting a message, weakening resistance resources and its ability to support Locksmith. In Cairo, as early as the start of February, it was feared that the operation had been compromised.

On the scene, Mike pushed ahead. By then, judging by his messages to Cairo, he realised that the inhabitants in this part of the Peloponnese coast were fearful of German reprisals and an element of the population was actively pro-German. However, on 4 February, an agent from Athens, Spyros Kotsis, finally made contact with Mike. Kotsis later wrote that Cumberlege had startled him with a resounding 'Hullo!' in English instead of the pre-arranged password, was hatless, in summer white naval uniform, and wearing a pistol and a pair of binoculars. He also noted Mike's gold earring. Two villagers observed this encounter and Kotsis had to pass Mike off as an Italian officer searching for British soldiers. He thought they were not convinced. Remaining with the Locksmith commandos for five or six days, he became fearful about their behaviour—for example, floating weather balloons twice a day, which nearby shepherds were bound to see. Communication proved difficult, but a basic understanding was reached in French. After another promised caïque failed to turn up, Kotsis returned to Athens on 9 February to try to find something suitable. Eight days later, Kotsis and an English-speaking colleague, Fotios Manolopoulos, returned and options were reviewed. Both Kotsis and Manolopoulos were now being hunted for arms smuggling by the Gestapo in Athens. SOE Cairo, which knew this through radio intercepts, wanted other partisans to work with Mike and his party, but the alternatives were limited and the lack of a Greek speaker in the party was proving a real handicap—in particular, restricting contact with any sympathetic locals. So Kotsis and Manolopoulos remained. Manolopoulos, an engineer called Michael Morakeas, and a third Greek, Kiriakoulis Sideris, were to take part in the actual canal mining operation.

It was Sideris, a resourceful young sailor from a farming background, who eventually turned up with a caïque from Piraeus on 3 March. This was a 20-ton vessel he had recently acquired named the *Aghia Varvara*, with a dubious background and disputed documents. However, legitimate papers for passage through the canal had been acquired from the Germans despite the *Abwehr* (military intelligence) having the *Aghia Varvara* under observation for her part in a weapons' smuggling operation. Unaware of this background, the Locksmith party loaded the mines and explosives on the vessel on 4 March. Mike had already been concerned about the reliability of the mines in Alexandria and now left one behind. He was accompanied by Jumbo Steele. The following day at dawn, close to the entrance to the canal, holes were drilled near the waterline of the caïque to attach the mines before dropping them. At about 9 a.m. on 5 March, as the process was going on, Mike was in the water attaching the counter mines to the *Aghia Varvara*'s bottom. A German patrol vessel suddenly turned up and he managed to scramble onboard unseen and hide with Jumbo Steel in a space behind a false bulkhead. The primed mines were still on deck disguised as petrol cans, but the Germans failed to spot them. The three Greeks acted normally, gave an explanation for their presence in the area, and the Germans left. It was a bruisingly narrow escape and Mike later praised the coolness displayed by Sideris during the search. His messages to Cairo, according to Nancy writing in August 1945, are 'amongst the most amusing in the whole Naval files and put the *Boys Own Paper* to horrid shame'.[8]

The three Greeks were now left to carry out the actual mining operation since it was feared that the Italian guard, who was to join the *Aghia Varvara* during the crossing of the canal, might well question Mike or Jumbo in Greek or Italian if he saw them on board. Disembarking some 7 miles from the entrance to the canal, they climbed a hill to watch the operation unfold. For security reasons (unexplained), Manolopoulos now decided to ditch three of the four mines with their counter mines before entering the canal.[9] Mike never knew this. The remaining mine was dropped some 700 yards east of a bridge across the canal without drawing the attention of the Italian guard. After a two-hour stop at the other end of the canal, the *Aghia Varvara* returned through it to take on a load of fish to solidify its cover story before returning to Piraeus. Meantime, Cumberlege and Steele returned the 40 miles overland to their hide near Tselevina, reaching it undetected on 11 March to await word that the raid had succeeded or failed and new instructions from Cairo.

Within four days, Mike knew the explosives had failed to go off. He immediately proposed a new raid, provided new supplies could be sent to him and also capturing a caïque and using it to destroy the many Axis sailing vessels near Cape Skyli. However, a German–Italian dragnet was now drawing ever-tighter around the Locksmith team. As the days went by following the canal raid, locals began to talk openly about the presence of a 'sabotage group' somewhere nearby. Italian secret police arrived at the home of Dimitros Sambanis demanding to know the 'whereabouts of Englishmen in the vicinity' according to a signal Mike sent to Cairo on 19 March. 'Every precaution' was taken, including destroying all previous telegrams sent. Even Sambanis had begun to question their credentials: 'Our position here depends largely on their goodwill' Mike observed two days later. By 28 March, Cumberlege (in his 114th signal) suggested that the team be resupplied with mines and explosives by air despite realising that such supplies would first have to be flown out from England. In London, questions had begun to be asked about whether another canal operation was necessary in view of the changing strategic situation. With the advantage of hindsight, it seems clear that the *Abwehr* by this stage (early April) realised that an Allied commando group was at work somewhere in the area.

Around noon on 8 April, a party of five Germans landed near Boufi Cove, guided by a close friend of Sambanis. It began searching the area. About 50 yards from the Locksmith shelter, it ran into Cumberlege and Thomas Handley. Mike reacted first, drawing his pistol and shooting one of the Germans in the thigh. The Germans retreated after an exchange of gunfire. Cumberlege ran back to the hut, grabbed a submachine gun and escaped as fast as he could. What Handley did is unknown, but in the panic, the pair left their codebooks and a transmitter behind. About an hour later, the Germans came back and found the transmitter, two machine guns, a pistol, a camera, three exposed films, and the codebooks. Sambanis saw the gunfight, soon met up with Mike, and was urged to escape with him, but responded that he would need first to round up his whole family—eighteen persons. Six days after the gunfight, another German force landed at Boufi Cove to search for the Locksmith party, followed the next day by an Italian unit in a boat, which removed everything from the Sambanis house. After the war, Sambanis, who had received £1,000 (£45,000 today) in Greek currency from Mike for safekeeping, came under suspicion of betraying the group. No actual evidence was ever found.

The Locksmith team now set up a new base in the village of Damala and cabled Cairo to report its predicament. Mike attempted to pass himself off as a Greek called Tsabis or Cabelis, but his inability to speak more than kitchen Greek hugely limited his ability to convince. A signal from the team was then intercepted by the *Abwehr* in Athens, which then decided to set a trap using the SOE codebooks and transmitter it had captured. Sometime around 23 April, Mike met up with Sambanis and the group recovered some stores that Sambanis had hidden, but they failed to locate 2,000 gold sovereigns that had been buried before the gunfight. Another local, Theodoros Philippopoulos, immediately came under suspicion, not least because he had told Sambanis about the cache and disappeared soon after with a friend. Mike's ability to operate was now limited, with both money and weapons in short supply. On 26 April, Handley received two signals purporting to be from Cairo stating that a submarine would arrive to fetch them from a location off Boufi Cove on 29 or 30 April. Cairo had already detected signals allegedly from the group that seemed bogus, but Handley failed to do so. On 29 April, the Locksmith team assembled, but poor weather prevented the three German patrol boats assigned to the trap from reaching the location. Next night, Cumberlege signalled out to sea with his torch and was incorrectly answered. This went on for three hours before Mike, hesitant and suspicious, finally decided to risk it and the team rowed out in a rubber boat. About ten minutes later, machine-gun fire was heard on shore. Mike and his loyal partners had no choice but to surrender. Sambanis, who had accompanied Mike to the shore, heard the gunfire, returned to his house, and fled to the hills with his family, eventually reaching Athens and remaining in the shadows until the German withdrawal from Greece seventeen months later. In an attempt to exploit their coup, the Germans then tried twice with false messages to lure an RN submarine to Poros. Cairo sent several 'test' messages, which cannot have been answered correctly and no vessel was ever despatched.

The catalogue of mistakes in this saga make painful reading and Mike himself, based on the few of his messages smuggled out of captivity, realised this full well after the event. The very human failing of over-confidence clearly was a factor throughout. Right from the outset at Lyneham airfield, Mike had been forced to compromise and ditch 850 lb of the carefully- calibrated supplies simply to seat three unexpected VIPs on the aircraft. The magnetic mine devised in Havant failed to go off; its design proved to be faulty and it had floated rather than sunk to the bottom of the canal. The lack of a Greek speaker in the group, despite Mike's specific request for one, proved to be a crippling and entirely avoidable handicap. Arrests of Greek resistance agents in Athens around the time the Locksmith team reached Boufi Cove added a further problem by disrupting both timings and logistics.

Once the German hunt for the group began, Handley and Cumberlege probably should have realised that all communication with Cairo was suspect since their codebooks had been captured. Even before then, Mike had shown an almost reckless disregard for security by signalling Cairo so often and at the length he did—140 messages in all over the course of 107 days, not to mention the weather balloons. No attempt was made by the team to move away from the wider Poros area after the failure of the canal operation; with Mike's seagoing skills, contacts in Nea Epidavros, intimate knowledge of the Aegean, available weaponry, and considerable cash and jewellery resources (Operation Locksmith began with 4,000 sovereigns, 28 diamonds and 250,000 drachmae[10]), he probably could have seized a caïque and reached Turkey or Lebanon. Treachery was evidently a factor. After the war, efforts were made by SOE to discover what had gone wrong. The most exhaustive, by the Balkan Counter Intelligence Service (BCIS), visited Poros, and a Greek Air Force officer called P. Prossalendis spent a couple of weeks interviewing locals. Although highly suspicious of Dimitros Sambanis, he found nothing clear-cut against him. Instead, he concluded that the Locksmith team had been betrayed either for money—Cumberlege's cache—or by pro-German sympathisers among the mainly Arvanite (Hellenised Albanians) population. Suspects, including several who had splashed out in ostentatious ways in the 1943–45 period buying caïques or new suits or generally 'disporting themselves', were arrested as the Greek civil war began in 1946.[11] They were never tried.

Despite this chapter of accidents, some self-induced, most not, the daring, heroism, and tenacity of the Locksmith team—Mike Cumberlege, Jumbo Steele, Jan Kotrba, and Thomas Handley—in infiltrating behind enemy lines, carrying out a sabotage mission, and evading capture for more than three months remains remarkable even many decades later. As Paddy Ashdown, the former leader of the Liberal Democrat party and member of the Royal Marines Special Boat Section, reflected on a BBC *Timewatch* programme about the wartime raid on Axis shipping in the Gironde a few months before Operation Locksmith, the personal sacrifice involved in such operations was total: 'In an age of easy living, where we are seldom asked to choose between ourselves and the greater good, they should be seen as an inspiration to us all'.[12]

Points of No Return

The Locksmith team were taken by their captors to Averoff jail in Athens. Run by the Italians, it had a notorious reputation, and a number of war crimes trials were held after the war of its officers and guards, including that of Lt F. D'Allessio, the chief torturer, and the chief warder Cesar Romero. Just before Italy surrendered to the Allies in 1944, all 800 prisoners then in the prison where handed over to the Germans by the Italians. Few survived, some were shot and most were sent as slave labour into the concentration camp system.[1] A number of Allied servicemen had ended up there prior to Mike's arrival and described being denied the status of POWs, flogged with 'a long wire-lined rubber truncheon' while tied to a telegraph pole, kept in solitary confinement without food or water, and roughly interrogated round the clock in the part of the prison across the street occupied by the Carabinieri. At least three are known to have been executed on trumped-up charges, such as 'attempting to organise a revolution in the Peloponnese'.

The *Abwehr* in Athens took a close interest in captives in Averoff, and it is known that one of the heads of its various units in the city, by the name of Hoffmeister, resorted to 'unlawful' means to extract information from the Locksmith team. In theory, as had happened to the four captured commandos who were part of the 'Cockleshell Heroes' attack on Axis shipping in the Gironde in December 1942, after the interrogation, 'with no holds barred', Hoffmeister should have handed the group over to the *Sicherheitsdienst* (SD, Security Service) to be shot in line with Hitler's infamous *Kommandobefehl* (Commando Order) of October 1942.[2] This secret directive, which applied to any Allied commandos encountered by German forces in Europe and Africa, whether in uniform or not, had caused divisions within the German High Command—Rommel refused to relay the order to his troops—and was later ruled at the Nuremberg Trials to be a direct breach of the laws of war. Any German officer who failed to carry it out, on the other hand, was liable to be shot himself. By the end of the war, more than 100 Allied personnel had been executed under the order.[3] Nevertheless, it is possible that there was some hesitation in the Greek capital at this time where Axis commanders were uneasily aware, following the fall of Tunisia, that they needed all the intelligence they could get about future Allied intentions in the Mediterranean.

Mike was, in any case, a prize catch for the Germans who knew of him (or so he wrote once) through his exploits (and gold earring) in Crete. A Greek naval officer, Lt Cdr Charalambos Koutsoyannopoulos, held in Averoff at the same time, later escaped, reached Smyrna in Turkey at the end of June, and brought with him the first word to reach SOE about the fate of the Locksmith team. He stated that the party had been brought to the prison in uniform and had apparently been well treated after being captured. In any event, on 10 May Mike was allowed to write a message of twenty-five words to Nancy through the Greek Red Cross: 'My darling love, in this first letter to you, my Marcus and Bira [the Siamese cat] all is well with me. Don't worry. Your loving husband Michael'. Handley's relatives received a Red Cross cable from him on similar lines dated 11 May. Steele and Kotrba's families never heard from them. The *Abwehr* withheld the messages and it was only on 3 August that they reached the British Red Cross. By then, the Admiralty had informed the relatives in England that the men were missing in action, something Nancy had already learnt unofficially at the start of July through her sister, Nora—'known for her shapely legs' according to Platon Alexiades, who was a Wren (Women's Royal Naval Service) officer working in the same building as the Director of Naval Intelligence. The apparent security breach was followed up by the Navy but no action was taken against Nora.

In Cairo, the SOE was informed by the Admiralty sometime in June that no effort should be spared to get the release of the Locksmith party and to buy it out if necessary. By then, it was already too late. On 11 May, the team was transferred to Austria and imprisoned in Mauthausen concentration camp for the next eight months according to enquiries made by the Swedish Red Cross after the war. Meantime, *Abwehr* attempts to capitalise on the capture of the group continued in a series of false radio messages sent to the SOE in Cairo using Locksmith's captured codebooks. One of them, on 16 May, contained a security check known only to Cumberlege and Handley, so either of them may have talked under interrogation. Another, twelve days later, claimed that Mike had been shot by an Italian patrol before the others were captured. Further messages allegedly from the group were transmitted into June, but were regarded suspiciously in Cairo and ceased on 3 June. No rescue submarine was ever sent to the Poros area.

Not until April 1945 was any definite information received about the Locksmith party's time in Mauthausen, when Mike managed to smuggle a message out through a fellow prisoner in Sachsenhausen concentration camp, Lt-Col. Jack Churchill, who was being released. It stated: 'Oberst Hofmeister [*sic*.] Defence [Abwehr] Athens Herr Seidl Gestapo Vienna both used unlawful means to press a conviction'. Seidl may have been a man who was later in charge of Theresienstadt concentration camp. More likely, he was Fritz Seidler, an SS thug who operated for some years with impunity at Mauthausen. His objective seems to have been to get Mike or his companions to admit that Locksmith's Greek contacts were civilian saboteurs.

Mauthausen, sited near several granite quarries that needed slave labour to be mined, was set up in 1938. It soon became a leading dumping ground for so-called misfits and criminals—'social outsiders' who could be worked to death. In his definitive book *KL: A History of the Nazi Concentration Camps*, Nikolaus Wachsmann describes it as 'the most punitive camp' in the system. From the invasion of Poland in 1939, it also began to take foreign political prisoners as Nazi conquests in Europe increased. Before long, 'here the dead are no news, they appear daily' as a fortunate survivor put it later. More than 90,000 people are estimated to have been murdered in the camp. Mass killings of invalids began in 1941. The next year, some 18,000 Russians were shot. Above the camp entrance gate, the words *Du Kommst Niemals Raus* (You Will Never Come Out) were engraved in stone. An affidavit signed in 1945 by John Starr, an SOE agent arrested in France and jailed in Mauthausen, described the place as 'not so much a concentration camp as an extermination camp'.[4]

Ernst Kaltenbrunner, the Austrian-born head of the SS in the country, had helped to set up Mauthausen in 1938. Later, he became head of the SD and personally ordered the execution of fifteen members of an Anglo-American military mission that parachuted into Slovakia in 1945. Tried at Nuremberg, he was hanged in 1946. In a celebrated article for *Collier's* magazine, 'The Paths of Glory', written after observing the trial, the American journalist Martha Gellhorn vividly caught the essence of Kaltenbrunner 'whose face was terrifying even now when it could bring fear to no one ... a face of really deadly evil'. Many years later, evidence emerged to suggest that he had ignored a few of Hitler's most extreme latter commands. Now, having gone along with the transfer of the Locksmith party from Averoff prison, in effect, he became complicit in its survival and it seems possible that he acquiesced in the group's imprisonment in Mauthausen and transfer to Sachsenhausen. We will never know for sure; no record of any sort was ever found relating to the team's time in this hellhole.

More, however, can be gleaned about Fritz Seidler, or 'Captain Notorious' as the inmates called him. He is thought to have shot his family and himself in May 1945. He had arrived at Mauthausen from Auschwitz in 1942 and soon became known for his brutality. According to the camp commandant, Franz Ziereis, in a death-bed confession in 1945, it was Seidler who was the person responsible for having the skins of the executed made into satchels, lamps shades, and book covers.[5] A survivor, Stanisław Dobosiewicz, said later of him: 'He didn't shout or get excited in public. He was cold-blooded, deliberate and systematic. He found everyone repugnant without exception. Before talking to an inmate, he would give him a hefty clout. He loved to hit, kill and injure people, particularly favouring a punch in the face to break a victims' jaw. He had enormous strength'. The drawing in the plate section by Stanislaw Walczak, now in the Mauthausen Memorial Archives in Vienna, shows him conducting an interrogation at the linked camp in Gusen in 1944.[6]

Under duress, and to his lasting chagrin, Mike was made to sign a confession that the Locksmith team were saboteurs even though German reports confirmed that they had been captured in uniform and were on a military mission. After the war, Nancy Cumberlege received a letter from a woman who had acted as an interpreter during her husband's 'severe' interrogation in Mauthausen. This person confirmed that Mike had been held there until December 1943. Cumberlege supported this when he confided to Jack Churchill, saying that the group had reached Sachsenhausen concentration camp in Germany in January 1944. Ernst Kaltenbrunner, by then head of the Reich main security office, including the SD, Gestapo, and Police, had signed the transfer document to Sachsenhausen himself. This declared that the four were 'Enemies of the State'—part of an elaborate ruse being prepared by the *Abwehr* to stage a mock trial in Berlin of ninety-seven Allied commandos then in German hands as a counter to the Soviet trial and public execution before 40,000 'working people' in Kharkov in mid-December 1943 of three Germans and one Ukrainian found guilty of war crimes in Ukraine.[7]

Sachsenhausen, some 22 miles north-west of Berlin, was one of four pre-war concentration camps in Germany. Its construction dates from 1936. More than 200,000 people were imprisoned here during its existence and it became a hub of the local economy. Used as a model for other camps and a training centre for guards, it is estimated that at least 30,000 inmates perished inside its barbed wire perimeter between 1936 and 1945 and tens of thousands more outside in various work details.[8] The original commandant, Baranowski, lasted to the end of 1939 and was described as a 'pathological sadist'. His equally corrupt successor, Lohritz, did nothing to curb the cruelty, left all power in the hands of the SS, and devoted himself to making money. In 1942, he was replaced by the bespectacled Anton Kaindl, more of a manager in the extensive camp system than a killer, who nevertheless was known in Sachsenhausen for his lethal inspection tours, during which he would point out prisoners he did not wish to see again. They would promptly 'be disposed of'. Under Kaindl, in reality, the institutionalised violence continued largely unabated. In 1943, it was refined with the construction of a crematorium and gas chamber inside the camp that was capable of routinely killing 300 people a day.

Shaped like a triangle, Sachsenhausen fanned out from a main gate into a large semi-circular assembly area with huts radiating from it (see map taken from *Moonless Night* by Plt Off. 'Jimmy' James). Each hut was daubed with a single word in white paint. Taken together, they read: 'There Is Only One Way to Freedom—Through Labour, Obedience, Sobriety, Order, Cleanliness, Self-sacrifice and Patriotism'. A typical day for most prisoners began at 4.15 a.m. in the summer, 5.15 a.m. in the winter, with a quick splash in cold water, an apology of a breakfast of ersatz coffee and a slice of thin bread, and an interminable roll-call on the assembly ground. Then the majority of prisoners were marched off to factories near the camp. From 1940, these included the largest brickworks in the world where the average life expectancy of the workers was three months, small armaments factories, and a nearby aircraft plant. Other 'enterprises' involved a counterfeiting operation in Barrack 19 run by about 140 Jewish men, and a 600-metre track inside the camp used to test military boots on nine surfaces; half-starved prisoners were made to walk 40 km a day carrying 15-kg sandbags.[9] Many died.

Violence, indeed, was ever-present at Sachsenhausen and totally random, much of it centred on the *Industriehof* or punishment block. Here torture was standard treatment followed by death by machine-gun shooting outside in a purpose-built sandpit/execution trench. Some 9,000 Soviet officers had been massacred at the site in the autumn of 1941, but matters were no better after that. A total of 100 Dutch resistance fighters were shot later that year. It was here at the end of May 1942 that the SS machine gunned 250 Jews who had been rounded up in Berlin in retaliation for the assassination of Reinhard Heydrich in Prague. Then, in May 1943, a German communist, Willi Feiler, witnessed eighty to 100 British and American airmen held in Sachsenhausen being sent to the sandpit and shot.[10] To cover up the crime, all the dead were recorded as 'escaped'. In the icy winter of 1944–45, 5,000 starved Russian POWs captured in the spring of 1944 were made to stand on parade from 7 a.m. until 5 p.m. in short sleeves, and shot on the spot if they moved; only 400 were alive by April 1945. At his post-war trial in 1947, Kaindl, true to his anaesthetised bookkeeper mentality, admitted matter of factly that 'more than 42,000 prisoners were exterminated under [his] command; this number included 18,000 killed in the camp itself'. He added that another '8,000 prisoners died by starvation during this period'.[11]

A structure of particular significance was the *genickschussbaracke* or neck-shooting barrack. Victims were told by the SS that they were being taken to a medical examination. Inside the building was a large room where prisoners were made to undress. They were then taken individually to an adjacent, smaller room and greeted by an SS guard dressed as a doctor and checked to see if they had gold fillings. Those that did were marked with an X. Led to a third room that resembled a bathroom with shower heads on the ceiling, the victim was ordered to stand against a measuring pole fixed to a wall. A sliding, porthole-like door behind the prisoner's neck then opened and another SS guard pulled the trigger. According to Nikolaus Wachsmann in his book *KL* 'judging by the gaping holes in the victims' skulls, the SS used special dumdum bullets'. A gramophone played cheerful music in the first waiting room to disguise the sound of the shot. Once the body slumped to the floor, orderlies from the crematorium dragged the corpse to a makeshift morgue where they ripped out any gold teeth before throwing the corpse into an oven. Back in the execution room, other orderlies hosed down the blood-stained execution site, 'Then the next prisoner was led in'.[12]

Sachsenhausen had originally been set up to incarcerate German political opponents of the Nazis. Thousands of communists, social democrats, former trade union leaders, and religious believers (such as Jehovah's Witnesses and members of the banned Bible Society) ended up here as well as Jews. By the end of 1939, the camp held about 11,000 prisoners. A typhus outbreak cut the population substantially at that point and led to the construction of the first crematorium. After the Nazi invasion of Poland and later of the Soviet Union, the camp expanded to include tens of thousands of POWs from the Eastern Front. By 1944, it also included a mixed bag of Danes, Norwegians, French, Belgian, Dutch, British, Irish, Italian, and many other nationalities who, for one reason or another, had ended up in the Nazis' clutches. A few well-known individuals called *Prominenten*, such as a one-time Chancellor of Austria, a recalcitrant German arms manufacturer, the former commander-in-chief of the Greek Army, and two members of a minor European royal family, were locked up in separate prison villas. Most 'elite' non-Germans, however, were held in two special barracks, Sonderlager A and Sonderlager B, sited inside the perimeter behind a 12-foot-high electrified barbed-wire fence and brick walls higher than the fence. Never sure of their fate, these inmates included two colourful Russian generals who the Germans hoped to turn against the Soviets, and a number of Allied POWs, such as Capt. Peter Churchill, an SOE officer captured in France who survived thanks to his name and the mistaken Gestapo belief that one day he could be made to broadcast from Berlin on behalf of the Nazis.

About 300 yards away from Sonderlager A was the so-called Zellenbau, or cell block described in Chapter 1. Built of ferro concrete and red brick, its walls had been doubled in thickness in 1942 so that the noisier incidents of torture could be carried out without unsettling other prisoners. T-shaped in design, the two top sections were known as the 'A' and 'B' wings with the stem 'C'. Sited alongside the punishment compound, this block was surrounded by its own electrified wire. Its eighty cells were reserved mostly for deserters, spies, saboteurs, commandos, persistent Allied POW escapers, and individuals or small groups of men seen as potentially high tariff in terms of hostage-taking or prisoner swapping. The whole of Europe was represented in the block, including Poles, Ukrainians, French, British, Romanians, Bulgarians, Serbs, and Croats, as well as Germans and Austrians. Extreme torture and midnight interrogations before execution were routine in underground cellars below the block. So were suicide attempts by the prisoners. Escape was out of the question. The steel cell doors opened outwards and were secured by two bolts and a lock, the window was barred, and the floor and ceiling were made of concrete. Cells were numbered and prisoners known only by numbers rather than names.

Mostly, the inmates never met and were let out only for fifteen or thirty minutes a day for solitary exercise in an adjoining yard. The Zellenbau, in other words, was essentially the end of the road for almost all who reached it. The only real unknown was the timing of that end. Inmates in other parts of the camp, some of whom survived in Sachsenhausen for several years, knew nothing about it—and nor did the inmates of the Zellenbau know anything about what went on in the main camp unless they had to visit the dentist on the other side of the compound. This dentist was a brave Dutch prisoner with an equally brave Dutch assistant who was prepared to share what he knew of the atrocities going on all around him with patients from the Zellenbau while drilling away at diseased molars.[13] Nevertheless, whatever records that were kept were destroyed before the end of the war, and for years after, the full horror of this cruel and evil place remained a dark secret. Even *KL*, the recent definitive history of the concentration camps, makes no mention of the Zellenbau.

This was the destination of the Locksmith team who arrived on or about 23 January 1944. From the moment of their appearance, the four men were treated as common criminals and accorded the toughest conditions and the worst and smallest food rations. As far as is known, none of them ever received a Red Cross parcel. Condemned to 'full arrest' status—the lowest of three categories assigned to the prisoners in the Zellenbau—they dragged out their days in darkened cells deprived of reading material, made to stand for much of the time, and always afraid for their lives. Little is known about how Steele, Handley, and Kotrba endured this regime, but for various reasons, Mike Cumberlege was able to establish communications with several other prisoners, which allow some sort of picture to be drawn. Initially, it seems, he was put in a cell (probably numbered 75) next to a Ukrainian resistance leader called Taras Bulba-Borovets. In 1981, the year he died, the Ukrainian diaspora in Canada published Bulba-Borovets' autobiography *Army Without a State*, written in Ukrainian and largely from memory. A resourceful researcher in Kiev unearthed the text of this book in 2016, so adding more detail about Mike's existence in the camp.

Bulba-Borovets and a dozen or so of his compatriots had been imprisoned in Sachsenhausen at the start of December 1943 while the Germans attempted to persuade them to fight against the Soviets in a specially-formed brigade on the Eastern Front. Coincidentally, the Allies had begun a mass air campaign against Berlin the month before their arrival in Sachsenhausen, which was sustained through most of 1944 and into 1945. As Cumberlege and his three companions reached the camp in January 1944, the raids had become a daily occurrence. Sachsenhausen was not hit directly, except by incendiary bombs, which caused a lot of fires. Bulba-Borovets recalled:

> We passed endless days. The sleepless nights were even longer. The Zellenbau swayed, like a ship on waves, but remained intact. While SS troops hid in a bunker, the prisoners sat in cages.... The roar of engines, bombings, gunfire, the howling sirens, the cries and laments of the slain and wounded mingled in such a terrible cacophony that was harmful to damaged people even those with the strongest nerves.

He added:

> The Ukrainians were permitted a one-hour walk most days. This allowed us to set up a rudimentary communication system.... There is nothing worse for the lone prisoner than isolation. All prison inmates fight this curse. Yet even with a strict regime of isolation prisoners always find ways for friendly contact.

In his book, Bulba-Borovets goes on to describe the day-to-day atmosphere in the Zellenbau block:

> The 'machine' carried out shootings all the time. We all await our turn at any moment.... Long summer days [in 1944] flew by like lightning but the short nights seemed an eternity. The quietest mouse rustling in the corridor sounded to us like a step taken by an SS boot. And when a guard did reach our corridor, for us all it was an eternity as we guessed which cell. Was it for us or not for us?

Escape plans were hatched, then discarded:

> Once a plan, again some new hope for a few days. Then complete hopelessness. Sachsenhausen is a city with dozens of walls covered with electrified barbed wire, tower guards with machine guns, searchlights and patrols with hundreds of dogs.

This might be followed by apathy—'the severest of threats to a prisoner'.

The Allied bombing of Berlin and the area around it was, indeed, ferocious for much of the period from March 1943 to May 1945. By one estimate, Berlin eventually received 67,000 tonnes of bombs, the most of any German city and more than twice the total dropped on London during the Blitz.[14] Three huge flak towers and 100 anti-aircraft batteries ringed the capital, but even so, some 50,000 people are thought to have died and millions made homeless. At the height of the bombing, there might be four major Allied raids a week, each involving 750 planes. During the final year of the war in Europe, the USAF and the RAF were effectively unopposed by the Luftwaffe over the Berlin area. Fear became widespread, but German morale held firm.

Communication among the Zellenbau prisoners in this period was possible in a variety of ways, according to Bulba-Borovets, although speaking to other prisoners directly was prohibited. One favoured method was to write in the margins and spaces of Nazi propaganda newspapers like the *Völkischer Beobachter*, which were distributed among some of the prisoners by their jailors and shared around. Sometimes, small scraps of this paper with bits of news were thrown into a cell by those taking exercise near a cell window or concealed in the buckets used for toilet needs that were taken out by orderlies. Another method involved tapping on the thick, inter-connecting cell walls and echoing radiator pipes in Morse code or using Morse code by drumming messages on the palms of one's hand during exercise periods for other prisoners watching from their cells.

From somewhere in the camp, the Ukrainians acquired a supply of tobacco. This was turned into Vinnytsia shag (named after a tobacco factory in Ukraine) and rolled into large, rough 'cigars'.

> We passed them through the 'mail' to our British comrades together with scraps of news. I was the contact of a sailor called Michael Cumberlege, the son of a retired Admiral. Morse signs thanked us for the information from the press and for the 'Havana cigars'. Michael joked every time that once we got out of here we would immediately smoke two large, genuine Havanas.... He was an extremely good companion in distress. Always cheerful, occupied with new ideas, very friendly, inventive, honest, modest, steady and resistant to all prison torments and surprises.

At the end of October 1944, Bulba-Borovets was let out of the Zellenbau and told by the Nazis that he would be released from the camp on certain conditions, in particular that the Ukrainians would agree to 'mount a common front against communism'. Negotiations dragged on until early-March 1945 when the German government issued a permit for the organisation of a Ukrainian army. Bulba-Borovets' detachment surrendered to the western Allies in May 1945, and he was interned in Italy. Mike Cumberlege and Jumbo Steele (in Cell 5) remained in Bulba-Borovets' memory more than thirty years later:

> Of all our English friends in the Zellenbau, only one escaped [possibly a reference to 'Wings' Day of the RAF, but he names 'Falconer' or 'Faulkner']. The fate of the

rest is unknown. There is speculation that at the end of the war they were shot. No one knows. Maybe some of them are [still] alive. Every war has millions of different surprises. Thousands of people have been found alive since the war, many older than his [Mike's] age. So God may have protected our unforgettable friend Michael and his other comrades in trouble. All *katsetnyky* [Ukrainian slang for concentration camp prisoners] will forever be a separate large family of fraternal friendship—living witnesses to the nightmare of totalitarianism.

Bulba-Borovets emigrated to Canada in 1948 and died in Toronto in 1981.

Two other larger-than-life characters had some contact with Mike and bore witness to him after the war. The first was the redoubtable RAF officer Wg Cdr 'Wings' Day, the only British POW in the Second World War to be awarded the DSO for services during captivity. Captured in 1939, he became a five-time escaper and was fortunate not to be shot after the Great Escape from Stalag Luft 111 camp in Lower Silesia in 1944. He had ended up in the 'last-chance saloon' of the Zellenbau having been caught by the Germans following the only known escape from Sachsenhausen's Sonderlager A hut in September 1944.[15] The other was Lt-Col. Jack Churchill—stocky, good looking and 'the kind of man who led his commandos into action to the skirl of his own bagpipes' in the words of a biography of 'Wings' Day. Like his namesake in Sachsenhausen, Jack Churchill, a distant cousin of Winston Churchill, had probably been spared for his name when he was captured with a commando force in the Balkans. He, too, took part in the escape from Sonderlager A in Sachsenhausen, attempted to walk to the Baltic coast, and was caught close to the sea near the city of Rostok. Both Churchill and Day were later among 140 prominent concentration camp inmates transferred to the Tyrol in April 1945. Guarded by SS troops who had orders to shoot all of them, the group survived thanks to the intervention of German regular soldiers who discovered what was planned and surrounded the SS unit.

Jack Churchill became the main conduit for the few messages that Mike Cumberlege was able to send out of the Zellenbau. After the war, he was interviewed by an SOE officer and reported that he had once seen Jumbo Steele by mistake when the door opposite his cell was opened; he looked well. He only saw Mike's shadow on the frosted glass of his cell but knew from a pliant orderly that the group wore blue and white striped convict clothes and were fed the lowest grade food.[16] At the end of January 1945, Mike managed to write a brief report about his Locksmith activities and smuggled it to Churchill. Several other short messages concerned a former *Abwehr* officer and double agent named 'Johnny' Jebsen who was held in the Zellenbau on charges of high treason. Mike commendably sought help for the man, ending one message emphatically: 'All charges against us are baseless'. Another short message to Nancy was found to contain a concealed message about Jebsen in similar vein. Churchill hid these messages, and another long one to Nancy, and took them with him when he left Sachsenhausen with Day and the other VIP hostages at the end of February.

Another British inmate in the Zellenbau, Payne Best, should be mentioned given that in 1950 he published an extensive memoir about his time there. *The Venlo Incident*, which was republished in 2009, still attracts controversy. Best was a rather incautious British spy seized by the Nazis with a colleague in neutral Holland in November 1939. Imprisoned in the Zellenbau for the rest of the war, he occupied several cells including a three-year spell next to a lavatory. Twice a day, seventy to eighty prisoners would 'come at the double from their cells, each carrying his open pail which he emptied into one of the two toilets, hold his empty pail for a moment under a running tap and go back at the double to his cell'. Best found the noise and stench intolerable and eventually persuaded the commandant, Kaindl, to move him to another cell.

Best, as this vignette suggests, was not a typical prisoner. He wore his own clothes—a herringbone suit, shirt, collar, and tie—described his guards as 'my loyal friends' (one of them ended up sharing his cell), was provided with books and tobacco, received 'pay' to buy things including alcohol from the camp canteen and shops in Berlin, and managed to keep a diary throughout his incarceration by writing in pencil on rolls of toilet paper. Much of his time was spent accumulating tiny bits of knowledge about the Zellenbau, which he recorded, and plotting the Allied air offensive on the German capital from local radio broadcasts on a map he devised for the purpose. On one occasion, in June 1942, he was visited by the head of the SS Heinrich Himmler—'a little sandy coloured man with wobbly glasses on his nose and an absolutely expressionless face'—who wanted to enlist his support to counter British claims about conditions in Sachsenhausen. Best, courageously, declined to cooperate and told Himmler that things were worse than the British alleged but was not punished for his nerve. The Sachsenhausen commandant subsequently conducted long discussions with Best, organised favours, presented him with a potted hydrangea, and allowed him to have a wireless and listen to the BBC. On 20 February 1945, Kaindl confided that he had 'asked to be relieved of responsibility for some of my more important charges'. He had received no reply. The same day, he came to say goodbye as Best, with a suitcase and five cartons of possessions, left the Zellenbau to join the group of VIP prisoners being taken away to the Tyrol by the SS.

Nowhere in *The Venlo Incident* does Best mention Mike Cumberlege or any of his companions, although Best was one of the inmates mentioned by an orderly who described how some of their food had been smuggled by friendly orderlies to Cumberlege and his men 'who never received Red Cross parcels'. The orderly added: 'The health of these men can well be imagined on a diet of wurzels cooked in water'. Best was also aware of the killings and torture and violence going on around him. 'I was to spend many uneasy hours listening to the shrieks of the victims,' he wrote, but blotted out the reality of life in a Nazi concentration camp in order to sustain 'an equable frame of mind.... I always tried to pretend that I was free and to behave as though I was sitting at home.'

During the mass execution of 'political prisoners' in Sachsenhausen put in motion by Gestapo Chief Müller on Himmler's orders at the end of January 1945, which he knew about, Best simply assumed he was in a different category to others and would not be killed: 'Perhaps I was a little bit mad by then'. Later, when he encountered 'Wings' Day and Jack Churchill in the VIP group moved from Sachsenhausen, he stated: '... In my heart I felt very much ashamed that whilst they had broken out of prison time and again, I had done nothing but sit in my cell leading the well-fed life of a prize poodle'.

One SOE agent Best did have some contact with was a near-neighbour in Cell 74 called Hugh Mallory Falconer, a squadron leader in the RAF who spoke perfect French and had served in the French Foreign Legion before the war. Falconer was a skilled wireless operator and had been converted into an SOE agent in 1941 and sent on a hazardous mission behind enemy lines in Tunisia. Quickly captured by the Italians and handed over to the Gestapo, he was relentlessly interrogated, flown to Italy, and then moved on to Berlin where his papers were lost and no one knew anything about him. Soon after, he was sent to Sachsenhausen, placed in the Zellenbau, and treated as a potentially worthwhile hostage.[17] Falconer, too, developed a relationship with Kaindl, but a more antagonistic, high-handed one than Best fostered, complaining constantly to the camp commandant about his treatment and blackmailing Schmidt, one of his guards (who had got drunk in his cell), to good effect. A born linguist, he taught himself fluent, if grammatically flawed, German in six months by listening to the nightly war bulletins broadcast on the camp loudspeakers outside his cell and matching the words he heard to bits of German text on newspaper portions given to the prisoners to be used as toilet paper.

It was Falconer, with his communication skills, who devised the rudimentary Morse code system that was used by other prisoners he trusted to tap messages between cells. Another of his innovations, as his German language skill grew, was to put together a weekly newssheet that he named the *Orinienburg Echo*. This was based on the nightly war reports and his sceptical interpretation of them. Each issue consisted of a single thin sheet of the so-called 'toilet paper' with the latest news written in pencil (supplied by Karl, the barber, who worked in a nearby cell) in the margin of what had once begun life as the *Völkischer Beobachter* newspaper. To distribute this newssheet, he devised an ingenious method of passing it around, using soap to stick the wispy paper to the underside of one of the four washbasins in the washroom. No copy was ever discovered, and in June 1944, he achieved his 'Great Scoop' when he was able to inform his readers on 7 June that D-Day had taken place in Normandy the day before. Mike was one of his half-dozen favoured 'subscribers'.[18]

Falconer was one of the large VIP hostage group prisoners, including Best, Jack and Peter Churchill, who reached Allied lines at the end of April 1945 after a nerve-shredding journey via Dachau concentration camp and the SS-infested Tyrol. Together with Peter Churchill, he was quickly flown to Allied headquarters in Naples. Here the pair gave full accounts of the treatment of the Locksmith team and other British officers in Sachsenhausen to a Lt-Col. Heddon of the War Crimes Department and a one-time Inspector at Scotland Yard. Unfortunately, in the chaos of war, the report was lost.[19] In February 1946, Falconer, by then working as a Welfare Officer for the RAF in Germany, made a new statement.[20] In this, he recorded that Mike occupied Cell 59 'more or less, with Sgt Major Steele, a South African, in Cell 6 or 7 and another Warrant Officer [Handley].... Just after 23 February 1945 they were all moved to Flossenberg'. No mention was made of Kotrba, known to the Germans only as John Davies.

Writing from memory thirty-five years later in his book *The Gestapo's Most Improbable Hostage* (eventually published in 2018), Falconer came up with another version of Mike's fate. In this, he claimed: '[Cumberlege had been] shot in the back of the neck one Sunday afternoon while sitting in his cell—I expect they [the SS] needed the space'. Both explanations put the date of Mike's 'disappearance' from the Zellenbau as February 1945 rather than March or April 1945. Falconer's 1946 statement went on to claim confusingly that Peter Churchill had also been moved to Flossenberg on the same day as Cumberlege, but that he 'cannot be sure if they [the Locksmith team] were shot or hanged.... A certain Petersen [possibly Knud Pedersen, a Merchant Navy Captain] belonging to the Danish section of SOE says he witnessed the shooting'. Flossenberg was a concentration camp near the Czechoslovak border where many SOE agents were executed in March 1945; Pedersen may simply have mixed up the identity of the victims he saw there. According to Peter Churchill, following his debriefing in Naples, 'immediate steps were taken to apprehend, try and condemn all SS men of every rank whose names and addresses I had been able to collect'.

At the top of the list of names Churchill and Falconer passed on was that of Anton Kaindl. He fled west to the British zone as the war ended. Initially recognised in the town hall at Plön and formally identified by Hugh Falconer (by then back in the RAF and serving in Detmold), he was interrogated closely. At first, Kaindl denied who he was until Falconer 'belted' him over the ear and he feared he was about to be tortured. He then broke down, started snivelling, and admitted his identity. Years later, Falconer recalled the following:

We listened patiently to the usual spiel that he was only carrying out orders from above, that he had only joined the Nazi Party to keep his job and save his wife and family from starving, that he had never approved of the methods of the Gestapo and had, at great risk to his life, managed to avoid carrying out the more brutal of the directives he received, and so on ad nauseam.[21]

As Sachsenhausen fell within the Soviet Zone of Germany and many thousands of Russians had died at his hands, he was handed over to the Soviet authorities for trial. Eventually, the British were to transfer about thirty persons who worked at Sachsenhausen to Soviet custody; another thirteen supposed to be handed over had disappeared. Little effort was made to find them. Kaindl and fifteen others were tried in October–November 1947 and found guilty of war crimes. Most were sent for varying terms to work in the coal mines of the Vorkuta Gulag on the Polar Sea, above the Arctic Circle in Siberia. Few survived for long.

All registration and death records at Sachsenhausen were burned as the war was ending, defendants at various post-war trials gave contradictory evidence, and many of the principals concerned were killed or died during 1945 so it will never be possible to determine exactly when the Locksmith team was killed or by whom. What happened in Sachsenhausen itself is clearer. According to the War Crimes Section of the Judge Advocate General Branch in the British zone of occupied Germany, the population of Sachsenhausen was roughly 47,000 on 21 April.[22] The entire camp population able to stand was then marched in batches of 500 towards Schwerin, which remained under SS control. As explained in Kaindl's testimony, the plan was to load them on barges and sink the barges in the North Sea. As many as 6,000 persons were shot *en route*; 7,000 died from starvation. Meantime, the Red Army was advancing west too fast for sufficient barges to be found, so any prisoners still standing were then forced towards Wittstock. Thousands more died or were shot. The remaining 18,000 were eventually freed by tanks of the Soviet Army. About 3,000 prisoners, half of them women, and all starving and unable to walk, were still in the camp when the Red Army arrived on 22 April. Many of them died soon after, unable to adapt to being fed properly. Instead of destroying the camp, the Soviets turned it into a detention centre run by the NKVD (secret police) and called it Soviet Special Camp No. 7/No. 1. At its peak, it held 60,000 Germans. It was closed in 1950 and, eleven years later, the East German puppet regime founded the Sachsenhausen National Memorial. Only one wing of the Zellenbau remains extant today.

10

Living Not Long Enough*: A Postscript

The war in Europe ground to a halt messily during the first week of May 1945. On 2 May, the Battle of Berlin ended. Ten days earlier, Soviet forces had reached Sachsenhausen. The sixty-eight barracks were largely deserted; tens of thousands of inmates had been forced at bayonet point out of the camp on 21 April and herded north on a 'death march' in the direction of Schwerin and the Baltic coast. Some 3,000 prisoners, mostly sick or wounded, remained in the camp. The Zellenbau was empty.

For the next nineteen months, Nancy Cumberlege, aided and supported by her father-in-law, the Admiralty, Winston Churchill personally, friends and associates of Mike from across the armed forces spectrum, various Soviet officials and departments, former Sachsenhausen prisoners by then spread around the world, and numerous international bodies that were active in the immediate and chaotic aftermath of the war, all searched for clues as to Mike's fate and clear evidence that he was dead. It proved to be a frustrating endeavour.

Initially, the Allied authorities had no actual evidence that Mike or any of the Locksmith party had even been in Sachsenhausen. Later, as British officers who had also been in the Zellenbau reached Allied lines and were debriefed, they confirmed that he had been imprisoned there but treated as a common criminal rather than a POW. Yet nothing conclusive was ever found. All German records in the camp seem to have been burnt before the SS departed or were destroyed by Allied bombing, and those held by the Gestapo in Berlin went the same way. Not until the end of 1946, when the circumstantial evidence had become overwhelming, did the Admiralty feel able to confirm Mike's death officially in a letter to Nancy.

The precise circumstances of his final moments, including the date, will never be known for sure. At first, Nancy clung to the hope that Mike had either escaped from the camp and reached Soviet lines or somehow been taken into captivity by the Soviet authorities as happened to many Polish and Ukrainian prisoners. Yet in May 1946, Rudolf Höss, an SS officer and former commandant of Auschwitz, who at the end of the war ran the organisation responsible for the administration of all concentration camps, testified that in late January 1945 he received a call from the head of the Gestapo, Heinrich Müller, requesting a list of 'potentially dangerous inmates' under his control so that these could be killed before the camps were evacuated. Kaindl, at Sachsenhausen, quickly supplied such a list and when Höss inquired soon after if the order had been carried out Kaindl's adjutant, the brutish Heinrich Otto Wessel, confirmed that it had been.[1] In Platon Alexiades' words: 'It is certain that the executions in February 1945 [when the Zellenbau population was drastically culled] were a direct result of this order'. More than likely, the actual date was 23 or 27 February 1945 as indicated by a notebook found after the Russians reached Sachsenhausen—the most concrete evidence there is. However, other testimony subsequently blurred the precise date of Mike's death and for a long time it was accepted as 10 April 1945.

The first definite news of the fate of the Locksmith party reached London via Maj. Johnny Dodge—a very distant relative of Prime Minister Winston Churchill—who had been part of the Great Escape from Stalag Luft 111 when seventy-six Allied POWs tunnelled out of that camp in March 1944. He was recaptured, taken to Sachsenhausen, escaped again, and was then chained to the floor in the Zellenbau before being released as a gesture of goodwill by the increasingly desperate Germans at the start of February 1945. Interviewed in London at the end of April, he revealed the whereabouts of the Locksmith party—the first firm news of the four men since an August 1943 message from the Greek Red Cross. However, he knew little more since he had had no direct communication with any of the group.

A more in-depth pointer to Mike's fate emerged a month later via Lt-Col. Jack Churchill who reached Allied lines in May 1945. At the end of that month, Churchill was debriefed and revealed a mass of information about the treatment of the Locksmith party, war criminals in the camps that he had been in, and the conditions in the Zellenbau. He handed over the two coded messages from Mike about 'Johnny' Jebsen and another about his time in Mauthausen in which Mike stated that he had been 'treated very severely' and gave the two names mentioned earlier—Hoffmeister, an 'extremely unpleasant' SS officer, and Seidl, probably Fritz Seidler, a guard known for his brutality. The pair, Mike wrote, had 'used unlawful means to press a conviction' based on the allegation that Locksmith's Greek contacts were civilian saboteurs. He eventually signed a record that stated that his party had been engaged on 'a military mission'. All its equipment was RN issue, he stressed, and it had had no sabotage materiel. The SS changed this to read that Locksmith was 'a sabotage mission' and tortured him until he signed the new version.

Jack Churchill also carried a personal note addressed to Nancy Cumberlege. This was written by Mike at the end of January 1945 and eventually reached her sometime later in the year. It was Mike's final communication with Nancy and read:

> My beloved Nan. I think I have forgotten how to write but will try it for it is really almost the one opportunity of direct contact I will get. Well sweetheart it has been perfectly bloody, no chance to write and always wondering if you are perfectly happy with Master Marcus and Bira. I must admit I had expected to be able to have heard of you in some way but it really seems there is no hope and I have quit trying to kick against fate. You will be happy darling to hear something of me and please do not worry. I am absolutely fine, a bit thin damn it and never have quite enough to eat. I had not expected anything else anyway. I have forgotten what they mean, things like jam and fresh pastries and sugar cakes! Never mind, our time is coming unless I am mistaken sooner than ever you would expect. I only hope everything is quite okay with you sweetheart and wonder if you have sufficient coming in for your needs. Fortunately, there is always (illegible) allotment which keeps you very kindly thank you! Really that is being such a relief, you can't think. Always to have felt that that help was there paving the way for you and others. Well, oh well so long as they haven't struck me off the Navy List altogether. Never forget that my thoughts are continuously with you and his Lordship! The Man from Far will need considerable cosseting on his return. Abrazos and caresses, Mike

By the time this note reached her, Nancy had returned to Sussex and rented a house five minutes away from her father-in-law. At the start of May, she wrote to the Paines in America that 'Life has been a little confused for the last two months.... I never want to go back to London. I suppose now that I hung on there with Mike in my mind'.[3] The month before, she had come across a copy of a Red Cross newspaper. In it, she spotted a photo of 'theatre staff' at Stalag Luft 111 (a POW camp for RAF officers) and 'identified one of the people as Mike'. On getting hold of the original photo, which had been taken in July 1944, she had it enlarged and concluded: '... There is no question to my mind that it is Mike'. The Red Cross investigated the matter but got nowhere. Nancy was undismayed. 'I still expect him to walk in any moment, and most likely before he gets here he will have done some fine work elsewhere,' she wrote.

In August 1945, however, she received a long hand-written letter from Wg Cdr Harry 'Wings' Day describing life in the Zellenbau.[4] In his letter, Day revealed in some detail about what life was like there: 'I never actually saw him [Mike] but we corresponded by passing notes through an intermediary'. Day went on to write about 'the intense boredom' of solitary confinement:

> After a time, perhaps three months, one gets used to doing nothing and the day passes somehow. I know your husband and his companions expected that

they would be shot as saboteurs when they were first captured. However, as the months passed and nothing happened, they thought the Germans would be merciful and not harm them and that they would all see their homes and families again. Your husband thought much of what he would do when he got back to England and I think that one of the main things was a good square meal. It was with those thoughts that I left him when I was removed from the prison in the beginning of March 1945.... I have the most intense admiration for the indefatigable spirit of your husband under the most severe mental and very trying physical conditions. Although the Germans offered to give him more food if he would do some work for them—he refused. I think with the help of a little imagination you can really appreciate what this refusal meant.

Day had previously given all the information about Sachsenhausen that he could to the Casualties Department in the War Office on his return to England in mid-July. In this debriefing, he offered his opinion that Mike had probably been liquidated by the SS or Gestapo because he had 'undergone severe treatment and would be a witness against various Germans'. Mike fell into this category, Day believed, because 'unfortunately [he] allowed himself to be forced to agree that he was a British agent'. Day assumed Mike had been executed in March.[5]

Day's account of the fate of the Locksmith group was echoed from an unexpected quarter at around the same time. In a lengthy letter to Nancy dated 12 August, a pre-war social friend of the Cumberleges then serving with the British Army of the Rhine, Lt-Col. Lennox Livingstone-Learmonth of the Royal Horse Artillery, typed out a chronological account of Mike's fate that he had put together from the day he had been taken prisoner in May 1943.[6] Much of the information was derived from a Willie L. Newell, described as 'the man in Berlin'.

In January 1945, according to one of Newall's informants, Mike had been escorted to hospital by two SS men for attention to 'something the matter with his mouth. Returned to the camp cured'. Throughout February, or so Livingstone-Learmonth's letter detailed, there had been mass prisoner liquidations in Sachsenhausen, including of British prisoners. This, too, was based on information from Newall. He, in turn, had acquired the details from 'a German who was a prisoner in the camp for four years' whom he had interrogated. In mid-March, Newall's informants told him that 'British uniforms were brought to the SS dressing rooms for re-issue to spies and agents. These included clothes belonging to Mike and [Jack] Churchill'.

Livingstone-Learmonth went on to describe his own efforts to discover more about the prisoners from contacts he had in Holland, Norway, and Belgium as well as in the Soviet zone of occupation in Germany. A ray of hope had emerged from Stavanger in Norway: 'Norwegians [imprisoned in Sachsenhausen] had a close liaison with the British prisoners and by bribing the guards were able to smuggle them food'. Livingstone-Learmonth promised to follow up this lead. At the same time, he worried that much of the information he was passing on would only bring 'more pain' to Nancy. He added: 'If he [Mike] is lying up somewhere with the Russians it is not getting him out any quicker'. Sachsenhausen, he revealed, was 'pretty well cleaned up now … I couldn't appreciate more your feelings about it all as you have written to me—that you can take it [bad news] but you can't take it for Mike and Marcus'. The letter ended 'My Darling, Darling Nan, as always—my love L'. A postscript at the top went: 'This has a typewritten envelope. You know my writing and when you see it you don't expect a letter like this. It is an attempt to break it gently that this is a bloody letter—a record of failure'.

There matters mostly rested for the next twelve months with one cul-de-sac succeeding another, but it was not for want of persistence. Nancy was tireless, chasing even the smallest clue as to Mike's fate. In July 1945, through a Conservative MP she knew called Arthur Marsden, a former Royal Navy officer, she contacted the Prime Minister Winston Churchill. Before going to the Potsdam conference, Churchill 'most kindly said that he would do all that he could, and so did Mrs. Churchill through her Russian contacts', Nancy informed Ellen Paine.[7] Then Churchill was voted out of power while at Potsdam and Nancy's hopes were dashed. Instead she bombarded the Admiralty Casualties section. By mid-August, its officials, kind and understanding to a fault, were conceding to her that the continuing lack of firm news about Mike's fate or whereabouts made it increasingly likely that he was dead. Nancy was not the least discouraged and placed advertisements in Dutch and Belgian newspapers seeking information from former POWs. These also proved to be dead ends.

Mike's father also pulled all the strings he could, personally contacting the admiral commanding the RNR, the UK naval Commander-in-Chief in Germany, and the Commandant of the British sector in Berlin Gen. Lewis Lyne, an old friend. The latter sent an intermediary to see his opposite number in the Soviet sector, Gen. Alexander Gorbatov, with a view to getting permission to go to Sachsenhausen. Nothing came of the approach, nor of a search made through the Soviet Repatriation Department in Moscow, nor of a third, which involved a visit by a British official to German prisoners (mostly ex-concentration camp guards) held by the Soviets at a hospital in Orienienburg. 'I regret these cases are almost hopeless,' the official reported to the Admiralty.[8] Still, the search went on. The Russians eventually allowed an Allied team to visit Sachsenhausen in the spring of 1946. It found nothing. Then, in May 1946, a Norwegian, Leif Jensen, who had been in Sachsenhausen until mid-March 1945 and by then was working in Shanghai for a UN agency in China, described in a letter to the Norwegian naval *attaché* in London how

Norwegian prisoners in the camp had managed to smuggle food to 'three or four' British men held in the Zellenbau. Jensen had previously informed British intelligence that 8,000 out of the 26,000 prisoners in the camp at the start of 1945 had been liquidated between early February and mid-April 1945.

Two letters Nancy received in this period caused her mixed emotions. One from Austria was the begging letter from the woman who had acted as interpreter in Mike's brutal cross-examination by the Gestapo in Mauthausen and wanted exoneration for her role in his treatment (presumably in case she was tried as a war criminal).[9] The other, from a displaced persons camp run by the British in Goslar in Lower Saxony, was addressed to Mike and dated 18 October 1945 and came from two Ukrainian partisans, Michael Moushynsky and Oleh Shtool. They asserted that they had occupied cells No. 77 and No. 68 in the Zellenbau adjacent to Mike's at the time. Shtool stated that he had communicated in cipher with Cumberlege using another name 'Lietenant [*sic.*] Lisovsky'. He went on to offer to tell Mike about their experiences under Taras Bulba-Borowets (known in the Zellenbau as 'Comrade Pfeife' and by then living in limbo in the American zone) after they left Sachsenhausen; the Nazis had tried to force them to fight the Russians on the Eastern Front. Both had married, had no work and no possibility of emigrating, and wanted to know how Mike had been released from Sachsenhausen and how he was doing: 'Are you cured from your kidney disease? How is doing your dear family and what is the matter [what has happened] with the comrades who were with us?'[10]

Finally, in July 1946, the redoubtable British intelligence officer Vera Atkins, while on a visit to Berlin for the War Crimes Sections to seek information about missing SOE (Special Operations Executive) agents who had disappeared in France, unearthed a reputable German witness called Paul Schröter. Born in 1903, Schröter was a labourer and car driver arrested by the Nazis in 1936 as a member of the outlawed Bible Society. He spent the next decade in various concentration camps, ending up as an orderly in the Zellenbau. After the war, he became a recognised 'Victim of Fascism' in East Germany. He was interrogated by Atkins three times between July and August 1946, made a good impression on her, and provided by far the most compelling and comprehensive account of the fate of the Locksmith quartet.

Schröter stated clearly, for instance, that Mike and his team 'were all transported by ambulance to the *Industriehof* [and] executed in the usual way'.[11] He gave a date 'on or about April 10th [1945]' but admitted to a poor memory for dates and stated he was not an eyewitness. The *Industriehof*, he explained, was the industrial-style execution area of the camp where bodies were disposed of *en masse* by cremation, having first been machine gunned in a sandpit or killed in other ways, including gassing. In the case of the Locksmith party, Schröter believed they had been executed next to the sandpit in the so-called neck-shooting barrack (*genisckschussbaracke*; see previous chapter). Schröter said he was 'quite sure' that the camp adjutant and 'chief executive' of the Zellenbau, Heinrich Wessel—'one of the most brutal of men'—attended the executions. As proof of their deaths, the prison garb of the men was handed back to the cell orderlies who later sent the clothes to the main camp stores. Schröter added: 'All papers, letters etc. belonging to the prisoners were afterwards taken by me and the camp boiler room attendant to the boiler house and burned'. Wrote Nancy (to Ellen Paine) when she received this distressing and final information at the end of August: 'Now that it has come [confirmation of Mike's death], I feel so miserable and unhappy. How can things like that happen to people as kind and generous as Mike?'

Schröter also added detail to the already grim outline known in London of prisoner treatment in the Zellenbau. In time, this was also passed on to Nancy by the Casualties Section in the Admiralty:

> They never received Red Cross parcels ... the health of these men can well be imagined on a diet of wurzels cooked in water. We orderlies managed, however, to converse with Allied prisoners of war in transit in the Zellenbau, tell them of the plight of the six [the Locksmith four plus two other SOE officers in the same block, Major Francis Suttill and Captain Williams]. From them we smuggled items from their Red Cross parcels to the six.

Despite this, the men were very emaciated. They had not required the attendance of the camp medical officer, although they had suffered from skin complaints and teeth ailments. All six were kept in strict solitary confinement in fairly dark, small cells with a glazed frosted glass window covered on the outside with fine wire mesh: 'Every morning they were allowed out for fifteen minutes exercise in the yard, but it was always avoided that they ever came together'.

In the Admiralty, Nancy's key contacts proved to be F. W. Kemp and F. Broughton, both of the Casualties Department at Queen Anne's Mansions (in the same building as Nancy's sister Nora Wooler who worked there at WRNS headquarters), and a personal friend Commander Bevan. Her letters to them can be found in the files of the National Archives.[12] They range from wild optimism—for months in 1945, she was convinced that Mike had been rescued by the Soviets and spirited to Russia—to deep despair. All were influenced by the false information (as it turned out) that Jumbo Steele, one of the Locksmith party, had been shot in February 1945 on the personal orders of the chief of the security police Ernst Kaltenbrunner. In one letter in early February 1946, she incautiously revealed that she knew Anton Kaindl, the Sachsenhausen camp commandant, had been arrested in the British zone in Germany—'Can't he give information?' she questioned Mr. Broughton, leading to a witchhunt to find out how she knew of this development (Nora had told her). At the end of 1946, she wrote another letter to the department thanking it for its efforts: 'I am not, of course, surprised at the unhappy ending of these long months of waiting but it doesn't lessen the unhappiness in any way'.

Kaindl was, indeed, in British hands having fled to the British zone as the fighting in Europe ended, carrying false papers. He had been arrested on 14 May 1945 and was being held in custody until the UK Judge Advocate General War Crimes Section decided whether or not to pursue a case against him and others associated with Sachsenhausen, or to hand them over to the Russians—the main victims numerically in Sachsenhausen—for trial in the Soviet zone in which the camp now lay. Vera Atkins interrogated him about the servicemen in the Zellenbau but failed to elicit anything useful. By early 1946, it had been decided to surrender Kaindl and about thirty others to the Soviets. Before a Soviet Military Tribunal in October–November 1947, he made the admission mentioned before that 'more than 42,000 prisoners were exterminated under [his] command [1942–45]; this number included 18,000 killed in the camp itself' and confirmed that 5,000 had been murdered from the start of February 1945 to the end of March on the orders of the chief of the Gestapo. He was found guilty of war crimes. The death penalty in the Soviet Union had been abolished a few months earlier. Instead, Kaindl was transported to the Vorkuta Gulag above the Arctic Circle and is believed to have died there a few months later.

Kaindl's name cropped up a final time in the Cumberlege context in February 1948 when a German judge, Alex Reichel, who had worked in the *Ausland* (foreign countries) department of the *Abwehr* (German military intelligence) during the war, was interviewed by the British. He recalled Mike's name, had studied his file, and had read a request that Mike had made to Kaindl to be allowed to have a wood-carving knife in prison to pass his time. Reichel claimed that he agreed and recommended to Kaindl that he grant the request 'to a man of distinction'.[13] But it seems unlikely anything happened. By a coincidence (or not), the head of the *Ausland* department, Count von Moltke, was one of the Nazi leaders who had opposed the execution of Allied commandos ordered by Hitler in 1942.

Others responsible for the Zellenbau regime fared somewhat better than Kaindl. The sadistic 'chief executive' Wessel, who, according to Schröter, 'often beat and kicked the prisoners', was tried for war crimes in the British zone and received a seven-year sentence. Eccarius, the chief guard, was one of the Sachsenhausen group handed over to the Soviets for trial with Kaindl despite being wanted by the Belgians. In some highly dubious testimony, he agreed to having been involved in fourteen of the forty or so killings that he said had taken place in the Zellenbau in 1944–45. He further claimed that Mike and his men had been fed SS rations, had all sorts of privileges such as reading material, and had been 'sent to Berlin' in the autumn of 1944 so he had no knowledge of their fate—all obvious lies to save his neck. He later contradicted himself and admitted that he had participated in the murders of Mike and his men in February 1945—the date confirmed by the 'Russian notebook' found in the camp. This had probably been written in April 1945 by someone in the camp records office before all records were destroyed. Eccarius was condemned by the Russians to life imprisonment in the Gulag. He survived and was repatriated to Germany in the Khrushchev 'thaw' along with other German POWs in 1956. Six years later, and again in 1969, he was tried in West German courts for various offences related to his time in Sachsenhausen. He received one sentence of four years and another of eight and a half years (serving only two years) before being released in 1971.

Higher up the chain of command, Ernst Kaltenbrunner, the chief of the SS Security Police who had been head of the SS in Austria in 1943 when the Locksmith party was captured and had also been responsible for the establishment of the Mauthausen camp, was incriminated in the murder of Jumbo Steele in a document found after the war. Kaltenbrunner, the senior SS official to be tried at Nuremburg (he was found guilty and hanged for his crimes), denied all knowledge of executions of Allied prisoners, including commandos caught in uniform. Someone in a position of high authority in Austria, however, must have decided to keep the Locksmith party alive once the men reached Mauthausen. Kaltenbrunner is the obvious person. He would not have been alone among leading Nazis in ignoring Hitler's notorious October 1942 *kommandobefehl*.

In England, Nancy attempted to pick up the strands of a life once the war in Europe came to a halt in May 1945. Much of her time, initially, was spent searching for news, any news, of Mike and his team. Often, she thought of what might have been. She wrote once to Mike: 'When I think about it, our [pre-war] life together was so lovely, all the things we saw and the things we did, all of them exciting and most of them together. Such lovely memories— they are a comfort now'.

Nancy, not surprisingly, also worried about money. Her husband was not declared dead by law until 2 April 1947, when probate was granted on his will. Until late November 1945, Mike—who was promoted to lieutenant commander on 22 November 1943—had received his full RN pay. The Admiralty decided to discontinue this from the start of December despite not having confirmed Mike's death officially. Nancy then received two-sevenths of the full pay plus a marriage allowance for three months. After that, from March 1946, she received only a widow's pension. During and immediately after the war, Mike had saved and inherited a sizeable amount. When his will was finally proved, he left Nancy £6,586 after tax paid, equivalent to some £250,000 today. Nancy, at that point aged thirty-one, was never a saver, lived in rented accommodation, and had a young son to bring up—a task that she found increasingly difficult. Before long, she needed help.

Once more, the Paines came to the rescue. Throughout the war, they had paid a stipend to Mike and sent Nancy and Marcus parcels of food and clothing. As post-war austerity and rationing gripped the UK, they continued to do so. Nancy moved back to London again and, late in 1946, thanks to the generosity of the Paines, was able to visit Cannes and go to Antibes. Here she unearthed a sad scene of neglect and dishonesty. The interior of La Gardiole, the house they had rented on Cap d'Antibes, had been '*cambrioled*' (burgled) and most of their carpets, pictures and silver stolen. The couple's beloved garden was a wasteland. 'It broke my heart,' she admitted to the Paines. 'It was the first and only house we ever had with all our things in it.'[14] In the harbour, Mike's small yacht *Sonneta* had been sunk by the retreating Germans in June 1944. Only the tip of her mast now protruded from the water. 'She has been underwater for two-and-a-half years and I doubt whether she is worth raising, save that being oak-built I think she ought not to deteriorate a lot,' Nancy wrote optimistically. The *Sonneta* was never recovered. The admiral nevertheless decided to return with his growing family to the villa he had built in 1938–39. He was soon disillusioned; the old carefree, expatriate pre-war world of the south of France had gone and ways of making a living were few and far between. After flirting with a move to South Africa, he decided to stay in the Mediterranean area, settled in Majorca, and eventually opened The Sea Club in a colonial-style villa on the seafront in Cala Ratjada. It is still owned and run by the Cumberlege family and advertises itself today as 'a home from home' for vacationers from middle-class southern England.

After Mike had been declared dead officially in November 1946, Nancy was free to think about her future. Earlier that year, she had remet Len Livingstone-Learmonth, by then a lieutenant-colonel aged thirty-six, unmarried and with an MC and Bar, and visited Ireland. Livingstone-Learmonth then retired from the Army, the couple married in 1947 and moved to County Cork in southwest Ireland near Mallow where he bought a smallholding. In a letter to the Paines at the start of September 1947, Nancy wrote that Len, a horse-mad huntsman but never a farmer, was helping with the harvest while she had begun a 'market garden' on a small scale to make ends meet, supplying shops in a nearby village. Very quickly, she was tiring of the 'priest-ridden, very rural' life in the republic and admitted to having to enjoy music and records and books 'by myself.... But it is a thousand times better than being as lonely as I was before.'

Numerous letters reached her from Mike's former comrades in arms and superiors in the SOE and the Navy. One, from John Godfrey in India, was hand-written after Mike had been reported missing in 1943. It had raised the prospect of him escaping from captivity: 'I know a little of the sort of work on which he was engaged and which he, pre-eminently, was bound to do so well'. Godfrey promised to do all he could: 'You know, Nan dear, that I will do anything to help you and Mike if it is in my power'. Hugh Bevan in the Naval Intelligence Division, who knew Mike well, described him as 'that rare combination, a man with vision, with patience, personality, organising ability and great courage'.[15] 'Wings' Day got in touch again to describe Mike as 'the most gallant person I have ever met. That opinion was shared by all who were in the prison [Zellenbau] ... he kept up [our] spirits more than anyone else'. Patrick Leigh Fermor wrote about 'that amazing buccaneerish figure—very funny, very well read, with a single gold earring ... a marvellous almost mythical figure'. Nicholas Hammond, who had accompanied Mike on several of his actions in Greece and escaped from Crete with him on the *Athanassios Miaoulis* in May 1940, wrote in July 1945: 'Mike showed more courage, character and determination in Crete than any man I have met in the war ... if it lies in any man's power to come through, Mike and Jumbo [Steele] will do it'.[16] Hammond went on to have a distinguished post-war career as a professor of Greek history at Cambridge and Bristol universities, headmaster at Clifton College, and prolific writer of books and articles on Ancient Greece.

By now, Marcus was away at preparatory school in England. He had been found to be blind in his left eye and so had no chance of getting into the Royal Navy. 'It is a bitter blow as Mike and I wanted it so much,' Nancy informed the Paines. Although the nine-year old proved to be 'crazy about his pony', Nancy usually packed him off to his grandfather in Antibes for the summer holidays. Before long, she had three more children, by Len. For the remainder of her life (she died in 1989), her relationship with Marcus was volatile. Marcus was to grow up alternatively blaming his absent father and idolising him, much influenced by the few stories of him that Nancy relayed, mostly about his bravery. In March 1948, he accompanied Nancy to Buckingham Palace to receive from King George VI the DSO and Bar awarded to Mike. After Sherborne School and Oxford University, he spent three years in Peru teaching English and sheep farming. In the 1960s, while working in London, he was attracted to Zen Budhism. Moving to Bruges in 1972, he became a prolific poet with forty published collections and a serious student of Shin Budhism.

Marcus has never forgotten the father he barely knew. In 2011, his poignant poem 'Mein Vater Lebt' (My Father Lives), written on his seventy-third birthday, vividly evoked Mike's memory:

> *Mike was a long time in the hut*
> *For his final interrogation*
> *By the German officers*
> *Before his release.*

When he finally came out
And I took him in my arms—
The thin young man in the pale brown sweater—
I knew at last death is an illusion.

Mein Vater lebt I proudly announced
To the plump female with the horsewhip
Who hadn't wanted to believe me,
As we turned and walked downhill.

'You must stick to your agreements
From now on papa' I warned him,
'no more unexplained disappearances
Into the nebulous atrophy of war.'

Although it was a dream,
I still feel him in my arms,
That warm young muscular body,
Glad to be in the land of the living.

In Germany, many of the structures at Sachsenhausen, including the Zellenbau, were razed to the ground in the 1950s. The remaining buildings are now open to the public as a museum and regular tours go there from Berlin. A plaque 'in memory of those brave members of the British and Commonwealth forces, many still unknown, who were interned in Sachsenhausen and perished here or elsewhere at the hands of their captors' was unveiled after the war. It lists the name of 'Lt. Cdr C. Cumberledge [*sic.*] RNVR' and his three companions on Locksmith—'Sgt Thomas Handley MM, Cpl Jan Kotbra [*sic.*] and CSM James Steele MM' as well as sixteen others. In 2015, the future German President and then Foreign Minister Frank-Walter Steinmeier was among dignitaries marking seventy years since the liberation of the camp. He described the site as representing 'the monstrosity of a regime which institutionalized horror'.[17] An estimated 200,000 people were imprisoned at Sachsenhausen between 1936 and 1945 and at least 30,000 murdered there. The final death toll in this camp will never be known. 'Remembrance has no expiration date,' Steinmeier said at the ceremony. In 1970, a striking memorial to the victims of Sachsenhausen, sculpted by Jean Baptiste-Leducq and made out of hammered copper, was inaugurated in Paris at the famous Père Lachaise cemetery. It portrays a deportee engulfed in barbed wire and flames. The base plate reads: '100,000 died in this Nazi concentration camp'.

For the rest of her life, Nancy Cumberlege carried a small brown leather wallet with her. It contained three photos of Mike, one of his cousin Cle, one of their son, Marcus, four childhood thank-you letters written by Mike to his grandmother and mother, a piece of Mike's hair when he was two, and a love letter Mike wrote Nancy from Alexandria on 11 August 1941. There was also a newspaper clipping of a short poem 'If You Should Hear' by Peter Railing:

If you should hear a flutter in the breeze
Or soft leaves tapping at the window pane
Or, standing in some distant country lane
Should hear the evening murmur through the trees;
Or if, at midnight, some discordant piece
Of music breaks your sleep, to swell and wane,
Then linger, echoing and full of pain.
A restless memory to mock your ease—
Softly you may remember one who sang
And suffered in the darkness many days;
Who in his eager heart nursed one sweet pang.
And had no secret fear or dark desire,
But sat in silence dreaming of your face
And to your praise wove fairylands of fire.

Also in the wallet were two messages from Mike written in captivity. One, 14 cm long and 1.5 cm wide and written on both sides of a scrap of dirty brown paper in some type of ink, was the one smuggled out of Sachsenhausen by Jack Churchill. To this, Nancy had added: 'Mike's note written 30 Jan 1945 from a Gestapo prison within Sachsenhausen Concentration Camp, Oranienburg, Germany and after 21 months of solitary confinement'. In pencil underneath: 'For thy sweet love remembered such wealth brings/That then I scorn to change my state with kings'—an excerpt from Sonnet 29 by William Shakespeare.

The second message from Mike is dated 17 January 1944 at a time when he might have been in transit to Sachsenhausen from Mauthausen. It reached Nancy sometime in September 1945. A typed note accompanying it, written from Vienna by a Capt. A. N. Weidenfeld of 376 Works Section, RE, CMF and dated 24 September 1945, states: 'The attached letter has been handed to me by an Austrian civilian who got it from a Herr Franz Weissenbock who allegedly was a fellow prisoner of your husband in a Gestapo prison. I hope that your husband [has] returned since. In case not, it might be of some assistance to you'. Written in (faded) pencil on both sides of a brown piece of paper 80 cm by 105 cm, with all four corners cut at a diagonal as if to fit into a secret hiding place, parts of it read as Mike's last will and testament. It seems to have accompanied some other communication:

My beloved Nan and Marcus. Important letter from sender [who] needs help. Do all you can [illegible] but under such conditions. Also please see this letter reaches wife exactly as written. Sender's signature of great importance. A just-in-case letter should I fail to make it out which is unlikely unless a bomb or something catches me for otherwise [illegible]. Greece was just heaven. I really was completely happy but our luck turned against us and we fell for a phoney situation. Tom H and his radio friends [lack of] experience and a pretty bloody one but could have been a damned sight worse. Very lucky to get out from under the longboat without all getting pipped. It's been unholy hell since, food appalling and solitary confinement for us all, no writing and no exercise and no books except my Golden Treasury. It's saved me and I quote [it] by the hours. But the hunger is what really gets you. It's bloody awful. My whole existence consists of questions revolving round it but even so I am very fit, I'll last out! My beloved sweetie heart everything I value in life depends on you. I pray to God that all my dreams are very soon realised. Such plans I've devised you simply won't imagine. I've designed something really very special. Such dream ships [illegible] you and I and Marcus [illegible] new boat from Pritchard is forming fast. How did Marcus [illegible] and you [illegible] for his fifth birthday and Xmas [illegible]? Wondered where and thought of virtually nothing else and was really miserable.

Overleaf (the top of the paper is cut off):

… just seem quite incapable of getting home for his birthday but I've really had some very bad luck. Maybe next year that will change for the better. Reckon you should be quite an affluent person now, getting all the cash and me nothing! I hope we are getting what should be coming to us and that the Navy [illegible]. Just send 'He's missing & left you penniless.' I hope and feel perfectly sure you're getting almost everything okay. Oh well, sweetie, no use worrying. I'm sure you'll make out. My promotion to Lt. Cdr should be automatic as from 7/11/43. I wonder so much where you are, where you are making our home. I hoped you might have gone to Bosham or Brixham for the summer. I am full of home and boat plans and I expect you are too. Let's hope we think alike! My problem Bira? I've thought about all our years together if I go down—I go down [illegible] … my love for you and Marcus—make him into a fine Englishman, a gentleman, and a real Cumberlege. If he lives up to these three you will be magnificent—such a fine good fellow and cheerful as maybe. Our [illegible] in a mess but we are forging ahead and I am prepared for my fate but hope to be with you by the end of the summer. You know I have thought of you all— my mistakes and my [illegible] and have been [illegible] and all my dear friends, Nora and Nick S and John etc etc and to you and Marcus my most precious thoughts and darling caresses. To have such a wonderful wife has given all the courage I needed. With such a fine little boy, may your future be as happy as my past. Think of me with love. Time has proved my love—Michaele. CMB Cumberlege.

In August 1945, before she received this message, Nancy had written to Ellen Paine:

> I would count myself as the luckiest person I know [even if Mike is confirmed dead] because of the ten years, lovely and unforgettable, that we had together. In this stricken world, I don't see that it has been given to many to have, for as long as that, the perfect happiness that we had together. [If Mike is dead] I would grieve for Marcus that he would miss so terribly much in not having known Mike, and I would grieve for Mike <u>who loved life so dearly</u>. It [life] was never anything but beautiful and exciting for him and he made it so for others. He was the most perfect person in it [life], and we will love him for ever and always, completely and never less. Had it only been six months of memories I would still think myself more than lucky. But ten years—that's a fair share of heaven for anybody, don't you think, and I don't ask for more. Thank God memories can never be taken from us. They warm me and cheer me every time I think of them.[18]

Mike was a hero of his time—charismatic, imaginative, resourceful, deeply interested in other cultures and people, anything but a Little Englander. Four of the five men he chose originally to accompany him on his second mission to blow up the Corinth Canal were not English. He did what he saw as his duty and betrayed no one. Those who betrayed him would, in Nancy's opinion, have been forgiven by him. The sea, the wind, the stars, the tides, the sails on his boats, the freedom that sailing offered and the way of life it gave him and Nancy framed his adult years. So did his great courage and drive and flair and determination in the face of overwhelming odds. His love of literature and poetry grew with age and sustained him in his darkest hours. Others admired him almost without exception and he proved to be a born leader of men whether they were British, Palestinian, Irish, Greek, French, Serbian, Croat, Rhodesian, or Czechoslovak. He also wore his heart on his sleeve, never forgetting the painful death of his cousin or others who fell in battle alongside him. He was human in many ways—never a machine—with a low boredom threshold, little time for those he regarded as fools, often outspoken, poking fun at the pompous, and only occasionally diplomatic. War suited his can-do, egalitarian, sometimes belligerent temperament, but so did peace with the many opportunities it offered to his adventurous, questing, culturally-acquisitive, and more sensitive nature.

In *The Log* of his old school, the Nautical College Pangbourne, in the Spring 1946 issue, Mike's life was summed up by an anonymous contributor. After describing Mike's wartime exploits and his fate as far as it was known publicly at that point, the correspondent wrote:

> He knew the risks and what the outcome might be if he were caught, but loved Greece and the Greeks. The months he spent ashore were wonderful and made

anything that might happen later more than worthwhile. I know of no other case of such varied qualities combined in one person. He was truly Elizabethan in character—a combination of gaiety and solidity and sensitiveness and poetry with daring and adventurousness and great courage.

Nearly twenty years after Mike was executed, Svetlana Alliluyeva, Stalin's troubled daughter, ended her book *Twenty Letters to a Friend* in 1963 with words that must have resonated with Nancy if she ever read them: 'What is Good never dies.... Everything on our tormented earth that is alive and breathes, that blossoms and bears fruit, lives only by virtue of and in the name of Truth and Good'. Svetlana's biographer Rosemary Sullivan added: 'Perhaps when human beings are tested to the depth that they [Russians] were tested, they find other dimensions of the inner self.... It has less to do with Western notions of goodness, the absence of evil, than with the will to affirm good in the face of evil'. Michael Cumberlege spent the last two years of his short life enduring extreme brutality entirely in solitary confinement with only his own thoughts for company. His positive, courageous spirit, by every account, endured to the very end. He would, one imagines, agree with Svetlana Alliluyeva.

---

*from a poem Mike wrote

Mike Cumberlege and his Poetry

It is only Poetry can make us be thought living men when we lie among the dead.

Giles Fletcher (1586–1623)

Now swarm many versifiers that need never answer to the name of Poets.

Sir Philip Sidney (1554–1586)

During the turbulent 1930s and his war years beyond, Mike Cumberlege had a passion for writing verse. Some fifty typed pages of his work survive. A short selection from these is presented below. What matters most is perhaps what they say about the man, rather than how we might rate them in an exercise of literary criticism. The family bookshelves Mike left behind were full of the English, French, and Spanish poets he admired. His poetic gene was passed on to his only son, Marcus (my contemporary at school), who won a coveted Eric Gregory Award for his own published poetry in 1967 at the age of twenty-nine and has written and published poetry all his life.

If I compare Mike's work with my own father's verse (they were born the same year) written over exactly the same period with a similar post-Georgian and late-romantic flavour, what stands out is Mike's high-voltage energy, which is expressed in a surge of alternating mood shifts: by turns mock-heroic, funny, flippant, yearning, ebullient, lonely, loving, sad, and even at times almost manic in his eager contrivances and imaginative bursts.

His neologism 'Mycholia' (a pun, I think, on 'Mike's melancholia'?) occurs on several pages of the surviving poems. This may be an important key to his work (and life?). From the context, I deduce that he may also have intended it as a possible title for a published collection of his work in due course. His five prose lines of introduction to the poem 'The Halibut' are consistent with this reading ('the winter of Mycholian discontent').

Among other poems gathered here, the opening 'A Limerick' works beautifully. 'To a Black Cat' seems to end on a slightly sinister note of unresolved ambiguity. Poems to or about his wife Nancy recur, some full of a sense of loss or longing, others ('To My Beard and My Darling Wife') suggesting that their life together could also be quite feisty. Mike's spoken French was obviously fluent, and I have included a couple of his short poems in French: the little squib 'L'Eléphant' is a saucy tease; the short poem 'Tout le Monde a son Carcassonne' as a metaphor for unfulfilled life ambitions is the more poignant now set against the background of Mike's tragic early death. The jaunty 'Benjamin Bounce' is an irresistible non-stop paean in praise of his new baby son, Marcus.

But perhaps the poem that works best is his thirty-two-line 'Mare Cantabrico' (the Cantabrian Sea being the southern part of the Bay of Biscay). Mike was, of course, a skilled sailor, and this poem captures the wild excitement of that notoriously stormy coast, and the colours and starkness of the coastal cliffs. It brings to mind Dylan Thomas's 1934 poem 'The Force That Through the Green Fuse Drives the Flower'. Indeed, I think Mike's use of the phrase 'the rain's wet winding-sheet' may even be a deliberately doffing of his poetic hat to Thomas, whose own poem includes the words 'The hand that whirls the water in the pool/stirs the quick sand, that ropes the blowing wind/ hauls my shroud sail...'

His son, Marcus, of course, should have the last word:

Memories of Mike
'Mein Vater Lebt'

Although it was a dream
Your imagination once ran wild
I still feel him in my arms

Sir John Weston
Richmond 2017

'A LIMERICK'

There once was an extraordinarily unfortunate old lady of Itchenor,
Who had the misfortune to have to have a doctor put a stitch in her.
She remembered the reason
But not the month or the season,
Except that it was round about the time of the death of Lord Kitchenor.

'To a Black Cat'

Black distillation of primeval night,
Culled from the crucible of some dead Mage,
Child of the darkest arts, what mystic page
Of magic hieroglyphics gave thee light?

What ebon bubble from the depths of hell
Enclosed thy soul? By what strange track
And glossy aeons of perpetual black
Did your dark path pass through before you fell

Here at my doorway with your sleek black coat?
High priest of her, the ancient goddess Set,
Alone you stand, a god incarnate yet,
A band of onyx jewels about your throat.

Inscrutable you are, your dreaming gaze,
The half-veiled emeralds of your blazing eyes
Tell nothing; but that life within you lies
Only the movement of your tail betrays.

Tameless and cruel your pitiless black heart
Has naught with Love, nor may the sadist see
Pleasure in love where pain can never be.
But still my sweet—Ah what a cat thou art!

SONNET FOR MY FATHER

Living again beneath the sculptor's hand
A fair slim boy stands dreamily alone,
A passioned, cold soliloquy in stone.
As though in hope, by his wild fancy fanned,
White Aphrodite yet might understand,
And from the high Uranian throne
Show him the favour that she once had shown
To proud Pygmalion in another land.

Ah had the sculptor Love for his defence
He had not asked so bold a recompense.
Daily we see how mortal 'tis to err;

Or had he used some little common sense
He would not quite do pointedly prefer
This stony him to some more mortal Her.

To My Beard and My Darling Wife

Give me the sound of the thunder
Of surf on a rock-strewn sea,
Of my ship with her sails torn asunder,
But give not, ah give not to me
The voice of my wife in the morning
With words that I know may be feared—
'Michael! You're simply disgusting,
Oh Michael there's egg on your beard.'

There's many a grim situation
I've faced in my long life at sea,
But never I've faced a face with a face
Of my wife when she's saying to me—
'Michael I've spoken before now,
Just think of the children I've reared,
The trouble, the trials, tribulations
And dammit there's egg on your beard.'
Oh hold with the tale of a sailor,
And if your course truly be steered
And you'd marry a girl and would nail her
Don't do so by growing a beard.
For there's naught to my mind so distressing,
No nothing so much to be feared
As the voice of your love in the morning
With—'Look at you, egg on your beard.'

Writeen in Loneliness 1935. For Nan

I lost you sweet, I lost you through the day
So hot, so hot the pavement's brazen glare,
Deserted streets and silence everywhere,
You were not there.
No more the fountains play soft liquid tunes.
Where is the green oasis of the square?

Lost in a fitful mirage of thin air
I lost you sweet.
Now evening comes in long and slanting lines
And magically peopled is the square
With voices, voices everywhere
And yours as well, I'm sure I heard it there.

ON A LACK OF LETTERS

The golden shower of silence falls
With steady pelt. Her deluge drowns
In thickening vapours, towers and walls,
This mansion that my being owns.
All, all about it does enfold
The silence that is more than gold.

No more the arrowy GPO
Her swift-flown missiles fires at me.
To what new target do they go,
To what strange hand, across which sea?
What use to watch the anxious clock
Since now it brings no postman's knock

There was a time—how long it seems;
A happy period past alas,
Or was it maybe only dreams
That like the fancy flit and pass?
Avaunt foul thought, no it was true,
I often used to hear from you!

Ah golden silence, why repeat
Your drumming threnody whose noise
Is nothing now the postman's feet
No more their customary joys
Sound welkin with a lovely note
That only recently she wrote?

What key, what sesame, what lamp,
What djinn, what witch, what magic art
Shall bring a letter with the stamp
That sends a flutter to my heart?

What sword shall pierce this curtain through
Dividing me from lovely you?

What flattery with double barb,
What winsome word with flitting dart,
What thought in black disguising garb
Shall pierce the armour of your heart?
Ah, had I but some new spun line
How soon answer would be mine!

ANOTHER SONNET

Worlds are not wide enough, nor seas so broad.
Skies are not high enough, nor depths so deep.
Living not long enough, nor deathless sleep
Ever was sound enough, if that one word
Up from your heart then should finally creep.
You that might utter it, give it accord,
Out of the soul of you where it is stored,
Offer it up that perchance it might keep
Lighter the memory, brighter the hour,
Sweeter the perfume and whiter the flower
Of love we forebore and words left unsaid.
Better to bury them; we that have power
O'er moments like these, and since they have fled,
Better to let the dead bury their dead.

L'ELÉPHANT

L'Eléphant est formidable
Comme il fait ses trucs.
Toujours assez convenabe,
L'amour à grand luxe.

Dis moi, Monsieur Eléphant,
Quand tu fais La Lutte,
Es tu assez délicat
Ou fais tu La Brute?

MY DREAMS

My dreams!
Tremendous as the sky,
As thronged with stars.
Whilst a mad destiny
Now urges, hastening me on.
What is this flight?
Of fancy? Or oblivion?

TOUT LE MONDE A SON CARCASSONNE

Je me fais vieux, j'ai soixante ans
J'ai travaillé toute ma vie
Sans avoir, durant tout ce temps,
Pu satisfaire mon envie.
Je vois qu'il n'est, ici bas,
De bonheur complet pour personne.
Mon voeu ne s'accomplira pas:
Je n'ai jamais vu Carcassonne,
Je n'ai jamais vu Carcassonne!

THE HALIBUT*

I

The Halibut, I've sung before,
Keeps closely to the ocean floor
Yes close against the ocean bed,
Ah never let it then be said
That Halibuts at times eschew
What larks and linnets like to do.

One does not see the little lark
Upon the ocean bed embark,
I think you also will agree
No linnets troll beneath the sea.
But do not think the Halibut
Stays stuck in some dull fishy rut,
Nay check the flow of tears dear friends
These simple fish serve useful ends.

While Halibut don't hop on legs
They lay a shocking lot of eggs.

II

Once years ago, at dead of night,
By lonely single candlelight
I noticed winging round my head
A Halibut which now lies dead.

Like Icarus she did aspire
To reach my urge, my mental fire,
But I on love had thought apace,
A body and a lovely face
(This Halibut no doubt as well)
But let us not the incubus
Twixt halibut and Thought discuss.

For downward falling, flaming fell
This fish which had this fateful night
Aspired too high by candlelight.

*The Halibut is a wild bird of the Mycholian imagination, a migratory creature that does not always stay flies to warmer climes when Mycholia grows cold, so that you may be sure when he is here that it is full summer and gone is the winter of Mycholian discontent.

MARE CANTABRICO

Rock frothed with spume flecks
Foot set in gasping water whorls,
Soon shattered into filigree tossed foam flecks
Transmuted emeralds. All upward hurls
In mad abandon, the green treasure,
To craggy jut and cleft,
Encrusting the rain-bediamonded seabirds
That cling there tired and windreft.

Here where the cliffs' green bosses
Press to the wind their scanty mosses

Trembling the pale harebell cowers.
And that yellow-tongued mauve crocus,
Frailest of Autumn's flowers,
Shivers to hear wild Boreas' rude trumpets,
Where from the North barbarian
Come the fierce passion blasts!

Windswept the bloodstained heather
Paints the stark mountain's side,
And each gully and cranny to the weather
Gapes open gash and scar full wide.
Higher the rabbit-haunted gorse-shocks
Cloak the cliff's rocky shoulder
With tattered and rocky shards,
Darkly, between each tumbled boulder.

In the wide bay's curved arm
The village sleeps—Barquero.
Only the wet sand shivers
To hear the tossed pine's alarm.
And the dervish squall sweeps on Vivero
Wrapped in the rain's wet winding sheet
Stamping the earth with bloodstained feet
Till the streams dun red rivers.

A SAILOR'S SONG

Oh I shall buy a sailboat for to sail across the sea
With bacon and eggs for breakfast and bacon and eggs for tea.

Oh I shall have a sailor in a lilywhite suit of duck
And I shall ask him questions whenever I get stuck.

And I shall have a kitbag and a brand-new sailor's knife
And I shall climb the great tall mast a-hazarding my life.

And when I steer my sailboat I'll make for Caribbee,
And there'll be bacon and eggs for breakfast and bacon and eggs for tea.

BENJAMIN BOUNCE

What, not met Ben?
Not met our Bounce?!
Oh Gee he's a
Pound in an Ounce.

Tight as a top,
High as a hop,
With the sure fire appeal
Of a Catherine wheel.

Here, there, everywhere.
Mind your step
You'll need that pep
When Bounce is around.

The crazy coot
Flashing a foot
In a neat boot
(Ben's boots button)
Frisky? So's young mutton.

Cute as the tin toot
And fussy funnel,
As into a tunnel
Pops the train
Rumble, fumble, grumble,
Sunshine, we're out again.

He's the cat's ankle
And the hot rankle
In a bee's thankyou.

The first slick tick
Of a may dawn in Benny
He don't miss any
He's time's rhyme
Tick tock of a clock.

He's got IT
And THEM too,
The whole crew
And then a bit
He's Pan's man.

Bounce has got 'em all beat
By a long mile.
Not a smile or a laugh
But a grin
That's Benjamin!

Endnotes

Chapter 1

1. Falconer, H. M., *The Gestapo's Most Improbable Hostage* (London: Pen & Sword Books, 2018).
2. Best, S. P., *The Venlo Incident* (London: Hutchinson & Co., 1950; Pen & Sword Books, 2009).
3. Smith, S., *'Wings' Day* (London: Pan Books, 1970).
4. Bulba-Borovets, T., *Army Without a State: A Memoir* (Winnipeg, 1981).
5. *Ibid.*

Chapter 2

1. Fermor, P. L., *Three Letters from the Andes* (London: John Murray, 1991).
2. Nautical College Pangbourne, *The Log*, Spring 1946.
3. Cumberlege, C. L., *Master Mariner* (London: Paul Davies, 1936).
4. Cumberlege, C. L., *Salt Horse* (unpublished memoir, 1938), p. 189, Book 1.
5. Cumberlege, C. L., *Salt Horse* (unpublished memoir, 1938), p. 1, Book 2.
6. *Ibid.*, p. 29.
7. Cumberbatch Family History, *Collections & Connections* (2015).
8. Cumberlege, C. L., *Salt Horse* (unpublished memoir, 1938), p. 46, Book 11.
9. Jose, A. W., *The Royal Australian Navy 1914–1918* (Sydney: Angus & Robertson, 1928).
10. Cumberlege, C. L., *Salt Horse* (unpublished memoir, 1938), p. 6, Book 3.
11. *Ibid.*, p. 46.
12. Cumberlege, Marcus, *Part One of a Short Memoir* (unpublished).
13. *Op. cit.*, Cumberbatch Family History.
14. *Op. cit.*, Cumberbatch Family History (personal letter Claude Cumberlege).
15. National Archives, AIR/80/55.
16. John Smith, (Naval Historical Society of Australia, 2017).
17. Aunt Gwen's letter to Nancy Cumberlege (1943).
18. Knight, R. I. E., *Pangbourne College: Spirit in Changing Times* (London: Profile Books, 2016).
19. Bryer, R., *Jolie Brise* (London: Martin Secker & Warburg Ltd., 1982).
20. Cumberlege, C. L., *Salt Horse* (unpublished memoir, 1938), pp. 41-42, Book 4.

21. *Ibid.*, p. 41.
22. Maillart, E., *Gypsy Afloat* (London: W. Heinemann, 1942).
23. Cumberlege, C. L., *Salt Horse* (unpublished memoir, 1938), p. 70, Book 4.

Chapter 3

1. Letter to Ellen Paine 29.10.40.
2. Bryer, R., *Jolie Brise* (London: Martin Secker & Warburg Ltd, 1982).
3. Letter to Ritchie Paine, (undated, 1938).
4. Outhwaite, L., *Atlantic Circle* (New York: Charles Scribner's & Sons, 1931).
5. Fielding, X., *Hide and Seek* (London: Secker & Warburg, 1954).
6. '*Jolie Brise*—a Famous Ship Completely Refitted', *Yachting Monthly*, 25 September 1935.
7. Cumberlege, C. L., *Salt Horse* (unpublished memoir, 1938), p. 61, Book 5.
8. *Ibid.*, p. 59.
9. *Ibid.*, p. 116.
10. *Ibid.*, p. 124.
11. Cumberbatch Family History, May 2015.
12. Cheltenham Ladies College records.
13. Peregrine, A., *Basking in France's ultimate celebrity resort* (London, Daily Telegraph 25.2.17).
14. Letter to Ellen Paine 17.12.38.
15. Letter to Ellen Paine 27.7.39.
16. Letter to Ellen Paine 17.12.38.
17. Letter to Ellen Paine 27.7.39.
18. Letter to Ritchie & Ellen Paine 2.1.39.

Chapter 4

1. Paine, W., 'About Landfall' (unpublished paper, 2016).
2. Undated newspaper clipping from Malta.
3. Walter Paine (author interview 4.11.16).
4. Moffat, D., '*Landfall*': Adriatic Cruise 1939 (published privately in USA: 1939).
5. Walter Paine (author interview 4.11.16).
6. Paine, W., 'About Landfall' (unpublished paper, 2016).
7. CMBC letter to Ritchie Paine 1937.
8. CMBC letter to Ritchie Paine 17.6.39.
9. Walter Paine interview 4.11.16.
10. Walter Paine interview 4.11.16.
11. CMBC letter to Ritchie Paine 17.6.39.
12. Moffat, D., '*Landfall*': Adriatic Cruise 1939 (published privately in USA: 1939).
13. Denham, H., *Inside The Nazi Ring* (London: Holmes & Meir, 1985).
14. Moffat, D., '*Landfall*': Adriatic Cruise 1939 (published privately in USA: 1939).
15. *Ibid.*
16. Walter Paine interview 4.11.16.
17. CMBC letter to Ellen Paine 13.11.40.

18. CMBC letter to the Paines 15.5.42.
19. *Ibid.*
20. CMBC letter to Ellen Paine 8.11.40.
21. Paine, W., 'That Business at Brioni' (unpublished paper, 2016).
22. Moffat, D., *'Landfall': Adriatic Cruise 1939* (published privately in USA: 1939).
23. CMBC Letter to Ritchie Paine 5.9.39.
24. Cowan, C. G., *The Voyage of the Evelyn Hope* (London: Cresset Press, 1946).
25. *Ibid.*
26. CMBC Letter to Ritchie Paine 29.12.39.
27. Chaney, L., *Elizabeth David* (London: Macmillan, 1998).
28. Paine, W., 'About Landfall' (unpublished paper, 2016).

Chapter 5

1. CMBC letter to Ritchie Paine, 17.2.40.
2. CMBC letter to Ellen Paine, 20.4.40.
3. CMBC letter to Ellen Paine, 31.10.39.
4. CMBC letter to Ellen Paine, 1.4.40.
5. *Ibid.*
6. *Ibid.*
7. CMBC letter to Ritchie Paine, 4.5.40.
8. CMBC undated letter to the Paines, August 1940.
9. *Ibid.*
10. Arlette letter to Nancy Cumberlege 4.5.1941.
11. CMBC letters to the Paines, 6 and 7 August 1940.
12. Fenby, J., *The General* (London: Simon & Schuster, 2010).
13. National Archives, ADM 199/813.
14. *Ibid.*
15. CMBC letter to Paines, 6.8.40.
16. CMBC letter to Ellen Paine 28.10.40.
17. CMBC letter to Nancy Cumberlege 26.8.40.
18. CMBC letter to Nancy Cumberlege 1.9.40.
19. CMBC letter to Nancy Cumberlege 24.8.40.
20. CMBC letter to Nancy Cumberlege 19.10.40.
21. CMBC letters to Nancy Cumberlege 4.9.40 and 16.9.40.
22. CMBC letter to Nancy Cumberlege, undated.
23. CMBC letter to Nancy Cumberlege 1.9.1940.
24. CMBC letter to Ellen Paine, 13.10.40.
25. CMBC letter to Ritchie Paine, 11.9.40.
26. CMBC letter to Ellen Paine, 13.11.40.

Chapter 6

1. Alexiades, P., *Target Corinth Canal 1940–44* (London: Pen & Sword Books, 2015), p. 33.
2. Beesly, P., *Very Special Admiral* (London: Hamish Hamilton, 1980).

3. Golomb, Y., *This is the Way It Was* (Oral history project, Israel: 2001).
4. Agayev, J. *Mariners* (Maariv Week, 6.10.89).
5. Nancy Cumberlege to Mike 24.2.41 and at the end of February 1941.
6. Ritchie Paine letter to Nancy Cumberlege, Spring 1941.
7. Nancy Cumberlege to Mike, 26.4.41.
8. Ernest F. Saunders, Diary of a British Sailor 1941 (unpublished, 1941).
9. National Archives, ADM 199/806.
10. *Ibid.*
11. Hammond, N., 'Memories of a British Officer in Greece 1941', *Balkan Studies*, vol. 23, No. 1, Thessaloniki, Greece, 1982.
12. Hammond, N., *John Pendlebury in Crete* (published privately by Cambridge University Press, 1948).
13. Letter to author 9.2.15.
14. See Chaney, L., *Elizabeth David* (London: Macmillan, 1998) and Cooper, A., *Writing at the Kitchen Table* (London: HarperCollins, 1999).
15. Alexiades, P., *Target Corinth Canal 1940–44* (London: Pen & Sword Books, 2015), pp. 58-59.
16. Nancy Cumberlege letter to Mike (between 26.5.41 and 4.6.41).
17. Nancy Cumberlege letter to Mike, 10.6.41.
18. Nancy Cumberlege letter to the Paines, 12.7.41.
19. Both letters dated 12.6.41.

Chapter 7

1. Chaney, L., *Elizabeth David* (London: Macmillan, 1998), p. 163.
2. Cooper, A., *Writing at the Kitchen Table* (London: HarperCollins, 1999), p. 85.
3. Elizabeth David Archive, (Schlesinger Library, Harvard University, USA).
4. Chaney, L., *op. cit.*, p. 163.
5. Nancy Cumberlege letter to Mike 9.9.41.
6. Elizabeth Gwynne to Charles Gibson-Cowan 8.10.41 (Elizabeth David Archive, Schlesinger Library, Harvard University, USA).
7. Email to author January 2018.
8. Nancy Cumberlege letter to Mike 3.10.41.
9. Nancy Cumberlege letter to Mike 14.10.41.
10. Nancy Cumberlege letter to Mike 28.10.41.
11. National Archives, WO 201/2756.
12. Caption material written by CMBC on back of photo.
13. Fielding, X., *Hide and Seek* (London: Secker & Warburg, 1954).
14. National Archives, HS 5/678.
15. New Zealand Electronic Text Collection, *Prisoners of War: The Cretan Campaign* (Victoria University of Wellington Library).
16. CMBC letter to Nancy Cumberlege 8.1.42.
17. CMBC letter to Nancy Cumberlege 11.1.42.
18. CMBC letter to Nancy Cumberlege 15.3.42.
19. National Archives, ADM 1/12409.
20. CMBC letter to Nancy Cumberlege 15.3.42.
21. Beesly, P., *Very Special Admiral* (London: Hamish Hamilton, 1980), p. xv.
22. CMBC letter to the Paines 15.5.42.

Chapter 8

1. Alexiades, P., *Target Corinth Canal 1940–44* (London: Pen & Sword Books, 2015).
2. CMBC personal record Locksmith Planning.
3. In the Cumberlege Locksmith planning file.
4. National Archives, HS5/346.
5. The letters date from 5 October 1942 to 12 January 1943.
6. CMBC letter to Nancy Cumberlege 21.12.42.
7. National Archives, HS 5/531.
8. Nancy Cumberlege letter to the Paines 2.8.45.
9. Fotios Manolopoulos escaped to the Middle East. Kiriakoulis Sideris survived the war and was compensated by the British for the assumed loss of his caïque.
10. National Archives, HS 5/531.
11. *Ibid.*
12. First shown on UK television in November 2011.

Chapter 9

1. National Archives, WO 311/370.
2. National Archives, WO 309/352 and 353.
3. Hitler's Commando Order, 18.10.42 (Wikipedia.org/wikicommando_order).
4. National Archives, WO 311/279.
5. *Ibid.*
6. Fritz Seidler entry (Mauthausen Memorial Archive).
7. Kharkov trial December 1943 (Axis History Forum).
8. Wachsmann, N., *KL: A History of the Nazi Concentration Camps* (London: Little Brown, 2015).
9. Moorhouse, R., *Berlin at War* (London: The Bodley Head, 2010).
10. National Archives, WO 309/2040.
11. Anton Kaindl testimony to Soviet Military Tribunal 23 October 1947.
12. National Archives, WO 309/1589 and 109 and Wachsmann, N., *KL: A History of the Nazi Concentration Camps* (London: Little Brown, 2015).
13. Falconer, H. M., *The Gestapo's Most Improbable Hostage* (London: Pen & Sword Books, 2018).
14. Moorhouse, R., *Berlin at War* (London: The Bodley Head, 2010).
15. Smith, S., *'Wings' Day* (London: Pan Books, 1970).
16. Alexiades, P., *Target Corinth Canal 1940–44* (London: Pen & Sword Books, 2015).
17. Falconer, H. M., *The Gestapo's Most Improbable Hostage* (London: Pen & Sword Books, 2018).
18. *Ibid.*
19. National Archives, HS 9/496/6 and HS 8/881.
20. National Archives, HS 9/314 and 9/315 and eighteen files in WO 311 and WO 309.
21. Falconer, H. M., *op. cit.*
22. National Archives, WO 309/853.

Chapter 10

1. National Archives, WO 309/438.
2. National Archives, FO 371/48935.
3. Letter to Ritchie & Ellen Paine 4.5.45.
4. Letter from 'Wings' Day 2.8.45.
5. National Archives, ADM1/28910.
6. Letter from Lennox Livingstone-Learmonth 12.8.45.
7. Letter to Ellen Paine 2.8.45.
8. National Archives, ADM 1/28910.
9. *Ibid.*
10. Letter dated 16.10.45 received by Nancy Cumberlege 29.11.45.
11. National Archives, WO 309/438.
12. National Archives, ADM1/28910.
13. Alexiades, P., *Target Corinth Canal 1940–44* (London: Pen & Sword Books, 2015).
14. Nancy Cumberlege letter to Mike Cumberlege 12.1.42.
15. Letter to the Paines undated (late 1946).
16. Letter to Nancy Cumberlege 30.6.43.
17. Letter to Nancy Cumberlege 10.7.45.
18. Letter to Ellen Paine 2.8.45.

Bibliography

Books and Articles

Agayev, J., *Mariners* (Israel, Maariv Week, 6.10.89)

Alexiades, P., *Target Corinth Canal 1940–44* (London: Pen & Sword Books, 2015)

Beesly, P., *Very Special Admiral* (London: Hamish Hamilton, 1980)

Beevor, A., *Crete* (London: John Murray, 1991)

Best, S. P., *The Venlo Incident* (London: Hutchinson & Co., 1950; Pen & Sword Books, 2009)

Bryer, R., *Jolie Brise* (London: Martin Secker & Warburg Ltd., 1982)

Bulba-Borovets, T., *Army Without a State: A Memoir* (Winnipeg, 1981)

Chaney, L., *Elizabeth David* (London: Macmillan, 1998)

Cheltenham Ladies College, *Archives* (Cheltenham: 2017)

Cooper, A., *Writing at the Kitchen Table* (London: HarperCollins, 1999)

Cowan, C. G., *The Voyage of the Evelyn Hope* (London: Cresset Press, 1946)

Cowan, C. G., *Loud Report* (London: 1928)

Cumberbatch Family History, *Collections & Connections* (2015)

Cumberlege, C. L., *Master Mariner* (London: Paul Davies, 1936)

Cumberlege, C. L., *Salt Horse* (unpublished memoir, 1938)

Cumberlege, C.M.B., '*Jolie Brise*—a Famous Ship Completely Refitted', *Yachting Monthly*, 25 September 1935

Denham, H., *Inside The Nazi Ring* (London: Holmes & Meir, 1985)

Doron, A., *Jewish Ghost Commando* (Israel: Maariv 'Week', October 1989)

Evans, R. J., *The Third Reich in Power* (London: Allen Lane, 2005)

Falconer, H. M., *The Gestapo's Most Improbable Hostage* (London: Pen & Sword Books, 2018)

Farran, R., *Winged Dagger* (London: 1948)

Fenby, J., *The General* (London: Simon & Schuster, 2010)

Fielding, X., *Hide and Seek* (London: Secker & Warburg, 1954)

Golomb, Y., *This is the Way It Was* (Oral history project, Israel: 2001)

Haag, M., *Alexandria, City of Memory* (Yale: Yale University Press, 2004)

Hammond, N., 'Memories of a British Officer in Greece 1941', *Balkan Studies*, vol. 23, No. 1, Thessaloniki, Greece, 1982

Hammond, N., *John Pendlebury in Crete* (published privately, Cambridge University Press, 1948)

Helm, S., *A Life in Secrets* (London: Little Brown, 2005)

James, B. A. 'Jimmy', *Moonless Night* (London: William Kimber, 1983)

Jose, A. W., *The Royal Australian Navy 1914–1918* (Sydney: Angus & Robertson, 1928)

Knight, R.I.E., *In Search of Mike Cumberlege* (London: Knightwrite Ltd, 2015)

Knight, R.I.E., *Pangbourne College: Spirit in Changing Times* (London: Profile Books, 2016)

Fermor, P. L., *Three Letters from the Andes* (London: John Murray, 1991)

Maillart, E., *Gypsy Afloat* (London: W. Heinemann, 1942)

Moffat, D., '*Landfall*': *Adriatic Cruise 1939* (published privately in USA: 1939)

Moorhouse, R., *Berlin at War* (London: The Bodley Head, 2010)

Nautical College, *The Log*, Pangbourne (Spring 1936)

Ogden, A., *Sons of Odysseus* (London: Bene Factum Publishing, 2005)

Outhwaite, L., *The Atlantic: A History of an Ocean* (New York: Coward-McCann, 1957)

Outhwaite, L., *Atlantic Circle* (New York: Charles Scribner's & Sons, 1931)

Outhwaite, L., 'Biscay Gales' in *Harper's Magazine* (USA: 31 January 1931)

Parish, M. W., *Aegean Adventures 1940–1943* (London: The Book Guild, 1993)

Paine, W., 'About Landfall' (unpublished paper, 2016)

Paine, W., 'That Business at Brioni' (unpublished paper, 2016)

Psychoundakis, G., *The Cretan Runner* (London: John Murray, 1955)

Roberts, J. A. G., and Farquharson-Roberts, M., *Royal Navy Officers from War to War 1918–1939* (London: Springer, 2015)

Rogers, A., *Churchill's Folly* (London: Cassell, 2003)

Scott, N., 'Brotherhood of Veterans of the Greek Campaigns', ww2greekveterans.com/

Smith, J., *Archives* (Naval Historical Society of Australia, 2017).

Smith, S., '*Wings' Day* (London: Pan Books, 1970)

The National Archives, Kew, England

Wachsmann, N., *KL: A History of the Nazi Concentration Camps* (London: Little Brown, 2015)

Index